1. The 24-Hour City Challenge: $20.
2. Ultimate Home Makeover: Tı......
3. Mystery Box Cooking Challenge: Creating gourmet meals from random ingredients.
4. The Great Urban Treasure Hunt: Solving clues across the city to find a hidden prize.
5. Extreme Sports Compilation: Showcasing breathtaking stunts from around the world.
6. The Kindness Challenge: Performing 100 acts of kindness in a day.
7. Zero Waste Week: Living sustainably and cutting out all waste.
8. The Ultimate Road Trip: Documenting a cross-country journey with daily challenges.
9. Behind the Scenes of a Movie Set: An exclusive look at how films are made.
10. World Record Attempts: Trying to break quirky world records.
11. Unbelievable Magic Tricks Revealed: Magicians sharing their most guarded secrets.
12. DIY Tiny House Build: Documenting the creation of a tiny house from scratch.
13. The Blindfolded Shopping Challenge: Buying complete outfits blindfolded.
14. Abandoned Places Exploration: Discovering and exploring abandoned wonders.
15. Celebrity Prank Wars: Celebrities pranking each other in elaborate ways.
16. The 30-Day Fitness Transformation: Documenting a full month of fitness progress.
17. Cooking with Grandparents: Traditional recipes made with love.
18. Reacting to Fans' TikToks: YouTubers react to and recreate fan-made TikToks.
19. The Ultimate Scavenger Hunt: Teams compete in a city-wide scavenger hunt.
20. Learning a New Skill in 24 Hours: From zero to hero in one day.
21. The $100 Startup: Launching a business with only $100.
22. The Ghost Town Series: Exploring and uncovering the stories of ghost towns.

23. The One Color Food Challenge: Eating only one-colored foods for 24 hours.
24. The Extreme Survival Challenge: Thriving in the wilderness with minimal supplies.
25. The International Candy Taste Test: Trying candies from around the world.
26. Transforming My Pet's Life: A complete makeover for a pet.
27. The Silent Vlog: A day in the life, but without speaking.
28. Underwater Room Challenge: Spending 24 hours in an underwater room.
29. High Adrenaline Sports: Showcasing extreme sports from skydiving to cliff jumping.
30. The Great Bake Off: A baking competition with a twist.
31. The Secret Life of Toys: Creating a stop-motion adventure.
32. The Flash Mob Surprise: Organizing a massive flash mob in a public place.
33. The Ultimate Puzzle Challenge: Solving the world's most complicated puzzles.
34. The One-Man Band: Creating a song using only homemade instruments.
35. The Ice Hotel Experience: Spending a night in an ice hotel.
36. The Blind Taste Test: Identifying foods while blindfolded.
37. The Budget Travel Challenge: Traveling to a destination on a shoestring budget.
38. The Drone Racing League: High-speed drone races through challenging courses.
39. The Art of Illusion: Creating mind-bending optical illusions.
40. The Great Outdoors Survival Guide: Tips and tricks for surviving in the wild.
41. Parody Music Video: Creating a parody of a popular music video.
42. The Unboxing Frenzy: Unboxing the weirdest products available online.
43. The DIY Space Experiment: Launching a homemade rocket into the stratosphere.
44. The Thrift Store Fashion Show: Creating high-fashion looks from thrift store finds.
45. The Homemade Roller Coaster: Building and riding a backyard roller coaster.

46. The Ultimate Food Challenge: Competitive eating with a gourmet twist.
47. The Time Capsule Project: Burying a time capsule for future generations.
48. The Human Domino Chain: Setting up and toppling a record-breaking domino chain.
49. The 360° Travel Experience: Exploring exotic locations in 360-degree videos.
50. The Zero Gravity Challenge: Experiencing and performing tasks in zero gravity.
51. The Virtual Reality Adventure: Taking viewers on a VR journey.
52. The Underwater Sculpture Park: Exploring underwater art installations.
53. The Biggest Bubble Ever: Attempting to create the world's largest soap bubble.
54. The Silent Retreat: Documenting the experience of a silent meditation retreat.
55. The Global Dance Party: Coordinating a dance video with participants worldwide.
56. The Homemade Submarine: Building and testing a DIY submarine.
57. The Ultimate DIY Treehouse: Constructing a dream treehouse from scratch.
58. The Giant LEGO Build: Creating a life-size structure out of LEGO.
59. The Backyard Waterpark: Transforming a backyard into a waterpark for a day.
60. The Animal Whisperer: Communicating with animals in unique ways.
61. The Cross-Country Race: Documenting a cross-country race on foot.
62. The Fantasy Cosplay Competition: Bringing fantasy characters to life.
63. The Microscopic World: Exploring the unseen world through a microscope.
64. The Ultimate Hide and Seek: A massive game of hide and seek in an unusual location.
65. The International Street Food Tour: Sampling street food from around the globe.

66. The DIY Rocket League: Building and playing a real-life version of Rocket League.

67. The Secret Garden Makeover: Transforming a neglected space into a beautiful garden.

68. The Abandoned Amusement Park: Exploring a deserted amusement park.

69. The Homemade Hovercraft: Designing and riding a hovercraft.

70. The Extreme Weather Challenge: Documenting life in extreme weather conditions.

71. The Lost City Exploration: Uncovering the mysteries of a lost city.

72. The Ultimate Trick Shot Compilation: Showcasing incredible trick shots in various sports.

73. The Eco-Friendly Home Challenge: Making a home sustainable in one week.

74. The Deep Sea Adventure: Exploring the depths of the ocean.

75. The Skydiving Chess Match: Playing chess while skydiving.

76. The International Sign Language Challenge: Communicating in different sign languages.

77. The 100-Layer Challenge: Applying 100 layers of various products.

78. The Ancient Skills Revival: Mastering skills from ancient civilizations.

79. The World's Largest Paintball Battle: Organizing a record-setting paintball game.

80. The Superhero Stunt School: Learning to perform superhero stunts.

81. The Ultimate DIY Race Car: Building and racing a homemade car.

82. The Haunted House Overnight: Spending the night in a reputedly haunted house.

83. The Ultimate Sandcastle: Constructing an elaborate sandcastle.

84. The DIY Jet Pack: Attempting to create and fly a homemade jet pack.

85. The World Music Tour: Exploring the musical traditions of different cultures.

86. The Virtual Escape Room: Designing and solving a virtual escape room.

87. The Super Slow Motion Compilation: Capturing mesmerizing slow-motion footage.

88. The International Language Challenge: Learning to say 'hello' in 100 languages.

89. The Around the World in 80 Dishes: Cooking and tasting dishes from 80 countries.

90. The Underwater Music Video: Shooting a music video entirely underwater.

91. The DIY Wind Turbine: Building a wind turbine to power a home.

92. The Ultimate Obstacle Course: Designing and completing a challenging obstacle course.

93. The Zero to Hero Chess Challenge: Learning chess from beginner to expert.

94. The Homemade Spacesuit: Designing and testing a DIY spacesuit.

95. The Desert Island Survival Challenge: Surviving on a deserted island.

96. The 360° Skydiving Experience: Capturing a skydive in 360-degree video.

97. The Homemade Arcade: Building and playing in a DIY arcade.

98. The World's Largest Domino Setup: Attempting the largest domino setup ever recorded.

99. The Firewalking Challenge: Learning the art of firewalking.

100. The Global Meditation Event: Coordinating a meditation session with participants from around the world.

101. The Blindfolded Drawing Challenge: Competing to create the best artwork blindfolded.

102. The One-Song Lip Sync Battle: Groups battle it out lip-syncing to the same song in different styles.

103. Around the World in 24 Hours: Virtual travel challenge visiting as many countries as possible via video calls.

104. The DIY Invention Challenge: Creating new gadgets from household items.

105. The Backwards Day: Doing everyday activities backward for a day.

106. The Ultimate Recycling Project: Turning trash into functional art.

107. The 1,000 Miles Challenge: Walking, running, cycling 1,000 miles as fast as possible.

108. The Human Statue Challenge: Posing as statues in public and trying not to move.

109. The Secret Recipe Contest: Chefs create dishes based on secret ingredients from viewers.

110. The Longest Echo: Finding locations with the most impressive echoes.

111. The Deep Fake Movie: Recreating a classic movie scene using deep fake technology.

112. The 24-Hour Live Stream: Documenting life non-stop for a full day.

113. The Shadow Puppetry Show: Telling stories through shadow art.

114. The Ancient Game Revival: Playing games that were popular in ancient civilizations.

115. The DIY Natural Beauty Challenge: Making cosmetics from natural ingredients.

116. The Smartphone Film Festival: Creating short films using only smartphones.

117. The Historical Reenactment Vlog: Bringing historical events to life through reenactment.

118. The Public Art Installation: Creating and displaying art in public spaces.

119. The 100 Different Sports Challenge: Trying 100 different sports or physical activities.

120. The Virtual Reality Time Travel: Experiencing different historical periods through VR.

121. The Ice Sculpture Challenge: Competing to carve the best sculpture out of ice.

122. The 48-Hour Film Project: Producing a short film in just 48 hours.

123. The World's Smallest Art Gallery: Creating and curating a miniature art gallery.

124. The Cultural Exchange Program: Sharing and learning traditions from different cultures.

125. The Paper Plane Contest: Designing and flying paper planes for distance and style.

126. The Urban Farming Experiment: Growing as much food as possible in a small urban space.

127. The Secret Handshake Workshop: Inventing unique handshakes and teaching them to strangers.

128. The Homemade Musical Instrument: Building and performing with DIY musical instruments.

129. The Underwater Clean-Up: Diving to clean up a local water body and showcase the impact.

130. The DIY Theme Park Ride: Designing and constructing a backyard theme park attraction.

131. The 100 Strangers Portrait Project: Photographing and telling the stories of 100 strangers.

132. The Virtual Choir: Assembling singers from around the world for a virtual performance.

133. The Instant Play: Writing, directing, and performing a play in 24 hours.

134. The Drone Light Show: Choreographing a light show with drones.

135. The No-Gadget Day: Documenting the experience of living a day without any gadgets.

136. The Homemade Rocket Launch: Designing, building, and launching a model rocket.

137. The One-Color Art Challenge: Creating artwork using only one color.

138. The Silent Movie Challenge: Making a short film in the style of old silent movies.

139. The Mystery Ingredient Cooking Show: Chefs create dishes using a surprise ingredient.

140. The Zero-Gravity Dance: Choreographing and performing a dance in zero-gravity conditions.

141. The International Folklore Festival: Showcasing folklore tales and traditions from around the world.

142. The Future City Design: Imagining and designing a city of the future.

143. The Rube Goldberg Machine Contest: Building complex machines to perform simple tasks.

144. The Digital Detox Challenge: Spending a week without the internet and documenting the experience.

145. The Mindfulness Marathon: Practicing 24 hours of continuous mindfulness activities.

146. The Balloon World Tour: Sending a camera attached to a weather balloon to capture views from the stratosphere.

147. The Multilingual Song: Creating a song that incorporates multiple languages.

148. The Ancient Cooking Challenge: Preparing meals using only ancient cooking methods.

149. The Stop Motion Road Trip: Documenting a road trip using stop-motion photography.

150. The Living History Project: Spending a week living as people did in a specific historical period.

151. The Extreme Weather Survival Guide: Tips for surviving and thriving in extreme weather conditions.

152. The Space-Themed Art Project: Creating art inspired by space and the universe.

153. The World's Longest Domino Line: Attempting to set up and topple a record-breaking line of dominos.

154. The Virtual Reality Game Creation: Developing and testing a new VR game.

155. The Cross-Cultural Wedding Traditions: Exploring wedding traditions from different cultures.

156. The 360-Degree Underwater Expedition: Exploring coral reefs and underwater life in 360-degree video.

157. The Microgravity Experiment: Conducting fun experiments in a microgravity environment.

158. The DIY Tiny Planet: Creating a "tiny planet" effect video showcasing local landmarks.

159. The Human Rights Awareness Campaign: Highlighting human rights issues through creative content.

160. The Global Yoga Session: Leading a yoga session with participants from around the world.

161. The Fantasy Map Making: Designing and illustrating a map of an imaginary world.

162. The Homemade Space Observatory: Building a backyard observatory to explore the night sky.

163. The Epic Food Journey: Tracing the origin and making of a famous dish across countries.

164. The Origami Challenge: Folding an intricate origami piece with a large group of people.

165. The Virtual Museum Tour: Guiding viewers through famous museums around the world.

166. The DIY Eco-Friendly Vehicle: Building and testing an environmentally friendly mode of transport.

167. The Interactive History Lesson: Teaching history in an engaging and interactive way.

168. The Biohacking Experiment: Trying different biohacks to improve health and performance.

169. The Aerial Photography Contest: Capturing stunning landscapes from the air.

170. The Public Speaking Marathon: Delivering inspirational speeches in public places.

171. The Homemade Planetarium: Creating a planetarium show at home.

172. The Time-Lapse World: Capturing the beauty of different locations in time-lapse.

173. The Ultimate Puzzle Room: Designing and solving an elaborate escape room.

174. The Living Sculpture: Creating and displaying living sculptures made from plants.

175. The Giant Mural Painting: Collaborating with a community to paint a giant mural.

176. The Virtual Dance Party: Hosting a global dance party with live DJ sets online.

177. The Wildlife Conservation Documentary: Highlighting efforts to protect endangered species.

178. The Historical Costume Challenge: Designing and wearing costumes from different historical periods.

179. The International Poetry Slam: Hosting a poetry competition with poets from around the world.

180. The Zero-Energy Home Challenge: Retrofitting a home to run on zero energy.

181. The Underwater House: Designing and simulating living in an underwater habitat.

182. The Global Cooking Marathon: Cooking 24 dishes from 24 countries in 24 hours.

183. The DIY Water Filtration: Building and testing a homemade water filtration system.

184. The Mind-Bending Illusion Art: Creating and explaining optical illusions.

185. The Homemade Arcade Game: Designing and building a working arcade game from scratch.

186. The Virtual Book Club: Discussing a book with authors and readers worldwide.

187. The Guerrilla Gardening Mission: Transforming unused urban spaces into green areas.

188. The Night Sky Time-Lapse: Capturing the beauty of the night sky over different landscapes.

189. The Interactive Art Project: Creating art that viewers can physically interact with.

190. The Extreme Makeover: Community Edition: Renovating a community center or public space.

191. The 100 Voices Choir: Assembling a choir of 100 people from different backgrounds.

192. The Homemade Telescope: Building a telescope to explore the stars and planets.

193. The Cultural Fashion Show: Showcasing traditional clothing from cultures around the world.

194. The Epic Bike Journey: Documenting a long-distance bike journey through diverse terrains.

195. The Virtual Reality Spacewalk: Experiencing a spacewalk through virtual reality.

196. The Global Handshake Project: Connecting people from different countries through a symbolic handshake.

197. The DIY Solar Oven: Building and cooking with a home made solar oven.

198. The Ancestral Skills Challenge: Learning and demonstrating skills our ancestors used daily.

199. The Ultimate Balancing Act: Performing extraordinary balancing feats.

200. The Cross-Continental Music Collaboration: Musicians from different continents create a song together.

201. The Silent Film Remake Challenge: Recreating modern movie scenes as silent films.

202. The Around-the-World Handstand Video: Performing handstands in iconic locations worldwide.

203. The One-Day Entrepreneur: Launching a pop-up business in just 24 hours.

204. The 100 Different Laughs Challenge: Imitating 100 different types of laughter.

205. The Historic Meal Preparation: Cooking a feast using only medieval kitchen tools and recipes.

206. The International Sign-Off: Saying "goodbye" in 100 different languages.

207. The Reverse Engineering Challenge: Taking apart gadgets to see how they work, then reassembling them.

208. The Urban Beekeeping Introduction: Starting an urban beekeeping project and documenting the journey.

209. The DIY Natural Swimming Pool: Building a chemical-free swimming pool in a backyard.

210. The Underwater Painting Challenge: Creating art underwater in a pool.

211. The VR Travel Log: Exploring and documenting virtual reality worlds.

212. The 24-Hour Backward Talking Challenge: Speaking in reverse for a whole day.

213. The 50 States, 50 Dishes Challenge: Cooking a signature dish from each state.

214. The Miniature Book Club: Discussing literature using only tiny, handcrafted books.

215. The Blindfolded Climbing Challenge: Climbing a wall or boulder blindfolded with guidance.

216. The Homemade Water Slide: Constructing and enjoying a giant, homemade water slide.

217. The Ancient Instrument Performance: Playing music on instruments from ancient civilizations.

218. The DIY Biodome: Creating a self-sustaining ecosystem in a homemade biodome.

219. The Sidewalk Chalk Art Festival: Creating and showcasing massive sidewalk chalk art.

220. The One-Button Fashion Challenge: Designing and wearing outfits with clothes that have only one button.

221. The Zero-Waste Art Project: Making art exclusively from recycled materials.

222. The Historical Figure Day-in-the-Life: Living a day as a historical figure, using period-accurate resources.

223. The Invisible Photography Exhibition: Displaying photos that use invisible ink visible only under UV light.

224. The 360-Degree Sports Match: Filming and experiencing a sports game in 360 degrees.

225. The Overnight Castle Build: Constructing a sand or snow castle overnight.

226. The Global Sunset Marathon: Documenting sunsets in different locations around the world in one day.

227. The Phone-Free Travel Challenge: Traveling to a new place without using any smartphones or GPS.

228. The Lego Stop-Motion Epic: Creating an epic story using Lego figures and stop-motion animation.

229. The World's Smallest Drone Race: Racing the smallest drones through obstacle courses.

230. The High Fashion Thrift Flip: Transforming thrift store finds into high fashion outfits.

231. The Backwards Running Race: Organizing a race where participants can only run backward.

232. The DIY Planetarium Show: Creating a show about constellations and the night sky at home.

233. The Underwater VR Experience: Exploring and documenting a dive using VR technology.

234. The 100-Puzzle Challenge: Solving 100 different puzzles as quickly as possible.

235. The Living in a Dome for a Week: Documenting life inside a geodesic dome.

236. The One-Sentence Story Contest: Telling the most compelling story in just one sentence.

237. The Citywide Game of Tag: Organizing a massive, citywide game of tag.

238. The Ultimate DIY Obstacle Course for Pets: Designing and building an obstacle course for pets.

239. The Smartphone-Free Day: Experiencing and documenting life without a smartphone for 24 hours.

240. The International Breakfast Tour: Sampling and making traditional breakfasts from around the world.
241. The One-Minute Silent Film: Creating compelling silent films that last only one minute.
242. The DIY Wind-Powered Car: Building and racing cars powered only by wind.
243. The 100-Hour Live Music Marathon: Streaming live performances for 100 continuous hours.
244. The Upcycled Art Exhibit: Showcasing art made entirely from upcycled materials.
245. The Vintage Tech Challenge: Using only technology from a certain decade for a day.
246. The Cross-Country Skateboarding Trip: Documenting a long-distance journey on a skateboard.
247. The Home made Soap Sculpture Contest: Crafting and judging sculptures made of soap.
248. The 24-Hour Barefoot Challenge: Going about daily activities without shoes for a day.
249. The Eco-Friendly Home Hackathon: Implementing sustainable living hacks in a home.
250. The Silent Disco Hike: Organizing a group hike where participants listen to the same music in headphones.
251. The One-Day Film School: Teaching the basics of film making in a single day.
252. The International Myth Busters: Exploring and debunking myths from different cultures.
253. The Reverse Cooking Show: Starting with the finished dish and guessing the recipe.
254. The Urban Survival Guide: Demonstrating how to thrive in a city with minimal resources.
255. The Backyard Bioblitz: Identifying as many species as possible in a backyard within 24 hours.
256. The DIY Arcade Cabinet: Building a working arcade cabinet from scratch.
257. The Self-Made Superhero Suit: Designing and creating a functional superhero costume.
258. The One-Week Wilderness Camp: Documenting a week of living and surviving in the wilderness.

259. The Indoor Cloud Project: Creating a cloud inside using scientific methods.

260. The Multisensory Virtual Gallery: Creating art that engages sight, sound, smell, and touch.

261. The Interactive Street Art: Designing street art that passersby can interact with.

262. The One-Hour Songwriting Challenge: Writing and recording a song in just one hour.

263. The Historical Reenactment Marathon: Participating in various historical reenactments around the world.

264. The DIY Solar Car Race: Building and racing solar-powered cars.

265. The Ultimate Chess Boxing Match: Competing in a combination of chess and boxing.

266. The One-Day Language Learning Challenge: Attempting to learn the basics of a new language in a day.

267. The Zero-Gravity Art Gallery: Imagining and designing art for a zero-gravity environment.

268. The Home made Ice Cream Flavors: Creating and taste-testing unique ice cream flavors.

269. The Virtual Reality History Lesson: Teaching history through immersive VR experiences.

270. The 100-Ingredient Smoothie: Making a smoothie with 100 different ingredients.

271. The Around-the-World Relay: Organizing a virtual relay with participants from every continent.

272. The Build-Your-Own Boat Race: Constructing boats from unconventional materials and racing them.

273. The International Folk Dance Compilation: Learning and performing folk dances from around the globe.

274. The DIY At-Home Escape Room: Designing and solving an escape room at home.

275. The Global Handwriting Project: Comparing handwriting and learning styles from around the world.

276. The One-Sheet Paper Challenge: Creating the most intricate design from a single sheet of paper.

277. The Home made Telescope Stargazing: Exploring the night sky with a DIY telescope.

278. The 100-Layer Clothing Challenge: Wearing 100 layers of clothing and documenting the experience.

279. The Time Capsule Voyage: Creating a time capsule and documenting predictions for the future.

280. The Ultimate Indoor Camping Experience: Setting up an elaborate camping site indoors.

281. The One-Day Animation Challenge: Creating a short animation film in 24 hours.

282. The DIY Mini Golf Course: Designing and playing on a homemade mini-golf course.

283. The Historical Documentaries Marathon: Watching and reviewing historical documentaries back-to-back.

284. The Zero-Waste Cooking Show: Preparing meals with absolutely no waste.

285. The International Kite Flying Festival: Making and flying kites with unique designs.

286. The 100-Kilometer Barefoot Walk: Walking a long distance barefoot to raise awareness for a cause.

287. The Solar System Model Project: Building an accurate model of the solar system.

288. The Underwater Hotel Stay: Documenting a stay in an underwater hotel room.

289. The One-Day Startup Launch: Creating and launching a startup business in 24 hours.

290. The Extreme Weather Camping: Camping in extreme weather conditions and documenting the experience.

291. The Around-the-World Virtual Marathon: Participating in a virtual marathon with international runners.

292. The DIY Hydroponics Farm: Setting up and maintaining a hydroponic farm at home.

293. The 100-Dance Moves Challenge: Learning and performing 100 different dance moves.

294. The One-Ingredient Recipe Challenge: Creating dishes using only one main ingredient.

295. The Cross-Platform Digital Scavenger Hunt: Organizing a scavenger hunt across various digital platforms.

296. The Home made Musical: Writing, directing, and performing in a homemade musical.

297. The International Puppet Show: Creating and performing a puppet show with global themes.
298. The One-Color Photography Challenge: Taking beautiful photos using only one color theme.
299. The DIY Underwater Camera: Building a camera capable of capturing underwater scenes.
300. The Ultimate DIY Tree Planting Drone: Designing a drone to plant trees in hard-to-reach areas.

301. The Back-to-Basics Camping Trip: Documenting a trip using only primitive camping techniques.
302. The International Dessert Bake-off: Baking and comparing traditional desserts from around the world.
303. The Self-Sustaining Aquarium Challenge: Creating an aquarium ecosystem that sustains itself.
304. The Reverse Engineering Toy Challenge: Disassembling toys to understand how they work, then reassembling.
305. The City-Specific Scavenger Hunt: Creating a scavenger hunt that highlights the unique features of a city.
306. The 24-Hour Public Transport Challenge: Exploring a city using only public transport for 24 hours.
307. The DIY Electric Skateboard: Building and testing a homemade electric skateboard.
308. The One-Act Play Competition: Writing, directing, and performing one-act plays within 48 hours.
309. The Ultimate Recycled Art Project: Creating large-scale art installations from recycled materials.
310. The Silent Retreat Experiment: Spending a week in silence and documenting the experience.
311. The Historical Fashion Revival: Recreating and wearing historical outfits in everyday life.
312. The Home made Pasta Shapes Challenge: Inventing and making new pasta shapes from scratch.
313. The Smartphone Photography Contest: Capturing and showcasing extraordinary photos taken with just a smartphone.
314. The 100 Different Sports Challenge: Trying out and documenting 100 lesser-known sports.
315. The DIY Vertical Garden: Building a vertical garden in an urban setting and documenting the process.

316. The One-Syllable Communication Day: Going through a day using only one-syllable words.

317. The Home made Rocket Stove Cooking: Building a rocket stove and cooking meals outdoors.

318. The Virtual Reality Art Gallery: Creating and touring art galleries in virtual reality.

319. The 360-Degree Nature Documentary: Capturing and sharing nature's beauty in 360-degree video.

320. The Eco-Friendly Transport Race: Competing in a race using only eco-friendly modes of transportation.

321. The One-Day Song Challenge: Writing, producing, and releasing a song in 24 hours.

322. The DIY Bioluminescent Project: Creating bioluminescent jars using natural or scientific methods.

323. The International Board Game Night: Playing traditional board games from different cultures.

324. The Zero-Input Garden Challenge: Growing a garden using permaculture principles with no external inputs.

325. The Handmade Paper Making: Creating and decorating paper from recycled materials.

326. The 48-Hour Film Noir Challenge: Creating a short film noir within 48 hours.

327. The Ultimate DIY Survival Gear: Crafting survival gear from scratch and testing its effectiveness.

328. The One-Week Barter Challenge: Living a week relying solely on bartering goods and services.

329. The Historical Cooking Show: Preparing meals exactly how they were made in historical periods.

330. The DIY Tiny Library: Building a tiny library for the community and documenting its use.

331. The Virtual Reality Space Mission: Simulating a space mission using virtual reality technology.

332. The Underwater Art Installation: Creating and documenting the installation of art pieces underwater.

333. The 100 Voices, One Song Challenge: Assembling 100 people to sing a song, each adding their voice.

334. The Around-the-World Fashion Show: Showcasing traditional and modern fashion from across the globe.

335. The One-Ingredient Diet Challenge: Eating foods made from one primary ingredient for a week.

336. The DIY Floating Habitat: Designing and constructing a floating habitat for waterways.

337. The Ultimate Book Swap: Organizing a massive, community-wide book swap event.

338. The Backyard Wildlife Documentary: Documenting the diversity of wildlife in a backyard over a season.

339. The One-Day Off-Grid Challenge: Living a day entirely off-grid and documenting the experience.

340. The Home made Natural Dye Workshop: Making and using natural dyes from plants and vegetables.

341. The Bicycle-Powered Inventions: Creating and showcasing inventions powered by bicycle.

342. The International Gesture Language Game: Communicating using only gestures learned from different cultures.

343. The DIY Solar Cook off: Hosting a cooking competition using only solar ovens.

344. The 100-Mile Local Food Challenge: Eating only food sourced from within 100 miles for a month.

345. The Zero-Waste Fashion Design: Creating fashionable outfits using zero-waste principles.

346. The Home made Instruments Orchestra: Crafting instruments from everyday items and performing music.

347. The Virtual Time Capsule: Creating a digital time capsule to be opened in the future.

348. The One-Color Living Challenge: Living a week using items of only one color.

349. The Home made Water Filtration Challenge: Designing and testing different methods of water filtration.

350. The 24-Hour Urban Foraging: Finding and preparing food by foraging in an urban environment.

351. The International Language Learning Marathon: Attempting to learn the basics of as many languages as possible in 48 hours.

352. The DIY Smart Home Gadgets: Creating smart home devices from scratch and integrating them into daily life.

353. The One-Hour Documentary Challenge: Creating a short documentary film in just one hour.

354. The Global Climate Action Project: Highlighting innovative climate action projects around the world.
355. The Ultimate Recycling DIY Challenge: Upcycling discarded items into useful products.
356. The Cross-Cultural Storytelling Circle: Sharing and interpreting stories from different cultures.
357. The Home made Kite Building and Flying: Crafting kites from scratch and hosting a kite-flying event.
358. The 100 Strangers Portrait Challenge: Photographing 100 strangers and telling their stories.
359. The DIY Eco-Friendly Cleaning Products: Making and testing homemade cleaning products.
360. The Virtual Reality Educational Tours: Creating immersive VR tours of historical and scientific sites.
361. The One-Day Micro adventure: Embarking on a spontaneous adventure close to home and documenting it.
362. The Home made Animation Film: Creating an animated short film using DIY techniques.
363. The Ultimate Upcycling Fashion Show: Designing and hosting a fashion show with upcycled materials.
364. The Community Mural Painting: Bringing together a community to paint a large-scale mural.
365. The 24-Hour Silence Challenge: Experiencing and reflecting on 24 hours of complete silence.
366. The DIY Musical: Writing, composing, and performing a short musical with homemade sets and costumes.
367. The One-Week Wilderness Photography Expedition: Documenting wilderness beauty and survival techniques.
368. The Global Dance Challenge: Learning and performing traditional dances from around the world.
369. The 100 Flavors Ice Cream Challenge: Creating and taste-testing ice cream with 100 different flavors.
370. The DIY Recycled Boat Race: Building boats from recycled materials and racing them on a body of water.
371. The Urban Guerrilla Gardening: Planting gardens in neglected urban spaces and documenting their growth.
372. The Home made Planetarium Project: Building a small planetarium to project the night sky indoors.

373. The International Cooking Marathon: Cooking a dish from every country over a set period.

374. The One-Song Dance Evolution: Choreographing a dance that evolves through different music genres.

375. The DIY Electric Bike: Converting a standard bicycle into an electric bike and documenting the process.

376. The Silent Movie Creation Challenge: Making a modern story into a silent film format.

377. The Backyard Biome Project: Creating a diverse ecosystem in a backyard and documenting its development.

378. The Home made Toy Hackathon: Innovating new toys from old or broken ones.

379. The One-Handed Living Challenge: Going about daily tasks using only one hand for 24 hours.

380. The Global Virtual Concert: Organizing a concert featuring musicians playing together from different locations.

381. The DIY Eco-Friendly Toy Challenge: Creating children's toys that are both fun and environmentally friendly.

382. The One-Day Local Adventure: Exploring hidden gems and attractions within a local area.

383. The Home made Natural Ink Making: Crafting inks from natural materials and testing them.

384. The International Mystery Box Cooking: Cooking meals with ingredients from international mystery boxes.

385. The Zero-Waste Journey: Documenting the transition to a zero-waste lifestyle over a month.

386. The DIY Backyard Observatory: Constructing an observatory to watch stars and planets.

387. The One-Week Minimalist Challenge: Living with the bare minimum for a week and documenting the experience.

388. The Global Virtual Jam Session: Musicians from around the world collaborate in a live-streamed jam session.

389. The Ultimate DIY Costume Challenge: Creating elaborate costumes using only household items.

390. The Home made Natural Beauty Regimen: Testing a beauty regimen using only homemade, natural products.

391. The Urban Exploration Series: Exploring and documenting abandoned buildings and urban spaces.

392. The One-Day Digital Detox Challenge: Spending a day completely disconnected from digital devices.

393. The DIY Off-Grid Living Experiment: Attempting to live off-grid for a period and documenting the experience.

394. The International Virtual Art Exhibit: Showcasing digital art from artists around the world in a virtual exhibit.

395. The Home made Board Game Creation: Designing and playing a completely original board game.

396. The 100 Different Handshakes Challenge: Creating and demonstrating 100 unique handshakes.

397. The One-Month Language Immersion: Documenting the journey of learning a new language in one month.

398. The DIY Solar Panel Project: Building and installing solar panels to power home appliances.

399. The Global Virtual Book Club: Reading and discussing a book with participants from different countries.

400. The Home made Natural Mosquito Repellent: Testing the effectiveness of homemade mosquito repellents.

401. The 24-Hour Urban Survival Challenge: Navigating a city's challenges with limited resources.

402. The Global Street Art Tour: Showcasing street art from cities around the world through a curated virtual tour.

403. The DIY Time Capsule: Creating a time capsule to capture today's world for future generations.

404. The One-Color Art Challenge: Creating artwork using shades of a single color for a week.

405. The International Folklore and Legends Series: Exploring and narrating folklore from different cultures.

406. The Ultimate Recycled Fashion Show: Designing and modeling outfits made entirely from recycled materials.

407. The 100-Hour Coding Marathon: Documenting the process of learning to code or build an app in 100 hours.

408. The Extreme Weather Vlog: Documenting life in extreme weather conditions around the globe.

409. The One-Week Vegan Challenge: Exploring veganism and its impact on health and the environment.

410. The DIY Tiny Home on Wheels: Building a tiny home on wheels from scratch and taking it on a road trip.

411. The Backyard Obstacle Course Challenge: Designing and completing a challenging obstacle course at home.
412. The Silent Communication Experiment: Exploring non-verbal communication methods for a day.
413. The One-Day Business Startup Challenge: Starting and launching a business in 24 hours.
414. The Historical Re-Creation Series: Re-creating and living a day in different historical periods.
415. The Urban Farm-to-Table Project: Growing food in an urban garden and preparing a meal.
416. The Home made Instrument Band: Forming a band using only homemade musical instruments.
417. The One-Minute, One-Take Film Challenge: Creating compelling one-minute films in a single take.
418. The 24-Hour Wilderness Survival: Documenting a survival experience in the wilderness with minimal gear.
419. The International Virtual Choir: Assembling singers from around the world to perform together online.
420. The Zero-Electricity Day: Spending a day without using any electricity and documenting the experience.
421. The DIY Paper Mache Sculpture: Creating large-scale paper mache sculptures and showcasing the process.
422. The One-Week Watercolor Challenge: Creating and sharing a new watercolor painting every day for a week.
423. The Virtual Reality Game Development Diary: Documenting the creation of a VR game from concept to launch.
424. The Eco-Friendly Transport Challenge: Exploring the most sustainable ways to travel in a city.
425. The 24-Hour Language Immersion Challenge: Immersing in a new language through various methods for 24 hours.
426. The Ultimate DIY Arcade Machine: Building a fully functional arcade machine from scratch.
427. The Global Meditation Experiment: Coordinating a simultaneous meditation session with participants worldwide.
428. The 100-Mile Diet Experiment: Eating only foods grown or produced within 100 miles for a month.
429. The Home made Candle Making Series: Crafting candles with unique scents and shapes.

430. The Virtual Reality Travel Vlog: Exploring and documenting virtual travel experiences across digital landscapes.

431. The One-Week Barefoot Challenge: Experiencing life going barefoot everywhere for a week.

432. The DIY Home Automation Project: Automating various home functions using DIY solutions.

433. The 24-Hour Comic Book Challenge: Creating a complete comic book from scratch in 24 hours.

434. The One-Month Minimalism Challenge: Documenting the journey of adopting a minimalist lifestyle for a month.

435. The Global Cuisine Cooking Marathon: Cooking and tasting traditional dishes from around the world in a marathon session.

436. The One-Shape Art Challenge: Creating artworks that incorporate a specific shape in various creative ways.

437. The Urban Treasure Hunt: Setting up and participating in a treasure hunt through city landmarks.

438. The Home made Beauty Products Series: Making and testing home made natural beauty products.

439. The 24-Hour No-Tech Challenge: Experiencing a day without any technology or digital devices.

440. The DIY Smart Garden Project: Creating a smart garden that monitors and waters itself using technology.

441. The One-Week Upcycling Challenge: Upcycling different items each day for a week and showcasing the results.

442. The Local History Documentary Series: Exploring and documenting the history of local neighborhoods or landmarks.

443. The International Sign Language Challenge: Learning and demonstrating basic phrases in different sign languages.

444. The One-Color Cooking Challenge: Preparing and eating meals that are all the same color for a day.

445. The DIY Natural Pool Project: Building a natural swimming pool that filters water without chemicals.

446. The 24-Hour At-Home Adventure: Creating an adventure experience within the confines of home.

447. The Historical DIY Project: Recreating historical artifacts, tools, or clothing using traditional methods.

448. The Zero-Waste Lifestyle Series: Documenting the challenges and successes of living a zero-waste lifestyle.

449. The One-Week Portrait Series: Painting or drawing a different portrait every day for a week.

450. The Global Virtual Dance Party: Hosting a live-streamed dance party with DJs and participants from around the world.

451. The Home made Natural Perfume: Crafting perfumes using natural ingredients and essential oils.

452. The One-Day Off-the-Grid Living: Spending a day living completely off the grid and documenting the experience.

453. The DIY Personal Drone Build: Building a personal drone from scratch and testing its capabilities.

454. The International Virtual Film Festival: Curating and hosting a virtual film festival with submissions worldwide.

455. The One-Month Fitness Challenge: Documenting a month-long journey of trying different fitness routines.

456. The DIY Green Roof Project: Installing a green roof to improve home insulation and biodiversity.

457. The One-Week Home made Music Challenge: Creating and sharing a new piece of music using home made instruments each day.

458. The Virtual Reality History Experience: Creating immersive VR experiences that transport viewers to historical events.

459. The 24-Hour Drawing Marathon: Drawing continuously for 24 hours and showcasing the results.

460. The DIY Tiny Aquarium: Building a tiny, self-sustaining aquarium and documenting its ecosystem.

461. The Global Virtual Cooking Class: Hosting a cooking class with participants preparing the same dish in real-time worldwide.

462. The One-Color Photography Project: Taking and sharing photos that focus on a single color for a week.

463. The DIY Recycled Art Installation: Creating a large-scale art installation using only recycled materials.

464. The One-Week Digital Art Challenge: Producing a different piece of digital art each day for a week.

465. The International Pen Pal Documentary: Connecting with pen pals around the world and sharing their stories.

466. The 24-Hour Fitness Challenge: Trying different workouts and fitness challenges over 24 hours.

467. The DIY Home Brewery: Documenting the process of brewing beer or cider at home from scratch.

468. The One-Day Silence Retreat: Spending a day in complete silence and reflecting on the experience.
469. The Ultimate DIY Playhouse: Designing and building a children's playhouse with unique features.
470. The 100-Song Music Challenge: Writing 100 short songs or musical pieces in a specific time frame.
471. The One-Week Wilderness Photography Challenge: Capturing the beauty of the wilderness with daily photography challenges.
472. The Global Virtual Poetry Slam: Organizing a poetry competition with poets performing live from different locations.
473. The One-Month Artistic Medium Experiment: Exploring and creating art with a new medium each day for a month.
474. The DIY Eco-Friendly Vehicle Project: Building and testing an eco-friendly vehicle using sustainable materials.
475. The One-Week Language Learning Diary: Documenting the progress of learning a new language intensively for a week.
476. The 24-Hour Animation Sprint: Creating an animated short film from concept to completion in 24 hours.
477. The Global Online Gaming Tournament: Hosting an online gaming tournament with players from around the world.
478. The One-Day Urban Foraging Guide: Foraging for edible plants in an urban environment and preparing a meal.
479. The DIY Container Home Project: Building a small, functional home out of shipping containers.
480. The One-Week Home made Toy Challenge: Creating a new, home made toy for children each day for a week.
481. The Cross-Cultural Virtual Reality Journey: Exploring and sharing immersive VR experiences of cultural sites around the world.
482. The DIY Biodegradable Plastics: Experimenting with and creating biodegradable plastics from organic materials at home.
483. The One-Day Historical Reenactment Challenge: Living a day according to the lifestyle of a specific historical period.
484. The Global Folk Music Collaboration: Musicians from different countries collaborate to create a fusion folk music piece.
485. The 24-Hour Zero-Waste Challenge: Attempting to produce zero waste for a full day and sharing tips and experiences.
486. The Homemade Natural Pesticide Project: Crafting and testing effective natural pesticides for home gardens.

487. The International Virtual Debate Tournament: Hosting a debate on global issues with participants from various countries.

488. The One-Week Mobile Photography Challenge: Capturing and sharing stunning photographs using only a smartphone.

489. The DIY Solar Water Heater: Building and installing a solar-powered water heater and documenting the process.

490. The One-Month Cultural Exchange Diary: Documenting the experience of learning about a new culture through virtual exchange.

491. The Homemade Air Purifier Project: Designing and creating an effective air purifier using accessible materials.

492. The 24-Hour Mindfulness and Meditation Challenge: Practicing mindfulness and meditation for 24 hours and sharing insights.

493. The DIY Smart Mirror Project: Building a smart mirror that displays news, weather, and personal updates.

494. The One-Week Wilderness Living Experiment: Documenting a week spent living in the wilderness with minimal supplies.

495. The Global Virtual Language Café: Hosting a virtual meeting space for people to practice and learn new languages together.

496. The 24-Hour Indoor Camping Adventure: Creating an indoor camping experience and documenting activities and challenges.

497. The One-Day Upcycling Furniture Workshop: Transforming old furniture into new pieces through creative upcycling techniques.

498. The Homemade Vertical Wind Turbine: Constructing and testing a vertical wind turbine for home energy generation.

499. The One-Month Fitness Transformation Diary: Documenting a month-long personal fitness journey, including routines and results.

500. The DIY Hydroponic Herb Garden: Setting up a hydroponic system for growing herbs indoors and sharing the progress.

501. The 24-Hour Back-to-Nature Challenge: Disconnecting from technology and spending a day immersed in nature.

502. The One-Week Vegan Baking Experiment: Baking a new vegan recipe each day for a week and sharing the outcomes.

503. The International Virtual Art Workshop: Conducting an art workshop with participants creating pieces inspired by different cultures.

504. The DIY Bicycle-Powered Generator: Building a generator powered by bicycle pedaling and testing its capabilities.

505. The One-Day Silent Film Festival: Curating and showcasing silent films, including modern takes on the genre.

506. The Homemade Natural Body Care Products: Crafting natural soaps, lotions, and balms and evaluating their effectiveness.

507. The 24-Hour Urban Gardening Project: Transforming a small urban space into a garden and documenting the process.

508. The One-Week Minimalist Living Challenge: Reducing possessions and living a minimalist lifestyle for a week.

509. The Global Virtual Cooking Showdown: Chefs from around the world compete in a virtual cooking competition.

510. The DIY Electric Longboard: Designing and assembling an electric longboard and testing its performance.

511. The 24-Hour Photography Challenge: Capturing photos that tell a story within 24 hours, focusing on a specific theme.

512. The One-Month Zero-Waste Journey: Documenting the challenges and solutions of living zero-waste for a month.

513. The International Virtual Knitting Circle: Gathering knitters from around the globe to share patterns and stories.

514. The Homemade Composting System: Creating and managing a composting system to reduce kitchen waste.

515. The 24-Hour Off-Grid Cooking Challenge: Preparing meals using off-grid cooking methods for a day.

516. The One-Week Digital Detox Retreat: Documenting the experience and benefits of a week-long digital detox.

517. The Global Virtual Choir Performance: Assembling a choir from singers worldwide to perform a piece remotely.

518. The DIY Rainwater Harvesting System: Building a system to collect and use rainwater at home, documenting the setup and benefits.

519. The One-Day Eco-Friendly Product Swap: Replacing everyday products with eco-friendly alternatives for a day.

520. The Homemade Natural Insect Repellent: Testing and sharing recipes for natural insect repellents that work.

521. The 24-Hour Homemade Boat Challenge: Designing, building, and testing a homemade boat within 24 hours.

522. The One-Week Artistic Collaboration Project: Artists collaborate on a piece remotely, sharing their creative process.

523. The DIY Home Insulation Techniques: Demonstrating ways to improve home insulation using DIY methods.

524. The One-Day Local History Hunt: Exploring and sharing lesser-known historical facts and locations in a community.
525. The Global Virtual Talent Show: Hosting a talent show with participants showcasing their skills online.
526. The 24-Hour Backyard Bio blitz: Identifying and documenting as many species as possible in a backyard within 24 hours.
527. The One-Week Handmade Gift Challenge: Crafting and giving a handmade gift each day for a week.
528. The DIY Smart Home Security System: Building and installing a basic smart home security system.
529. The 24-Hour Urban Exploration Marathon: Exploring and documenting hidden gems in a city over 24 hours.
530. The One-Month Craftsmanship Challenge: Learning and practicing a traditional craft for a month, sharing progress and products.
531. The International Virtual Book Reading: Authors and readers from around the world participate in a virtual book reading.
532. The DIY Natural Swimming Pond: Documenting the process of converting a backyard pool into a natural swimming pond.
533. The 24-Hour Zero-Carbon Footprint Challenge: Attempting to live with a zero-carbon footprint for 24 hours.
534. The One-Week Sustainable Fashion Challenge: Wearing and promoting sustainable fashion choices for a week.
535. The Global Virtual Science Fair: Students and hobbyists present their science projects in a virtual science fair.
536. The DIY Backyard Wildlife Sanctuary: Creating a sanctuary to attract and support local wildlife, documenting the process.
537. The 24-Hour Vintage Tech Revival: Using vintage technology for all tasks and entertainment for a day.
538. The One-Month Language Tutoring Exchange: Pairing up with a language tutor and documenting the learning exchange.
539. The International Dessert Baking Marathon: Baking and comparing desserts from around the world in a marathon baking session.
540. The DIY Wind-Powered Art Installation: Creating art installations powered by wind, showcasing the design and movement.
541. The 24-Hour Public Space Transformation: Revitalizing a local public space or park in 24 hours and documenting the process.

542. The DIY Miniature Greenhouse Project: Building a miniature greenhouse and tracking plant growth over time.

543. The Global Virtual Reality Adventure: Taking viewers on virtual reality adventures to explore wonders around the world.

544. The One-Week Zero Plastic Challenge: Avoiding all plastic use for a week and sharing alternatives and insights.

545. The Historical Document Deep Dive: Investigating and explaining the significance of a historical document in a fun, engaging way.

546. The International Virtual Jam Session: Musicians from different countries collaborate to create music together online.

547. The DIY Biofuel Experiment: Producing biofuel at home from waste and testing its use in engines or stoves.

548. The 24-Hour Homemade Toy Hackathon: Designing and creating innovative toys from household items in 24 hours.

549. The One-Month Meditation Journey: Documenting the effects of daily meditation on health and well-being over a month.

550. The Ultimate Recycled Robot Challenge: Building functional robots from recycled materials and showcasing their abilities.

551. The Global Cuisine Virtual Potluck: Participants from various countries prepare and share their traditional dishes online.

552. The DIY Off-Grid Solar System: Installing and testing a small, off-grid solar power system for home use.

553. The One-Week Living History Experiment: Living as if in a different historical era for a week and documenting the experience.

554. The 24-Hour City Bike Tour: Exploring and showcasing the highlights of a city by bike within 24 hours.

555. The International Online Film Club: Watching and discussing films from around the world with an online community.

556. The DIY Smart Gardening System: Creating a smart system for efficient home gardening, including automation and monitoring.

557. The One-Day Flash Fiction Challenge: Writing and publishing a piece of flash fiction within 24 hours.

558. The Global Handcraft Exchange: Crafting traditional handcrafts and exchanging them with participants from other countries.

559. The DIY Natural Makeup Challenge: Creating and applying makeup from natural, homemade ingredients.

560. The 24-Hour Virtual Museum Marathon: Visiting and reviewing virtual museums from around the world in 24 hours.

561. The One-Month Fitness and Nutrition Transformation: Documenting a comprehensive fitness and nutrition overhaul.

562. The Ultimate Upcycled Artwork: Creating a piece of art entirely from upcycled materials and documenting the creative process.

563. The 24-Hour Backyard Astronomy Event: Observing and documenting celestial events and objects from a backyard.

564. The One-Week Wilderness Craft Skills: Learning and practicing traditional wilderness crafts and survival skills.

565. The Global Virtual Choir and Orchestra: Assembling musicians and singers to perform a piece remotely, edited together.

566. The DIY Water Recycling System: Building a system to recycle greywater for home use and showcasing its impact.

567. The One-Day Digital Art Marathon: Creating and sharing digital art pieces on a specific theme for 24 hours.

568. The International Cooking Technique Tutorial: Teaching unique cooking techniques from various cultures.

569. The 24-Hour Mini Documentary Challenge: Producing a short documentary on a local topic or issue within 24 hours.

570. The DIY Tiny Eco-Home Build: Documenting the building process of a tiny, eco-friendly home from start to finish.

571. The One-Week Local Ingredient Cooking Challenge: Preparing meals using only ingredients sourced locally for a week.

572. The Global Virtual Craft Fair: Showcasing and selling handmade crafts from artisans around the world in a virtual fair.

573. The One-Month Renewable Energy Experiment: Using only renewable energy sources for a month and documenting the experience.

574. The 24-Hour Urban Permaculture Project: Starting and outlining the development of an urban permaculture garden in 24 hours.

575. The International Dance Tutorial Series: Learning and teaching dances from different cultures in a series of tutorials.

576. The DIY Aquaponics System Setup: Building and operating an aquaponics system to grow fish and plants together.

577. The One-Day Local History Road Trip: Exploring and sharing the history of local landmarks and sites in a day.

578. The Virtual Reality Space Exploration: Creating a VR experience that takes viewers on a tour of the solar system.

579. The 24-Hour Vegan Survival Challenge: Finding and preparing vegan food while camping or surviving in the wilderness.

580. The One-Week Handwriting Improvement Challenge: Practicing and improving handwriting with different techniques and tools.

581. The DIY Eco-Friendly Home Products: Making and using eco-friendly cleaning and personal care products at home.

582. The Global Virtual Yoga Retreat: Conducting a yoga retreat with participants joining from around the world online.

583. The One-Day Smartphone Film making Workshop: Teaching viewers how to create a short film using just a smartphone.

584. The International Virtual Language Learning Day: Learning basics of a new language with the help of native speakers online.

585. The DIY Home Energy Efficiency Audit: Conducting an energy audit at home and implementing changes to improve efficiency.

586. The One-Week Sustainable Living Vlog: Documenting a week of making sustainable choices in everyday life.

587. The Global Folk Tale Animation Project: Animating and sharing folk tales from different cultures.

588. The 24-Hour Micro adventure Challenge: Embarking on small, local adventures and sharing the experiences.

589. The One-Month Art Challenge: Creating a new piece of art every day for a month, using various mediums and techniques.

590. The Virtual Reality Educational Series: Developing VR content that educates on historical events, scientific concepts, or cultural practices.

591. The DIY Portable Solar Charger: Building a portable solar charger for devices and testing its effectiveness.

592. The 24-Hour Local Wildlife Documentary: Documenting the wildlife in a local area over the course of 24 hours.

593. The One-Week Water Conservation Challenge: Implementing water conservation techniques and measuring the impact.

594. The International Virtual Cooking Challenge: Cooking a meal with the same set of ingredients as someone from a different country.

595. The DIY Home Composting Guide: Starting and maintaining a composting system at home, with tips and troubleshooting.

596. The 24-Hour Zero-Emissions Day: Aiming to live a day with zero carbon emissions and sharing the experience.

597. The One-Week Cultural Immersion Project: Immersing in a different culture through food, music, language, and customs.

598. The Global Virtual Book Club: Reading and discussing a book chosen by international participants.

599. The DIY Bicycle Repair Workshop: Demonstrating how to perform common bicycle repairs and maintenance.

600. The One-Day Nature Photography Challenge: Capturing the beauty of nature in a local area within 24 hours.

601. The Urban Foraging Field Guide: Identifying and using edible plants found in an urban environment.

602. The 48-Hour Film Scoring Challenge: Composing a soundtrack for a short film within two days.

603. The One-Month Minimalist Fashion Experiment: Wearing a capsule wardrobe for a month and documenting the experience.

604. The DIY Solar Oven Bake-off: Competing to bake the best dish using only solar ovens.

605. The Virtual Reality Time Capsule: Creating a VR experience that captures life today for future generations to explore.

606. The 24-Hour Local Legends Investigation: Exploring and documenting the truth behind local myths and legends.

607. The International Virtual Pottery Class: Teaching and learning pottery-making techniques from around the world online.

608. The Zero-Waste Pet Care Guide: Tips and tricks for reducing waste while caring for pets.

609. The 360-Degree Wilderness Expedition: Documenting a wilderness adventure in 360-degree video.

610. The One-Week Homemade Musical Instruments Challenge: Creating and playing instruments made from everyday items.

611. The DIY Tiny Eco-Village: Starting a project to build a miniature sustainable community model.

612. The 24-Hour Street Art Creation: Designing and executing a piece of street art in a day.

613. The Global Virtual Magic Show: Magicians from different countries perform tricks and illusions online.

614. The One-Month Bodyweight Fitness Challenge: Documenting progress through a month-long bodyweight exercise routine.

615. The DIY Floating Garden Project: Building a floating garden for urban areas with limited green space.

616. The 24-Hour Off-the-Grid Challenge: Living a day without any connection to the grid and sharing the experience.

617. The One-Week Language Learning Bootcamp: Intensively learning the basics of a new language in a week.

618. The Global Virtual Reality Classroom: Teaching a subject in an immersive VR environment to students worldwide.

619. The DIY Eco-Friendly Furniture Design: Creating furniture from sustainable materials and showcasing the process.

620. The 24-Hour Wildlife Rescue Mission: Documenting the rescue and rehabilitation of local wildlife.

621. The One-Week Watercolor Landscape Challenge: Painting a different landscape every day for a week using watercolors.

622. The Virtual Reality Historical Battles: Recreating famous battles in VR to educate and engage viewers.

623. The 48-Hour Backpack Invention Marathon: Designing and creating a multifunctional backpack within two days.

624. The One-Month Plant-Based Diet Journey: Exploring the benefits and challenges of a plant-based diet for a month.

625. The DIY Backyard Observatory for Stargazing: Constructing a simple observatory for night sky observation and education.

626. The 24-Hour Urban Wildlife Documentary: Capturing the diversity of wildlife that thrives in urban settings.

627. The International Online Chess Tournament: Organizing a chess tournament with players from around the globe.

628. The One-Week Sustainable Transport Challenge: Using only sustainable modes of transport for a week.

629. The Virtual Reality Underwater Exploration: Creating a VR experience to explore coral reefs and marine life.

630. The DIY Natural Sunscreen Making: Crafting effective natural sunscreens and testing their sun protection factor.

631. The 24-Hour Guerrilla Gardening Mission: Secretly beautifying neglected urban spaces with plants and flowers.

632. The One-Month Coding Project: Learning to code by building a simple application or website from scratch.

633. The Global Virtual Reality Art Gallery: Curating a virtual reality art exhibit featuring artists from around the world.

634. The 48-Hour Wilderness Survival Guide: Documenting essential survival skills while in a wilderness setting.

635. The One-Week Upcycled Home Decor Challenge: Transforming discarded items into stylish home decor.

636. The Virtual Reality Space Station Tour: Offering an immersive VR tour of the International Space Station.

637. The DIY Wind Turbine Challenge: Building a small wind turbine to generate electricity and documenting the build.

638. The 24-Hour Vegan Gourmet Challenge: Preparing gourmet vegan meals over the course of a day.

639. The One-Month Mindfulness Meditation Experiment: Practicing mindfulness meditation daily and sharing insights and benefits.

640. The Global Virtual Reality Film Festival: Showcasing short films from around the world in a virtual reality format.

641. The DIY Bicycle-Powered Water Pump: Creating a water pump powered by pedaling a bicycle.

642. The 24-Hour Flash Mob Planning and Execution: Organizing and carrying out a flash mob in less than 24 hours.

643. The One-Week Zero-Electricity Living Challenge: Living without electricity for a week to explore alternative living practices.

644. The Virtual Reality Cultural Heritage Tour: Preserving and exploring cultural heritage sites in VR.

645. The DIY Sustainable Kitchen Guide: Implementing sustainable practices in the kitchen and reducing food waste.

646. The 24-Hour Backyard Biome Mapping: Identifying and cataloging the biodiversity found in a backyard.

647. The One-Month Fitness Tracker Experiment: Using a fitness tracker to monitor and improve health over a month.

648. The Virtual Reality Astronaut Training Experience: Simulating astronaut training exercises in virtual reality.

649. The DIY Rain Garden Project: Creating a rain garden to improve water drainage and support local ecosystems.

650. The 24-Hour Homemade Board Game Marathon: Designing and playing homemade board games for 24 hours.

651. The One-Day Urban Beekeeping Experience: Exploring the basics of urban beekeeping and its impact on local ecosystems.

652. The 48-Hour Tiny House Design Challenge: Designing and planning a tiny house using sustainable materials and methods.

653. The Global Virtual Reality Sports Tournament: Hosting a virtual sports tournament with participants competing from their own locations.

654. The DIY Eco-Friendly Toy Design: Creating and testing toys made from environmentally friendly materials.

655. The 24-Hour Local Folklore Podcast: Producing a podcast that explores local folklore, myths, and legends in 24 hours.

656. The One-Month Public Speaking Journey: Documenting the process of overcoming public speaking fears through daily challenges.

657. The Virtual Reality Deep Sea Exploration: Developing a VR experience that takes viewers on a journey to explore deep-sea environments.

658. The DIY Portable Solar Light: Building and testing a portable solar light for use in off-grid situations.

659. The 24-Hour City Park Biodiversity Survey: Conducting a biodiversity survey in an urban park and documenting findings.

660. The One-Week Handmade Paper Crafting: Exploring various techniques of handmade paper crafting and creating unique artworks.

661. The Global Virtual Reality Architecture Tour: Showcasing architectural marvels from around the world in VR.

662. The DIY Recycled Material Greenhouse: Building a functional greenhouse from recycled materials and documenting the process.

663. The 24-Hour Street Photography Marathon: Capturing the essence of a city through street photography over 24 hours.

664. The One-Month Alternative Energy Experiment: Using and evaluating different alternative energy sources for a month.

665. The Virtual Reality Ancient Civilization Exploration: Creating a VR experience that allows users to explore ancient civilizations.

666. The DIY Bicycle Camper Trailer: Designing and building a lightweight camper trailer towable by a bicycle.

667. The 24-Hour Local Artisan Collaboration: Collaborating with local artisans to create unique pieces within 24 hours.

668. The One-Week Wilderness Photography Expedition: Documenting a journey through wilderness areas to capture stunning landscapes and wildlife.

669. The Global Virtual Reality Cooking Class: Teaching traditional cooking techniques from various cultures in VR.

670. The DIY Urban Vertical Farm: Setting up a small-scale vertical farm in an urban setting and tracking its development.

671. The 24-Hour Zero-Waste Challenge in a City: Attempting to live a zero-waste lifestyle in an urban environment for 24 hours.

672. The One-Month Language Revival Challenge: Immersing in and learning a language that is endangered or less commonly spoken.

673. The Virtual Reality Planetarium Experience: Creating a VR experience that simulates a visit to a planetarium, showcasing constellations and celestial events.

674. The DIY Smart Irrigation System: Developing a smart irrigation system that conserves water by using IoT technology.

675. The 24-Hour Improvised Music Creation: Collaborating with musicians to create and record music using improvised instruments.

676. The One-Week Eco-Friendly Fashion Challenge: Wearing and promoting eco-friendly and sustainable fashion choices for a week.

677. The Virtual Reality Wildlife Safari: Designing a VR experience that simulates a wildlife safari in various ecosystems.

678. The DIY Natural Swimming Pool Conversion: Transforming a traditional swimming pool into a natural swimming pool and documenting the process.

679. The 24-Hour Historical Reenactment Vlog: Living as someone from a historical period for 24 hours and vlogging the experience.

680. The One-Month Tiny Living Experiment: Documenting the challenges and benefits of living in a tiny space for a month.

681. The Global Virtual Reality Music Festival: Hosting a music festival in VR with performances from artists across different genres and countries.

682. The DIY Compost Bin Design Challenge: Designing and building an efficient and easy-to-use compost bin.

683. The 24-Hour Urban Homesteading Project: Starting an urban homesteading project and documenting the initial steps and challenges.

684. The One-Week DIY Furniture Upcycling: Transforming old furniture into new, functional pieces through creative upcycling techniques.

685. The Virtual Reality Ocean Cleanup Game: Developing a VR game that educates players about ocean pollution and cleanup efforts.

686. The DIY Foldable Solar Panel Project: Creating a foldable solar panel for portable energy generation.

687. The 24-Hour Mini Documentary on Local Heroes: Producing a mini-documentary that highlights local heroes making a difference in the community.

688. The One-Month Artisanal Craft Mastery: Learning and mastering an artisanal craft, such as pottery or blacksmithing, over a month.

689. The Global Virtual Reality Art Collaboration: Artists from around the world collaborate on a piece of art in VR.

690. The DIY Sustainable Rainwater Harvesting System: Installing a rainwater harvesting system to collect and use rainwater efficiently.

691. The 24-Hour City Bike Repair Station Setup: Setting up temporary bike repair stations across a city and documenting the impact.

692. The One-Week Wilderness Survival Skills Course: Learning and practicing wilderness survival skills over a week-long course.

693. The Virtual Reality Spacewalk Experience: Creating a VR experience that simulates the feeling of a spacewalk outside the International Space Station.

694. The DIY Eco-Friendly Packaging Solutions: Designing and testing eco-friendly packaging solutions for everyday products.

695. The 24-Hour Local Cuisine Cooking Marathon: Preparing and showcasing local cuisine dishes within 24 hours.

696. The One-Month Fitness and Mindfulness Retreat at Home: Hosting a virtual retreat focused on fitness, mindfulness, and healthy living.

697. The Virtual Reality Historical Reenactment: Recreating a historical event or period in VR for educational purposes.

698. The DIY Bicycle Generator for Emergency Power: Building a bicycle generator that can be used to generate emergency power.

699. The 24-Hour Flash Fiction Writing and Publishing: Writing, illustrating, and publishing a piece of flash fiction in 24 hours.

700. The One-Week Portable Greenhouse Experiment: Building a portable greenhouse and documenting its effects on plant growth.

701. The DIY Air Quality Monitoring Station: Building a station to monitor air quality in your neighborhood and analyzing the data.

702. The 24-Hour Urban Accessibility Challenge: Exploring and documenting accessibility challenges in a city and proposing solutions.

703. The One-Month Sustainable Eating Plan: Documenting the journey of eating sustainably sourced food for a month.

704. The Virtual Reality Cultural Festivals Tour: Experiencing and showcasing cultural festivals around the world through VR.

705. The DIY Kinetic Energy Devices: Creating devices that convert kinetic energy into usable power and testing their efficiency.

706. The 24-Hour Homemade Natural Detergent Making: Crafting and testing the effectiveness of homemade natural laundry detergents.

707. The One-Week Alternative Transportation Experiment: Using only alternative forms of transportation for a week and documenting the experience.

708. The Virtual Reality Deep Space Exploration: Developing a VR experience that takes viewers on exploratory missions through deep space.

709. The DIY Upcycled Art Installation: Creating a large-scale art installation from upcycled materials and documenting the process.

710. The 24-Hour Local Heritage Video Project: Creating short videos that highlight the unique heritage and history of local communities.

711. The One-Month Eco-Friendly Living Challenge: Attempting to live as eco-friendly as possible for a month and sharing tips and experiences.

712. The Global Virtual Reality Language Learning: Using VR to immerse in language learning environments and documenting the progress.

713. The DIY Portable Clean Energy Generator: Building a portable generator that uses clean energy sources and testing its capabilities.

714. The 24-Hour Wildlife Conservation Awareness Campaign: Creating and executing a campaign to raise awareness about local wildlife conservation efforts.

715. The One-Week Digital Art Challenge Using Open Source Software: Creating digital art using only open-source software and sharing daily creations.

716. The Virtual Reality Ancient World Reconstructions: Reconstructing ancient world sites in VR and providing educational tours.

717. The DIY Bicycle-Powered Charging Station: Designing and building a charging station powered by pedaling a bicycle.

718. The 24-Hour Community Art Project: Engaging the community to create a collaborative art project in 24 hours.

719. The One-Month Zero-Waste Household Challenge: Documenting the journey towards achieving a zero-waste household in a month.

720. The Global Virtual Reality Science Lab: Conducting science experiments in a VR laboratory and sharing the educational content.

721. The DIY Smart Home Energy System: Creating a smart system for monitoring and optimizing home energy use.

722. The 24-Hour Vintage Tech Restoration: Restoring a piece of vintage technology and exploring its history and impact.

723. The One-Week Wilderness Ethnobotany Series: Learning and sharing knowledge about the use of plants for medicinal and nutritional purposes in the wilderness.

724. The Virtual Reality Ocean Conservation Experience: Creating a VR experience to educate about ocean conservation issues and efforts.

725. The DIY Sustainable Water Filtration System: Building and testing a water filtration system using sustainable materials.

726. The 24-Hour City Soundtrack Project: Capturing and composing a soundtrack that represents the sounds of a city within 24 hours.

727. The One-Month Fitness Challenge With Community Impact: Organizing a fitness challenge that also benefits the local community or a charity.

728. The Virtual Reality Astronomical Events Viewing: Offering a VR experience to view and learn about astronomical events like eclipses and meteor showers.

729. The DIY Recycled Material Sculpture: Creating sculptures from recycled materials and showcasing the creative process and outcomes.

730. The 24-Hour Local Unsolved Mysteries Documentary: Investigating and documenting an unsolved mystery in the local area.

731. The One-Week Living with AI Assistants Experiment: Integrating AI assistants into daily life for a week and documenting the experience and challenges.

732. The Virtual Reality Escape Room Design Challenge: Designing and creating an escape room experience in VR.

733. The DIY Eco-Friendly Insulation Materials Test: Experimenting with different eco-friendly materials for home insulation.

734. The 24-Hour Public Space Reimagining: Designing and presenting ideas to reimagine and repurpose a public space for community use.

735. The One-Month Homemade Beauty Products Experiment: Creating and using homemade beauty products for a month and evaluating the results.

736. The Global Virtual Reality Meditation Sessions: Hosting meditation sessions in VR settings from around the world.

737. The DIY Hand-Powered Water Pump: Constructing a hand-powered pump for water and testing its effectiveness in different settings.

738. The 24-Hour Flash Animation Challenge: Creating a short animation from concept to completion within 24 hours.

739. The One-Week Urban Gardening Bootcamp: Teaching viewers how to start and maintain an urban garden over the course of a week.

740. The Virtual Reality Cultural Immersion Experience: Creating a VR experience that immerses viewers in different cultural practices and environments.

741. The 24-Hour Urban Renewal Project: Documenting a rapid urban improvement project, from planning to execution, focusing on sustainability and community involvement.

742. The One-Month Craftsmanship Challenge: Mastering a new craft or traditional skill over a month, documenting the learning process, challenges, and final creations.

743. The DIY Bioluminescent Garden: Creating a garden that glows at night using bioluminescent plants or microbial lights, detailing the setup and maintenance.

744. The Virtual Reality Exploration of Microscopic Worlds: Developing a VR experience that takes viewers on a journey through microscopic environments, revealing the beauty of the unseen world.

745. The 24-Hour Local Myth Busting Marathon: Investigating and debunking or confirming local myths and legends within 24 hours, using science and research.

746. The One-Week Portable Solar Cooker Challenge: Designing, building, and cooking with a portable solar cooker for a week, testing different recipes and efficiency.

747. The Global Virtual Reality Geography Quiz: Hosting an interactive geography quiz in VR, challenging participants with locations and facts from around the world.

748. The DIY Smart Recycling Bin: Building a smart recycling bin that sorts recyclables automatically, documenting the technology and build process.

749. The 24-Hour Community Mosaic Artwork: Collaborating with the community to create a large-scale mosaic artwork in a public space, capturing the process and the story behind the art.

750. The One-Month Off-Grid Living Experiment: Living off-grid for a month, documenting the preparation, challenges, adjustments, and insights gained from the experience.

751. The Virtual Reality Time Travel Adventure: Creating a VR series that takes viewers on historical adventures, offering immersive experiences of different eras and events.

752. The DIY Water Filtration and Purification Experiment: Testing and comparing homemade water filtration and purification methods, analyzing effectiveness and practicality.

753. The 24-Hour Guerrilla Greening Initiative: Secretly transforming neglected urban spaces into green, plant-filled areas overnight, documenting the planning, execution, and community reactions.

754. The One-Week Traditional Boat Building Journey: Building a traditional boat using age-old techniques and materials, detailing the craftsmanship, history, and sailing capabilities.

755. The Global Virtual Reality Cultural Exchange: Facilitating a cultural exchange program in VR, where participants can share and experience different cultures, traditions, and stories.

756. The DIY Atmospheric Water Generator: Constructing a device that extracts water from the air, documenting the build process, the science behind it, and its effectiveness.

757. The 24-Hour Pop-Up Public Library Project: Setting up a temporary public library in a community, highlighting the importance of reading and access to books.

758. The One-Month Renewable Energy Challenge: Utilizing only renewable energy sources for all personal or household energy needs for a month, sharing experiences, challenges, and impacts.

759. The Virtual Reality Underwater Coral Reef Restoration Tour: Offering an educational VR tour of coral reef restoration projects, highlighting the importance of marine conservation.

760. The DIY Eco-Friendly Home Cleaning Products: Creating a range of homemade, natural cleaning products, demonstrating recipes, usage, and effectiveness comparisons.

761. The 24-Hour City-wide Scavenger Hunt for History: Organizing a scavenger hunt that guides participants through historical landmarks and hidden history in a city.

762. The One-Week Living Like a Historical Figure Challenge: Emulating the lifestyle, habits, and routines of a historical figure for a week, reflecting on the experience and historical insights.

763. The Global Virtual Reality Space Camp: Hosting an educational space camp in VR, teaching participants about astronomy, space exploration, and the science of space.

764. The DIY Vertical Axis Wind Turbine Project: Building a vertical axis wind turbine for residential use, documenting the design, construction, and performance analysis.

765. The 24-Hour Flash Gardening Makeover: Transforming a public or community space with a garden makeover in just 24 hours, promoting green spaces and community involvement.

766. The One-Month Culinary World Tour Challenge: Cooking and eating dishes from a different country each day for a month, exploring global cuisines and culinary traditions.

767. The Virtual Reality Exploration of Extinct Ecosystems: Creating VR experiences that allow users to explore ecosystems from Earth's past, understanding extinct species and lost environments.

768. The DIY Passive Solar Heating Solutions: Designing and implementing passive solar heating projects for home warmth, showcasing different techniques and their effectiveness.

769. The 24-Hour Art from Waste Challenge: Creating art exclusively from waste materials within 24 hours, promoting recycling and creativity in sustainability.

770. The One-Week Wilderness Tracking and Nature Observation: Learning and practicing wildlife tracking and nature observation skills in a wilderness setting, sharing findings and experiences.

771. The 24-Hour Urban Survival Skills Workshop: Teaching essential urban survival skills and hacks within a day, including navigation, resource finding, and emergency preparedness.

772. The One-Month Minimalist Art Challenge: Creating daily art pieces using minimalist techniques, focusing on the concept of "less is more" and documenting the creative journey.

773. The Virtual Reality Exploration of Future Cities: Designing and exploring futuristic city concepts in VR, emphasizing sustainability, technology, and community living.

774. The DIY Smart Window Farming System: Building a window farming system that uses IoT technology for urban agriculture, detailing setup, plant growth, and tech integration.

775. The 24-Hour Local Culture Immersion Experience: Immersing in a local culture through food, music, dance, and traditions for 24 hours and sharing insights and learnings.

776. The One-Week Portable Tiny Home Adventure: Documenting the experience of living in a portable tiny home for a week, exploring different locations and minimalist living.

777. The Virtual Reality Wildlife Tracking and Conservation: Creating a VR experience that teaches wildlife tracking skills and highlights conservation efforts.

778. The DIY Upcycled Musical Instruments Project: Crafting musical instruments from upcycled materials and demonstrating their sound and musical capabilities.

779. The 24-Hour Historical Costume Creation: Designing and creating historical costumes within 24 hours, showcasing the research, design process, and final fitting.

780. The One-Month Off-the-Beaten-Path Travel Vlog: Exploring lesser-known travel destinations for a month, focusing on culture, nature, and sustainable tourism practices.

781. The Virtual Reality Ancient Crafts Workshop: Offering VR workshops on ancient crafts, allowing users to learn and practice skills like pottery, weaving, or blacksmithing.

782. The DIY Bicycle-Powered Home Appliances: Developing home appliances powered by bicycle pedaling, such as a washing machine or grinder, and evaluating their efficiency.

783. The 24-Hour Eco-Friendly Product Design Sprint: Designing and prototyping an eco-friendly product in 24 hours, focusing on sustainability and practicality.

784. The One-Week Community Art Collaboration: Collaborating with local artists and community members to create a communal art project, documenting the process and community impact.

785. The Virtual Reality Deep Jungle Exploration: Guiding viewers on a VR exploration of deep jungle ecosystems, highlighting biodiversity and conservation issues.

786. The DIY Home Greywater Recycling System: Installing a system to recycle greywater for garden irrigation or other non-potable uses, documenting the process and impact.

787. The 24-Hour Heritage Craft Marathon: Learning and practicing a heritage craft for 24 hours, such as basket weaving, leather working, or traditional woodworking.

788. The One-Month Fitness Transformation with Local Sports: Engaging in different local sports and fitness practices around the world for a month, exploring cultural approaches to fitness.

789. The Virtual Reality Space Colony Design Challenge: Creating and touring virtual space colonies, focusing on architectural design, sustainability, and livability in space.

790. The DIY Natural Light Enhancement Solutions: Experimenting with ways to enhance natural light in homes using reflective surfaces, strategic placements, and DIY projects.

791. The 24-Hour Public Speaking and Storytelling Festival: Organizing a festival that showcases public speaking and storytelling talents, including workshops and live performances.

792. The One-Week Wilderness Craft and Art Project: Merging art and wilderness survival skills to create nature-inspired crafts and artworks, documenting the inspiration and process.

793. The Virtual Reality Time-Lapse Earth Journey: Offering a VR experience that showcases time-lapse changes of the Earth's landscapes, climate, and human impact over centuries.

794. The DIY Energy-Efficient Cooking Devices: Designing and testing energy-efficient cooking devices, such as solar cookers or insulated cooking bags.

795. The 24-Hour Community Skill-Share Event: Hosting a community event where people share and learn skills from each other, from cooking and gardening to coding and crafting.

796. The One-Month Cultural Exchange Diary with a Twist: Participating in a cultural exchange program with a focus on unusual or niche cultural practices, documenting the unique experiences.

797. The Virtual Reality Ocean Floor Exploration: Creating a VR journey to explore the ocean floor, including shipwrecks, marine life, and underwater geography.

798. The DIY Compact Home Office Solutions: Designing and building compact, multifunctional home office setups that maximize small spaces.

799. The 24-Hour Flash Nonfiction Writing Challenge: Writing and publishing a piece of flash nonfiction within 24 hours, focusing on personal stories, travel experiences, or cultural insights.

800. The One-Week DIY Eco-Friendly Beauty Routine: Switching to a completely DIY, eco-friendly beauty routine for a week, documenting the preparation, usage, and effects on skin and hair.

801. The 24-Hour Upcycled Fashion Show: Designing and hosting a fashion show featuring outfits made entirely from upcycled materials, highlighting creativity and environmental awareness.

802. The One-Month Micro green Gardening Journey: Documenting the process of growing various micro greens at home, sharing tips, recipes, and the health benefits observed.

803. The Virtual Reality Lost Civilizations Exploration: Creating a VR series that allows viewers to explore ancient, lost civilizations, uncovering their mysteries and achievements.

804. The DIY Backyard Biotope Creation: Building a backyard biotope to support local wildlife, documenting the design, construction, and the species it attracts over time.

805. The 24-Hour Community Help-a-thon: Organizing a day dedicated to community service, where participants help with various local projects and document the impact.

806. The One-Week Traditional Cooking Techniques Challenge: Learning and practicing traditional cooking techniques from around the world for a week, sharing the history and outcomes.

807. The Virtual Reality Extreme Weather Experiences: Developing VR experiences that simulate extreme weather conditions, educating viewers on weather phenomena and safety measures.

808. The DIY Solar-Powered Gadgets Project: Creating a series of small, useful gadgets powered by solar energy, showcasing the build process and their practical applications.

809. The 24-Hour City Beautification Project: Collaborating with local artists and volunteers to beautify a part of the city with murals, plantings, and clean-ups in just 24 hours.

810. The One-Month Sustainable Transport Experiment: Using only sustainable modes of transportation for all travel needs for a month, documenting experiences and environmental impact.

811. The Virtual Reality Dinosaur Park Adventure: Offering an educational VR adventure through a park filled with dinosaurs, combining fun with paleontological facts.

812. The DIY Rainwater Collection and Usage System: Setting up a system to collect and use rainwater at home, detailing the construction, benefits, and water-saving results.

813. The 24-Hour Zero-Electricity Cooking Challenge: Cooking without electricity for 24 hours using alternative methods like solar cookers, wood fires, or biogas.

814. The One-Week Handwritten Letter Exchange: Reviving the art of handwritten letters by exchanging daily letters with a friend or follower for a week, sharing the experience.

815. The Virtual Reality Space Repair Mission: Simulating a space repair mission in VR, teaching viewers about space technology, the challenges of spacewalks, and satellite maintenance.

816. The DIY Eco-Friendly Air Cooler Project: Building an eco-friendly, low-energy air cooler, demonstrating the DIY process, and evaluating its cooling effectiveness.

817. The 24-Hour Local Language Immersion: Immersing in a local or minority language for 24 hours, attempting to learn and communicate, and highlighting the importance of language preservation.

818. The One-Month Off-Grid Cooking Series: Preparing meals using off-grid cooking methods such as solar ovens and fire pits for a month, sharing recipes and techniques.

819. The Virtual Reality Coral Reef Restoration Tour: Creating a VR experience that takes viewers on a tour of coral reef restoration projects, highlighting conservation efforts.

820. The DIY Bicycle Repair and Customization Workshop: Hosting a workshop on repairing and customizing bicycles, encouraging cycling as a sustainable transport option.

821. The 24-Hour Public Art Installation Challenge: Designing and installing a piece of public art in a community space within 24 hours, focusing on themes of unity or environmentalism.

822. The One-Week Wilderness Film making Adventure: Documenting the challenges and beauty of wilderness film making, from capturing wildlife to adapting to unpredictable conditions.

823. The Virtual Reality Ancient Artisan Workshops: Crafting VR experiences that teach traditional artisan skills from ancient cultures, such as pottery, weaving, or metalworking.

824. The DIY Home Biofuel Production: Exploring the process of producing biofuel at home from waste materials, documenting the methodology, safety, and outcomes.

825. The 24-Hour Sustainable Living Vlog: Living sustainably for 24 hours, highlighting challenges, solutions, and the impact of small changes on daily environmental footprint.

826. The One-Month Cultural Documentary Series: Creating a series of short documentaries that explore different cultural practices, celebrations, and lifestyles around the world.

827. The Virtual Reality Under-the-Sea Music Concert: Hosting a music concert in a VR underwater setting, combining visual and auditory elements for a unique environmental message.

828. The DIY Vertical Windmill for Urban Energy: Building a vertical windmill suitable for urban environments, focusing on the design, efficiency, and potential energy savings.

829. The 24-Hour Flash Eco-Adventure Race: Organizing a race that combines physical challenges with eco-friendly missions, like planting trees or cleaning up natural sites.

830. The One-Week Living History Experience: Living according to the customs, technologies, and daily routines of a specific historical period for a week, documenting the insights gained.

831. The 48-Hour Silent Retreat in Nature: Documenting the experience of a silent retreat in a natural setting, focusing on mindfulness and nature's impact on well-being.

832. The One-Month Zero-Sugar Lifestyle Challenge: Trying a zero-sugar diet for a month, documenting the health effects, challenges, and creative recipe adaptations.

833. The DIY Portable Tiny Home on Wheels Tour: Showcasing the design, construction, and lifestyle in a self-built portable tiny home, including tips for living minimally and sustainably.

834. The 24-Hour Urban Foraging and Cooking Adventure: Identifying edible plants in an urban environment and preparing a meal with foraged ingredients, highlighting urban ecology.

835. The Virtual Reality Tour of the Human Body: Creating an educational VR experience that takes viewers on a journey through the human body, explaining physiology and health.

836. The One-Week Wilderness Living Skills Course: Sharing daily lessons on essential wilderness living skills, from fire-making and shelter-building to water sourcing and navigation.

837. The Global Online Music Collaboration Project: Bringing together musicians from different countries to collaborate on a song remotely, showcasing the creative process and cultural fusion.

838. The DIY Eco-Friendly Insulation Techniques for Homes: Demonstrating how to insulate a home using eco-friendly and sustainable materials, with a focus on DIY methods and cost-effectiveness.

839. The 24-Hour Back-to-Basics Farming Challenge: Spending a day living and working on a farm using traditional farming techniques, reflecting on the connection to food and land.

840. The One-Month Language Learning Sprint: Documenting the intensive process of learning as much of a new language as possible in one month, using various methods and tools.

841. The Virtual Reality Exploration of Mars: Offering viewers a VR journey across the Martian landscape, highlighting scientific discoveries and the potential for future colonization.

842. The DIY Solar Water Heating System Installation: Installing a solar water heating system from scratch, explaining the mechanics, benefits, and energy savings.

843. The 24-Hour City Bike Path Exploration: Exploring and reviewing the bike paths in a city within 24 hours, promoting cycling as a sustainable and healthy mode of transportation.

844. The One-Week Traditional Fishing Techniques Experiment: Learning and practicing traditional fishing techniques from around the world for a week, exploring cultural and environmental aspects.

845. The Virtual Reality Ghost Town Exploration: Creating a VR experience that allows users to explore and learn about abandoned ghost towns, their history, and the stories they hold.

846. The DIY Wind-Powered Generator Build: Constructing a wind-powered generator and documenting the build process, efficiency tests, and how it integrates into home energy use.

847. The 24-Hour Homemade Natural Cosmetics Workshop: Making a range of natural cosmetics from scratch in 24 hours, including soaps, creams, and makeup, highlighting health and environmental benefits.

848. The One-Month Off-the-Grid Solar Challenge: Living off the grid using only solar power for all energy needs for a month, documenting the setup, challenges, and lifestyle adjustments.

849. The Virtual Reality Antarctic Expedition: Taking viewers on a virtual expedition to Antarctica, showcasing its unique ecosystems, wildlife, and research activities.

850. The DIY Tiny Aquaponics System Setup: Building a small-scale aquaponics system suitable for urban homes or apartments, documenting the process, maintenance, and growth outcomes.

851. The 24-Hour Local Craftsmen and Artisans Tour: Visiting local craftsmen and artisans within 24 hours, showcasing their skills, products, and the importance of preserving traditional crafts.

852. The One-Week Sustainable Fashion Creation: Designing and creating sustainable fashion pieces over a week, using recycled materials and eco-friendly processes.

853. The Virtual Reality Space Station Life Simulation: Simulating life aboard the International Space Station in VR, including daily routines, scientific experiments, and the challenges of living in space.

854. The DIY Home Biogas System for Waste Recycling: Building a biogas system to recycle organic waste into energy at home, documenting the construction, operation, and benefits.

855. The 24-Hour Flash Animation Creation Marathon: Creating a short animation from concept to completion within 24 hours, focusing on a timely theme or social message.

856. The One-Month Clean Water Access Project: Documenting the process of improving access to clean water in a community, including the challenges faced and solutions implemented.

857. The Virtual Reality Deep-Sea Adventure to Sunken Ships: Exploring sunken ships and underwater mysteries in VR, combining historical facts with immersive visuals.

858. The DIY Permaculture Garden Setup: Establishing a permaculture garden, documenting the design principles, planting strategies, and the ecosystem's development over time.

859. The 24-Hour Urban Art Installation with Recycled Materials: Creating and installing a piece of public art using recycled materials in an urban setting, promoting sustainability and community engagement.

860. The One-Week Homemade Instrument Music Challenge: Crafting homemade musical instruments and using them to compose and record music over a week, showcasing creativity and innovation.

861. The Virtual Reality Journey Through the Solar System: Developing an educational VR experience that takes users on a tour of the solar system, providing detailed information about each planet.

862. The DIY Sustainable Home Cooling Solutions: Exploring and implementing sustainable cooling solutions for homes, documenting effectiveness, cost, and environmental impact.

863. The 24-Hour Wildlife Documentary in a Local Park: Producing a short documentary on the wildlife found in a local park within 24 hours, highlighting biodiversity in urban areas.

864. The One-Month Artisan Bread Making Journey: Documenting the process of learning to make various types of artisan bread from scratch, sharing techniques, recipes, and taste tests.

865. The Virtual Reality Reconstruction of Historical Battles: Creating VR experiences that reconstruct historical battles, offering educational content on military history and tactics.

866. The DIY Recycled Rain Garden Project: Constructing a rain garden using recycled materials to manage stormwater runoff, documenting the design, build, and environmental benefits.

867. The 24-Hour Zero-Waste Challenge in a Small Town: Attempting to live zero-waste for 24 hours in a small town, exploring local challenges and solutions to waste reduction.

868. The One-Week Digital Nomad Experiment in a Remote Location: Living and working as a digital nomad in a remote location for a week, documenting connectivity challenges, productivity, and lifestyle changes.

869. The Virtual Reality Exploration of Volcanoes: Offering an immersive VR experience that explores active and dormant volcanoes, educating viewers on geology and volcanic activity.

870. The DIY Home Energy Audit and Improvement Project: Conducting a home energy audit and implementing improvements to increase energy efficiency, documenting the process and results.

871. The 24-Hour Sustainable Urban Design Hackathon: Hosting a hackathon to generate sustainable urban design solutions within 24 hours, focusing on issues like green spaces, transportation, and housing.

872. The One-Month Cultural Dance Learning Challenge: Learning and practicing a new cultural dance every week for a month, exploring the history and significance of each dance.

873. The Virtual Reality Exploration of the Amazon Rainforest: Creating a VR journey through the Amazon rainforest, highlighting its biodiversity, conservation issues, and the impact of deforestation.

874. The DIY Mobile App Development for Social Good: Developing a mobile app from scratch that addresses a social or environmental issue, documenting the coding process, challenges, and user feedback.

875. The 24-Hour Edible Urban Garden Setup: Transforming a small urban space into an edible garden in 24 hours, focusing on container gardening, vertical farming, and sustainable practices.

876. The One-Week Wilderness Kayaking Expedition Vlog: Documenting a week-long kayaking expedition through wilderness areas, focusing on nature, challenges, and environmental awareness.

877. The Virtual Reality Journey Inside a Painting: Creating a VR experience that allows users to step inside famous paintings, exploring the art and the story behind it.

878. The DIY Eco-Friendly Personal Care Products: Making a range of eco-friendly personal care products, such as shampoo bars, deodorants, and toothpaste, sharing recipes and testing results.

879. The 24-Hour Citywide Kindness Campaign: Organizing and documenting a series of kindness initiatives across a city in 24 hours, from free hugs and compliments to community service projects.

880. The One-Month Journey of Building a Community Library: Documenting the process of creating a community library, from gathering donations and organizing books to the grand opening.

881. The Virtual Reality Exploration of Underwater Caves: Offering an immersive VR experience that takes viewers on explorations of underwater caves, emphasizing marine biology and cave formations.

882. The DIY Tiny Home Building Series for Sustainable Living: A series documenting the step-by-step process of building a tiny home for sustainable living, covering design, construction, and lifestyle adjustments.

883. The 24-Hour Homemade Wind Turbine Challenge: Designing, building, and testing a homemade wind turbine within 24 hours, focusing on renewable energy education and DIY skills.

884. The One-Week Culinary Herb Garden Project: Starting a culinary herb garden, documenting the selection, planting, care, and culinary uses of various herbs.

885. The Virtual Reality Ghost Hunting Experience: Creating a VR experience that simulates ghost hunting in haunted locations, blending history, folklore, and paranormal investigation.

886. The DIY Water-Saving Irrigation System for Gardens: Developing and installing a water-saving irrigation system for gardens, focusing on efficiency, cost-saving, and environmental impact.

887. The 24-Hour Public Space Transformation for Play: Transforming a public space into a playful, interactive area for children and adults within 24 hours, promoting playfulness in urban design.

888. The One-Month Off-Grid Internet Challenge: Exploring alternative methods of accessing the internet while living off-grid for a month, documenting connectivity solutions and lifestyle impacts.

889. The Virtual Reality Journey Through the Human Mind: Designing a VR experience that navigates through the human mind, illustrating concepts of psychology, consciousness, and mental health.

890. The DIY Natural Pest Control Solutions for Gardens: Testing and sharing effective natural pest control solutions for home gardens, focusing on organic and eco-friendly methods.

891. The 24-Hour Flash Volunteerism Event: Organizing a spontaneous volunteer event to address community needs within 24 hours, showcasing the power of collective action.

892. The One-Week Homemade Pasta Making Marathon: Making a different type of homemade pasta each day for a week, exploring various recipes, shapes, and sauces.

893. The Virtual Reality Tour of the International Space Station: Providing an educational VR tour of the ISS, detailing its modules, the life of astronauts, and the science conducted aboard.

894. The DIY Urban Cooling Solutions Project: Implementing urban cooling solutions, such as green roofs and shade structures, to combat heat islands, documenting the process and temperature differences.

895. The 24-Hour International Cuisine Cooking Challenge: Preparing dishes from a different country every hour for 24 hours, exploring global cuisines and cooking techniques.

896. The One-Month Journey to Self-Sufficiency: Attempting to live as self-sufficiently as possible for a month, covering food production, energy generation, and waste reduction.

897. The Virtual Reality Exploration of the Arctic: Creating a VR experience that takes viewers on an educational journey through the Arctic, focusing on climate change and ecosystem preservation.

898. The DIY Bicycle-Powered Home Systems: Building systems powered by bicycle pedaling, such as lighting or small appliances, to promote fitness and sustainability.

899. The 24-Hour Art Challenge Using Only Recycled Materials: Producing art pieces using solely recycled or repurposed materials within 24 hours, emphasizing creativity in sustainability.

900. The One-Week Living With Robots Challenge: Integrating various robots into daily life for a week, documenting interactions, efficiencies, and challenges faced.

901. The Virtual Reality Walk Through Historical Events: Creating immersive VR experiences that allow users to walk through key historical events, providing educational content in an engaging format.

902. The DIY Compact Living Solutions for Small Spaces: Designing and implementing compact living solutions to maximize space in small apartments or homes, including foldable furniture and smart storage.

903. The 24-Hour Sustainable City Design Marathon: Collaborating with architects, urban planners, and the community to design a sustainable city layout within 24 hours, focusing on green spaces, energy efficiency, and public transportation.

904. The One-Month Ethical Fashion Journey: Exploring ethical fashion by wearing, reviewing, and creating clothing that is sustainable, fair trade, and environmentally friendly for a month.

905. The Virtual Reality Brain Teasers and Puzzle Rooms: Developing VR puzzle rooms and brain teasers that challenge users' problem-solving skills in immersive environments.

906. The DIY Off-Grid Lighting Solutions: Creating and testing off-grid lighting solutions, such as solar lanterns or oil lamps, focusing on accessibility and sustainability.

907. The 24-Hour Local Wildlife Documentary Project: Filming and producing a documentary on local wildlife within 24 hours, highlighting biodiversity, conservation efforts, and urban wildlife interactions.

908. The One-Week Eco-Friendly Product Design Sprint: Designing and prototyping a new eco-friendly product each day for a week, focusing on innovation in sustainability.

909. The Virtual Reality Tour of Futuristic Homes: Showcasing futuristic home designs in VR, including smart technologies, sustainable materials, and innovative living spaces.

910. The DIY Bicycle-Powered Smoothie Stand: Setting up a smoothie stand powered by bicycle pedaling, promoting healthy eating and sustainable energy in a fun, interactive way.

911. The 24-Hour Indoor Microadventure Challenge: Creating an indoor adventure challenge, such as building a fort, indoor camping, or a treasure hunt, to encourage creativity and play.

912. The One-Month Journey Through Classical Literature: Reading and discussing a piece of classical literature each week for a month, exploring themes, historical context, and modern relevance.

913. The Virtual Reality Exploration of Microhabitats: Developing a VR experience that explores diverse microhabitats, educating viewers on ecosystems, biodiversity, and conservation.

914. The DIY Sustainable Pet Care Solutions: Creating sustainable pet care products and solutions, such as eco-friendly toys, bedding, and waste management, sharing DIY guides and benefits.

915. The 24-Hour Community Cooperative Setup: Documenting the setup of a community cooperative within 24 hours, focusing on collective resource sharing, community building, and sustainability.
916. The One-Week Wilderness Photography and Art Project: Combining wilderness photography with natural art creations, documenting the artistic process and the inspiration drawn from nature.
917. The Virtual Reality Trip to the Sun: Offering an educational VR experience that simulates a journey to the Sun, teaching about solar phenomena, energy, and the importance of the Sun to Earth.
918. The DIY Modular Furniture for Small Spaces: Designing and building modular furniture that can be easily reconfigured for various uses in small living spaces, sharing blueprints and assembly tips.
919. The 24-Hour Sustainable Cooking Fuel Challenge: Experimenting with different sustainable cooking fuels, such as biogas, ethanol, or solar, for 24 hours, comparing efficiency and environmental impact.
920. The One-Month Adventure in Learning a Musical Instrument: Documenting the journey of learning to play a new musical instrument from scratch in one month, sharing progress, challenges, and performances.
921. The Virtual Reality Walk Through Iconic Movie Sets: Creating a VR experience that allows users to explore and interact with sets from iconic movies, blending film history with immersive technology.
922. The DIY Water Conservation and Reuse in Gardening: Implementing water conservation and reuse strategies in gardening, such as rainwater harvesting and greywater systems, documenting setup and results.
923. The 24-Hour Build and Fly Your Own Kite Challenge: Designing, building, and flying kites within 24 hours, focusing on aerodynamics, creativity, and the physics of kite flying.
924. The One-Week Homemade Gourmet Pet Food Experiment: Preparing homemade gourmet meals for pets for a week, focusing on nutrition, pet preferences, and comparing it to commercial pet food.

925. The Virtual Reality Interactive Science Experiments: Developing interactive VR science experiments for education, allowing users to conduct virtual experiments in physics, chemistry, and biology.

926. The DIY Convertible and Multipurpose Furniture Project: Crafting furniture that can be converted for multiple purposes, such as a dining table that turns into a work desk, highlighting space-saving solutions.

927. The 24-Hour Pop-Up Community Garden Creation: Organizing and creating a pop-up community garden in an underused urban space within 24 hours, encouraging community involvement and green living.

928. The One-Month Exploration of Ancient Board Games: Learning and playing a different ancient board game each week, exploring their history, cultural significance, and gameplay mechanics.

929. The Virtual Reality Journey Through the Art World: Offering a VR experience that takes viewers on a journey through art history, visiting virtual galleries and learning about significant artworks and movements.

930. The DIY Energy-Efficient Appliance Modifications: Modifying existing home appliances to improve their energy efficiency, documenting the modifications, testing, and impact on energy consumption.

931. The 48-Hour Urban Microclimate Experiment: Documenting the creation and impact of microclimates through urban gardening techniques, such as green walls and roof gardens, within two days.

932. The One-Month Traditional Instrument Learning Odyssey: Picking up a traditional musical instrument and documenting the learning process, focusing on the cultural history and personal growth experienced.

933. The DIY Smart Composting System: Building a smart composting system that uses technology to optimize decomposition and reduce waste, including setup, challenges, and the composting process.

934. The 24-Hour National Park Photo Safari: Capturing the beauty and biodiversity of a national park through photography over 24 hours, highlighting conservation messages.

935. The One-Week Living as a Historical Explorer Challenge: Emulating the lifestyle of a historical explorer for a week, including diet, exploration techniques, and documenting discoveries in a modern context.

936. The Virtual Reality Guide to the Galaxy: Creating an immersive VR experience that guides viewers through the Milky Way galaxy, explaining astronomical phenomena and the scale of cosmic structures.

937. The DIY Bicycle-Powered Home Appliance Series: Designing and testing home appliances powered by bicycle, such as a washing machine or blender, focusing on sustainability and practicality.

938. The 24-Hour Eco-Friendly Product Hackathon: Developing eco-friendly versions of common household products within 24 hours, from concept to prototype, focusing on sustainability and innovation.

939. The One-Month Ancient Martial Arts Practice: Diving into the practice of an ancient martial art for a month, documenting the physical, mental, and spiritual journey encountered.

940. The Virtual Reality Prehistoric Earth Exploration: Offering an educational VR experience that takes users back to prehistoric Earth, showcasing dinosaurs, ancient plants, and the evolution of life.

941. The DIY Off-Grid Living Gadgets: Creating gadgets and tools that make off-grid living more comfortable and efficient, sharing DIY guides and life hacks.

942. The 24-Hour City Sound Mapping Project: Recording the diverse sounds of a city within 24 hours and creating an interactive sound map that highlights the city's acoustic environment.

943. The One-Week Zero-Electricity Living Experiment: Living without electricity for a week, documenting the challenges, adaptations, and insights gained from a simpler lifestyle.

944. The Virtual Reality Arctic Wildlife Expedition: Designing a VR experience focused on Arctic wildlife, educating viewers about species' adaptations, threats to their survival, and conservation efforts.

945. The DIY Thermal Energy Storage System: Building and testing a simple thermal energy storage system to regulate home temperatures, documenting the science, construction, and results.

946. The 24-Hour Underwater Clean-Up Vlog: Organizing and participating in an underwater clean-up effort, highlighting the impact of pollution on aquatic ecosystems and promoting marine conservation.

947. The One-Month Sustainable Wardrobe Challenge: Curating a sustainable wardrobe for a month, focusing on ethical fashion choices, thrifted finds, and DIY clothing projects.

948. The Virtual Reality Experience of Extreme Sports: Creating VR experiences that let users virtually try extreme sports, such as base jumping, deep-sea diving, or mountain biking, focusing on adrenaline and safety.

949. The DIY Portable Water Filtration Device: Designing and constructing a portable water filtration device for use in outdoor adventures or emergency situations, including effectiveness tests.

950. The 24-Hour Flash Theatre Production: Putting together a theatre production from scriptwriting to performance within 24 hours, focusing on creativity, teamwork, and the power of storytelling.

951. The One-Week Urban Survival Skills Series: Teaching essential urban survival skills over a week, from navigating without GPS to finding food and water in a cityscape.

952. The Virtual Reality Journey Through the Human Digestive System: Developing an educational VR journey through the human digestive system, explaining its functions, common issues, and health tips.

953. The DIY Green Energy Experiments for Kids: Creating simple green energy projects for children, such as solar ovens or water wheels, aiming to educate and inspire the next generation about renewable energy.

954. The 24-Hour Wilderness Art Challenge: Creating art in the wilderness using natural materials within 24 hours, exploring the intersection of art, nature, and environmental consciousness.

955. The One-Month Fitness Regimen With Historical Exercises: Following a fitness regimen based on historical exercise practices for a month, documenting the experiences, benefits, and historical context.

956. The Virtual Reality Exploration of the World's Caves: Offering an immersive VR tour of the world's most spectacular caves, highlighting geological formations, cave ecology, and the thrill of exploration.

957. The DIY Solar-Powered Entertainment System: Building a solar-powered system to power entertainment devices, such as TVs or gaming consoles, showcasing renewable energy in leisure activities.

958. The 24-Hour Backyard BioBlitz and Species Identification: Conducting a BioBlitz in a backyard or local park, identifying as many species as possible in 24 hours, and discussing biodiversity and conservation.

959. The One-Week Culinary Fusion Experiment: Mixing cuisines from different cultures to create innovative dishes for a week, exploring culinary diversity and creativity in food.

960. The Virtual Reality Walk Through the World's Forests: Creating a VR experience that takes users on walks through various types of forests around the world, emphasizing ecology, conservation, and the importance of forests.

961. The DIY Rain Barrel and Water Conservation System: Setting up a rain barrel system to collect rainwater for garden use, including tips on water conservation and sustainable gardening practices.

962. The 24-Hour Minimalist Filmmaking Challenge: Producing a short film with minimal equipment and budget within 24 hours, focusing on storytelling, creativity, and resourcefulness.

963. The One-Month Public Transportation Only Challenge: Using only public transportation for all travel needs for a month, documenting the experience, challenges, and impact on lifestyle and carbon footprint.

964. The Virtual Reality Journey Through the Circulatory System: Designing an educational VR experience that navigates through the human circulatory system, explaining its function, health, and diseases.

965. The DIY Eco-Friendly Air Conditioning Alternatives: Exploring and building alternative cooling solutions for homes, such as evaporative coolers or passive cooling designs, focusing on sustainability and efficiency.

966. The 24-Hour Local Language Challenge: Attempting to learn and communicate in a local or minority language for 24 hours, highlighting language preservation and cultural diversity.

967. The One-Week Handcrafting Traditional Toys Project: Crafting traditional toys by hand over a week, exploring historical playthings, their cultural significance, and the joy of handmade toys.

968. The Virtual Reality Exploration of Abandoned Spaces: Creating VR tours of abandoned buildings and spaces, combining exploration with stories of history, decay, and the passage of time.

969. The DIY Hydroelectric Power Experiment: Constructing a small-scale hydroelectric power generator and testing its ability to generate electricity, documenting the process and results.

970. The 24-Hour Pop-Up Guerrilla Gardening Event: Organizing a guerrilla gardening event to beautify neglected urban spaces with plants and flowers, promoting green activism and community involvement.

971. The One-Month Journey of Learning Sign Language: Dedicating a month to learning sign language, sharing the learning resources, progress, and interactions with the deaf and hard of hearing community.

972. The Virtual Reality Deep Dive into Ancient Civilizations: Developing VR experiences that immerse users in the daily life, architecture, and customs of ancient civilizations, providing an interactive learning experience.

973. The DIY Bicycle-Powered Washing Machine: Building a washing machine powered by pedaling a bicycle, focusing on off-grid living solutions and physical activity.

974. The 24-Hour Sustainable Living Documentary: Documenting a day in the life of individuals or families living sustainably, showcasing their practices, challenges, and impacts on the environment.

975. The One-Week Edible Wild Plants Exploration: Identifying, foraging, and cooking with edible wild plants for a week, sharing knowledge about foraging safety, plant identification, and nutritional benefits.

976. The Virtual Reality Simulation of Life in Microgravity: Creating a VR simulation that lets users experience life in microgravity, such as aboard the ISS, highlighting the challenges and adaptations required.

977. The DIY Natural Swimming Pond Project: Transforming a backyard into a natural swimming pond, documenting the planning, construction, and ecosystem development.

978. The 24-Hour Vintage Technology Challenge: Using only vintage technology for all tasks and entertainment for 24 hours, reflecting on the evolution of technology and its impact on daily life.

979. The One-Month Adventure in Guerrilla Filmmaking: Embarking on a guerrilla filmmaking project, using minimal equipment and resources to produce a short film, focusing on creativity and storytelling.

980. The Virtual Reality Tour of the Human Brain: Offering an immersive VR tour of the human brain, explaining its complex structures, functions, and the latest neuroscience discoveries.

981. The 36-Hour Wilderness Photography Challenge: Embarking on a wilderness adventure to capture the most breathtaking natural scenes within 36 hours, emphasizing the beauty and fragility of nature.

982. The One-Month Barter-Only Living Experiment: Navigating daily life using only bartering instead of money for a month, exploring alternative economies and community connections.

983. The DIY Smart Gardening Assistant Build: Creating a smart device or system to assist with gardening tasks, detailing the technology used and its impact on plant growth and garden efficiency.

984. The 24-Hour City Rooftop Gardens Tour: Exploring and showcasing various rooftop gardens in a city within 24 hours, highlighting urban agriculture and green space benefits.

985. The One-Week Ancient Board Games Revival: Learning, making, and playing ancient board games from different cultures over a week, uncovering the history and social significance behind each game.

986. The Virtual Reality Journey to the Center of the Earth: Offering an educational VR experience that simulates a journey to the Earth's core, explaining geological science in an engaging way.

987. The DIY Recycled Art Materials Challenge: Creating art exclusively using recycled materials for a week, promoting sustainability in the art community and showcasing creative recycling.

988. The 24-Hour Multilingual Vlog Challenge: Producing a vlog that involves speaking in as many languages as possible within 24 hours, celebrating linguistic diversity and the challenges of language learning.

989. The One-Month Off-Grid Internet Solution Exploration: Investigating and utilizing off-grid internet solutions for a month, documenting the setup, reliability, and overall experience.

990. The Virtual Reality Space Junk Cleanup Simulation: Creating a VR game or simulation focused on cleaning up space junk, raising awareness about space debris and its dangers.

991. The DIY Bicycle Touring Kit: Assembling a comprehensive DIY kit for bicycle touring, including homemade gear and hacks, promoting sustainable travel and adventure cycling.

992. The 24-Hour Sustainable Fashion Makeover: Transforming everyday wardrobes into sustainable fashion statements within 24 hours, highlighting ethical brands and upcycling techniques.

993. The One-Week Smartphone Filmmaking Workshop: Teaching viewers how to produce quality films using only smartphones over a week, covering scripting, shooting, and editing techniques.

994. The Virtual Reality Exploration of Microhabitats: Designing VR experiences that allow users to explore different microhabitats, emphasizing biodiversity and the importance of small ecosystems.

995. The DIY Portable Clean Energy Kit: Building a kit that harnesses solar, wind, or kinetic energy for portable use, showcasing the build process and potential applications.

996. The 24-Hour Heritage Craft Marathon: Spending 24 hours learning and practicing a heritage craft, documenting the skill's cultural importance and the craftsmanship involved.

997. The One-Month Minimalist Challenge with a Twist: Adopting a minimalist lifestyle with specific constraints or goals for a month, reflecting on consumer habits, simplicity, and personal growth.

998. The Virtual Reality Underwater Archeology Dive: Creating a VR experience that simulates diving into underwater archaeological sites, offering insights into maritime history and underwater preservation.

999. The DIY Wind Instrument Creation Series: Crafting various wind instruments from scratch, demonstrating the process, the science of sound production, and performing music with the created instruments.

1000. The 24-Hour Local Unsung Heroes Documentary: Producing short documentaries about local unsung heroes within 24 hours, showcasing community impact and inspiring stories.

1001. The One-Week Eco-Friendly Meal Prep Challenge: Preparing a week's worth of meals using eco-friendly practices, focusing on zero waste, local sourcing, and plant-based options.

1002. The Virtual Reality Time Capsule Project: Developing a VR time capsule that captures current events, culture, and daily life, to be revisited in the future for historical reflection.

1003. The DIY Solar-Powered Toy Car Race: Building and racing solar-powered toy cars, documenting the design and engineering process, and highlighting renewable energy principles.

1004. The 24-Hour International Folk Dance Challenge: Learning and performing different international folk dances within 24 hours, exploring cultural expressions through dance.

1005. The One-Month Wilderness Connection Experiment: Spending a month connecting with wilderness through various activities, documenting the mental, physical, and spiritual experiences.

1006. The Virtual Reality Ghost Towns of the World Tour: Offering VR tours of ghost towns around the world, telling the stories of their rise and fall, and preserving digital heritage.

1007. The DIY Eco-Friendly Water Filtration System: Designing and building a water filtration system using eco-friendly materials, testing its effectiveness and exploring the science behind it.

1008. The 24-Hour Vintage Film Camera Challenge: Capturing a series of photographs or a short film using only vintage film cameras within 24 hours, exploring the art of analog photography.

1009. The One-Week Living with Artificial Intelligence Experiment: Integrating AI into daily life for a week in various ways, documenting interactions, benefits, and ethical considerations.

1010. The Virtual Reality Lost Languages Revival: Creating VR experiences that introduce users to languages that are extinct or endangered, aiming to preserve linguistic diversity.

1011. The DIY Personal Mobility Device: Building a personal mobility device, such as a skateboard or unicycle, from scratch, focusing on design, functionality, and sustainability.

1012. The 24-Hour Flash Non-Profit Organization Launch: Launching a non-profit organization within 24 hours to address a specific community need or social issue, documenting the process and initial impact.

1013. The One-Month Digital Detox in Nature: Documenting the experience of a digital detox while living in close connection with nature for a month, sharing insights on technology, nature, and well-being.

1014. The Virtual Reality Ancient Trades and Crafts Exploration: Offering VR workshops on ancient trades and crafts, allowing participants to learn skills such as blacksmithing, pottery, or traditional woodworking.

1015. The DIY Home Biometric Systems Project: Implementing simple biometric systems for home use, such as fingerprint scanners for security, documenting the tech setup and applications.

1016. The 24-Hour City Soundtrack Creation: Composing a soundtrack inspired by the sounds of a city captured within 24 hours, blending urban soundscapes with music production.

1017. The One-Week Handmade Paper and Ink Making: Crafting paper and ink from natural materials over a week, exploring historical and sustainable methods of paper and ink production.

1018. The Virtual Reality Exploration of Future Technologies: Creating a VR experience that showcases potential future technologies and their impact on society, industry, and daily life.

1019. The DIY Thermal Cooking Devices Experiment: Building and testing thermal cooking devices, such as haybox cookers, to conserve energy and reduce cooking costs.

1020. The 24-Hour Improv Theater in Public Spaces: Organizing impromptu theater performances in public spaces within 24 hours, engaging with unsuspecting audiences and promoting performance art.

1021. The One-Month Journey Through Mythology and Folklore: Exploring myths and folklore from different cultures each day for a month, discussing their origins, meanings, and impact on contemporary culture.

1022. The Virtual Reality Exploration of the Earth's Extremes: Developing VR experiences that take users to extreme environments on Earth, such as the deepest oceans, highest mountains, and polar regions.

1023. The DIY Sustainable Pet Habitat Project: Creating a sustainable habitat for pets, focusing on eco-friendly materials, natural enrichment, and minimizing environmental impact.

1024. The 24-Hour Local Food Challenge: Only eating foods grown, produced, or sourced within a local area for 24 hours, documenting the experience, challenges, and benefits of local eating.

1025. The One-Week Portable Solar Power Station Build: Building a portable solar power station from scratch over a week, detailing the design, construction, and testing in various settings.

1026. The Virtual Reality Walk Through Historic Inventions: Offering an interactive VR journey through historic inventions, allowing users to explore the creations and their inventors' stories.

1027. The DIY Rainwater Harvesting and Purification Project: Setting up a system to harvest and purify rainwater for home use, sharing the construction process, purification methods, and usage tips.

1028. The 24-Hour Dance Marathon for Charity: Organizing a dance marathon to raise funds for a charitable cause, documenting the preparation, the event itself, and the community involvement.

1029. The One-Month Exploration of Natural Dyes and Textiles: Experimenting with natural dyes and sustainable textiles for a month, documenting the dyeing process, patterns, and environmental impact.

1030. The Virtual Reality Deep Dive into Quantum Physics: Creating a VR experience that simplifies quantum physics concepts, making them accessible and engaging for non-scientists.

1031. The 48-Hour Pop-Up Public Library Challenge: Creating a temporary public library in a community space, documenting the collection process, setup, and community reactions within two days.

1032. The One-Month Living History Experiment: Immersing in the lifestyle of a specific historical period for a month, from attire to daily routines, and sharing educational content about the era.

1033. The DIY Urban Heat Island Mitigation Project: Demonstrating ways to reduce urban heat through green roofs, reflective surfaces, and tree planting, including before-and-after temperature data.

1034. The 24-Hour Wilderness Skills Challenge: Testing survival skills in the wilderness over 24 hours, focusing on shelter building, fire starting, and foraging, with safety tips and lessons learned.

1035. The One-Week International Virtual Book Club: Hosting a book club that reads and discusses books from different cultures each day for a week, fostering global literary appreciation and discussion.

1036. The Virtual Reality Journey Through the Human Eye: Creating an immersive VR experience that navigates through the human eye, explaining vision science and eye health in an interactive format.

1037. The DIY Eco-Friendly Personal Transportation Device: Building a sustainable personal transportation device, like a skateboard or scooter, from recycled materials, documenting the design and build process.

1038. The 24-Hour Local Myth and Legend Exploration: Investigating local myths and legends within 24 hours, combining historical research with storytelling to uncover the truths and tales of a region.

1039. The One-Month Sustainable Water Use Challenge: Documenting efforts to reduce water usage to the minimum for a month, sharing tips, challenges, and the impact on water conservation awareness.

1040. The Virtual Reality Exploration of the World's Deserts: Offering an educational VR tour of various deserts around the globe, highlighting their ecosystems, conservation issues, and beauty.

1041. The DIY Solar-Powered Entertainment Area: Creating an outdoor entertainment area powered entirely by solar energy, including the setup of solar panels and energy storage solutions.

1042. The 24-Hour Zero-Waste Community Event: Organizing a community event focused on zero-waste practices, documenting the planning, execution, and waste diversion outcomes.

1043. The One-Week Traditional Pottery Making Journey: Learning the art of traditional pottery making from a local artisan, documenting the process from clay preparation to the final firing.

1044. The Virtual Reality Tour of Historic Battlefields: Developing VR tours of historic battlefields, offering insights into historical conflicts, strategies, and the significance of each site.

1045. The DIY Rain Garden and Sustainable Drainage System: Installing a rain garden and sustainable drainage solutions to manage storm water run off, detailing the environmental benefits and biodiversity.

1046. The 24-Hour Citywide Random Acts of Kindness Spree: Performing random acts of kindness across a city within 24 hours, inspiring positivity and documenting the reactions and impacts.

1047. The One-Month Carbon Footprint Reduction Challenge: Attempting to minimize personal or household carbon footprint for a month, tracking efforts, changes made, and overall impact.

1048. The Virtual Reality Deep-Dive into Renewable Energy Sources: Creating a VR experience that educates on different renewable energy sources, their workings, and their benefits for the planet.

1049. The DIY Upcycled Home Decor Series: Transforming discarded items into stylish home decor through upcycling projects, showcasing creativity and techniques for repurposing materials.

1050. The 24-Hour International Cuisine Cooking Marathon: Preparing and sharing dishes from a different country every hour for 24 hours, exploring global cuisines and cooking techniques.

1051. The One-Week Off-the-Grid Camping Adventure: Documenting a week-long off-the-grid camping trip, focusing on sustainable practices, nature connection, and survival skills.

1052. The Virtual Reality Space Exploration Series: Producing a series of VR experiences that take viewers on exploratory missions to different planets and moons in our solar system.

1053. The DIY Bicycle Repair and Maintenance Workshop: Hosting a workshop on bicycle repair and maintenance, promoting cycling as a sustainable mode of transportation and sharing DIY repair tips.

1054. The 24-Hour Urban Wildlife Safari: Exploring and documenting urban wildlife within 24 hours, highlighting biodiversity in city settings and the importance of urban green spaces.

1055. The One-Month Artisan Cheese Making Process: Diving into the world of artisan cheese making, documenting the process of making different types of cheese over a month.

1056. The Virtual Reality Underwater World Building Game: Developing a VR game that allows players to build and explore their own underwater worlds, emphasizing marine conservation.

1057. The DIY Energy-Efficient Cooking Methods Test: Experimenting with various energy-efficient cooking methods, such as pressure cooking and solar ovens, comparing energy use and cooking results.

1058. The 24-Hour Flash Fiction Writing and Publishing Marathon: Writing and publishing a piece of flash fiction within 24 hours, focusing on creativity under time constraints.

1059. The One-Week Mobile App Development for Social Impact: Developing a mobile app that addresses a social issue within a week, from idea generation to prototype, focusing on usability and impact.

1060. The Virtual Reality Exploration of Microscopic Life: Offering an immersive VR experience that allows users to explore the world of microscopic life, including bacteria, viruses, and microorganisms.

1061. The DIY Portable Greenhouse Project: Building a portable greenhouse to extend the growing season, documenting the construction, planting, and results of the greenhouse gardening.

1062. The 24-Hour Urban Greening Initiative: Initiating and completing an urban greening project, such as tree planting or creating pollinator gardens, within 24 hours to enhance city ecology.

1063. The One-Month Journey Through World Religions: Exploring the beliefs, practices, and cultural impacts of different world religions over a month, sharing insights and reflections.

1064. The Virtual Reality Time-Travel to Historical Inaugurations: Creating VR experiences that transport users to historical presidential inaugurations, offering a blend of history and immersive storytelling.

1065. The DIY Home Water Recycling System: Implementing a home system to recycle grey water for gardening or toilet flushing, documenting the process, challenges, and water savings.

1066. The 24-Hour Sustainable Community Kitchen Setup: Establishing a community kitchen focused on sustainability within 24 hours, highlighting community involvement, local food sourcing, and zero-waste practices.

1067. The One-Week Exploration of Folk Tales and Storytelling: Delving into folk tales from various cultures for a week, exploring storytelling traditions and their meanings, and sharing adaptations.

1068. The Virtual Reality Architectural Design of Future Cities: Designing futuristic cityscapes in VR, focusing on sustainable urban planning, green buildings, and innovative transportation systems.

1069. The DIY Solar-Powered Night Light Project: Creating solar-powered night lights for outdoor or indoor use, showcasing the build process, solar technology, and sustainable lighting solutions.

1070. The 24-Hour International Sign Language Learning Challenge: Attempting to learn basic phrases in different sign languages within 24 hours, promoting awareness and inclusivity for the deaf community.

1071. The One-Month Fitness Challenge Using Parkour: Taking on a parkour fitness challenge for a month, documenting the training process, progress, and the physical and mental benefits gained.

1072. The Virtual Reality Exploration of the World's Megacities: Offering VR tours of the world's largest megacities, examining urban challenges, cultural diversity, and innovative solutions to city living.

1073. The DIY Backyard Wildlife Habitat Creation: Building a wildlife-friendly habitat in a backyard, documenting the design, implementation, and the variety of wildlife attracted to the new habitat.

1074. The 24-Hour Recycled Materials Sculpture Contest: Organizing a sculpture contest where participants create artworks from recycled materials within 24 hours, emphasizing creativity and environmental consciousness.

1075. The One-Month Journey into Herbalism and Natural Remedies: Exploring the world of herbalism and natural remedies, documenting the learning process, preparation of remedies, and their effects.

1076. The Virtual Reality Walk Through Ancient Forests: Creating a VR experience that takes users on walks through ancient forests around the world, highlighting conservation and the importance of old-growth forests.

1077. The DIY Home Air Quality Improvement Projects: Implementing projects to improve indoor air quality, such as building plant walls or DIY air purifiers, documenting the methods and results.

1078. The 24-Hour Vintage Cooking Challenge: Preparing meals using only vintage cooking techniques and tools for 24 hours, exploring historical cuisines and cooking methods.

1079. The One-Week Immersive Language Learning with VR: Using virtual reality to immerse in a new language for a week, documenting the VR language learning experience and progress.

1080. The Virtual Reality Exploration of Iconic Historical Homes: Offering VR tours of iconic historical homes, providing insights into the lives of historical figures and architectural history.

1081. The DIY Water-Saving Garden Irrigation System: Designing and installing a water-saving irrigation system for gardens, focusing on efficiency, sustainability, and water conservation techniques.

1082. The 24-Hour Make-Do-and-Mend Challenge: Reviving the make-do-and-mend spirit by repairing and upcycling clothing and household items within 24 hours, promoting sustainability and resourcefulness.

1083. The One-Month Exploration of Mindfulness and Meditation Techniques: Practicing different mindfulness and meditation techniques each day for a month, sharing experiences, benefits, and challenges.

1084. The Virtual Reality Deep-Dive into the World's Coral Reefs: Developing a VR experience that explores the beauty and ecological importance of coral reefs, including threats like bleaching and conservation efforts.

1085. The DIY Bicycle-Powered Home Entertainment System: Building an entertainment system powered by pedaling a bicycle, including the setup and how it encourages fitness and sustainability.

1086. The 24-Hour Citywide Recycle and Reuse Drive: Organizing a drive to collect recyclable and reusable items across a city within 24 hours, highlighting community engagement and environmental impact.

1087. The One-Month Sustainable Living Experiment in a Tiny House Community: Living in a tiny house community focused on sustainability for a month, documenting the lifestyle, community dynamics, and environmental footprint.

1088. The Virtual Reality Simulation of Extreme Weather Events: Creating VR simulations of extreme weather events, educating on meteorology, preparedness, and the impact of climate change.

1089. The DIY Eco-Friendly Cooling Solutions for Homes: Exploring and implementing eco-friendly ways to cool homes, such as using natural ventilation, shading, and evaporative cooling, documenting effectiveness and comfort levels.

1090. The 24-Hour Cultural Exchange Marathon: Hosting a virtual cultural exchange marathon, where participants from different countries share aspects of their culture, traditions, and daily life over 24 hours.

1091. The One-Week Journey into the World of Bees: Diving into beekeeping and the world of bees for a week, learning about their importance to ecosystems, threats they face, and how to support them.

1092. The Virtual Reality Tour of the Solar System's Moons: Offering an educational VR tour of the moons in our solar system, highlighting unique features, scientific discoveries, and exploration missions.

1093. The DIY Sustainable Home Office Setup: Creating a sustainable home office, focusing on eco-friendly materials, energy efficiency, and ergonomic design, documenting the transformation and tips.

1094. The 24-Hour Local Sustainable Food Challenge: Eating only locally sourced, sustainable food for 24 hours, exploring local food systems, farm-to-table practices, and the impact on the environment.

1095. The One-Month Craft and Folk Art Revival Project: Reviving traditional crafts and folk art by learning and practicing a different craft each week, sharing the cultural significance and personal reflections.

1096. The Virtual Reality Exploration of Ancient Trade Routes: Developing a VR experience that takes users along ancient trade routes, exploring the goods traded, cultures connected, and the routes' historical impact.

1097. The DIY Portable and Renewable Energy System for Camping: Building a portable renewable energy system for camping, focusing on solar power and sustainable camping practices.

1098. The 24-Hour Urban Biodiversity Inventory: Conducting a biodiversity inventory in an urban area within 24 hours, documenting species found, habitat conditions, and biodiversity importance.

1099. The One-Month Fitness Challenge with Historical Workouts: Trying different historical workout routines for a month, exploring how fitness practices have evolved over time and their benefits.

1100. The Virtual Reality Exploration of Unseen Worlds: Creating VR experiences that take users into unseen worlds, such as the microscopic universe, deep-sea environments, or inside a volcano, blending education with immersive storytelling.

1101. The 36-Hour Innovation Marathon: Hosting a marathon where participants are challenged to come up with innovative solutions to everyday problems within 36 hours, documenting the brainstorming, creation, and testing phases.

1102. The One-Month Global Street Food Exploration: Virtually exploring street food from a different country each day for a month, attempting to recreate dishes at home, and diving into their cultural significance.

1103. The DIY Floating Aquatic Garden Project: Building a floating garden for aquatic plants and small fish, detailing the construction process, ecological benefits, and maintenance tips.

1104. The 24-Hour Urban Reclamation Project: Transforming a neglected urban space into a functional and attractive area for community use, documenting the planning, execution, and community response.

1105. The One-Week Wilderness First Aid Course: Sharing essential wilderness first aid skills over a week, including practical demonstrations, tips for preparation, and responding to common outdoor emergencies.

1106. The Virtual Reality Tour of Extinct Ecosystems: Creating a VR experience that takes viewers through ecosystems that no longer exist, educating on environmental changes and the importance of conservation.

1107. The DIY Eco-Friendly Party Planning Guide: Organizing a party or event following strict eco-friendly guidelines, showcasing sustainable decor, catering, and waste management practices.

1108. The 24-Hour Community Art Challenge: Inviting community members to contribute to a collaborative art project within 24 hours, highlighting the power of art to unite and express communal values.

1109. The One-Month Journey Into Precision Agriculture: Exploring the concepts and practices of precision agriculture, using technology to enhance crop yields and sustainability, documenting the learning process and practical applications.

1110. The Virtual Reality Reconstruction of Lost Monuments: Offering VR experiences that reconstruct historical monuments that have been lost or destroyed, providing a glimpse into the past and the significance of preserving history.

1111. The DIY Home Energy Monitoring System: Building a system to monitor home energy usage in real-time, focusing on identifying energy-saving opportunities and implementing efficiency measures.

1112. The 24-Hour Nature Connection Experiment: Spending 24 uninterrupted hours in nature, documenting the experience of disconnecting from modern life and reconnecting with the natural world.

1113. The One-Week Underwater Photography Challenge: Taking on the challenge of underwater photography, sharing techniques, challenges, and the stunning beauty of aquatic life captured over a week.

1114. The Virtual Reality Space Anomaly Exploration: Creating VR content that allows users to explore mysterious space anomalies, blending astrophysics with engaging storytelling to spark curiosity about the universe.

1115. The DIY Sustainable Pet Living Solutions: Crafting sustainable living solutions for pets, such as eco-friendly toys, bedding, and accessories, showcasing the making process and pet reactions.

1116. The 24-Hour Flash Documentary on Local Sustainability Efforts: Producing a short documentary within 24 hours that highlights local initiatives and individuals driving sustainability efforts in the community.

1117. The One-Month Traditional Storytelling Revival: Reviving the art of traditional storytelling, exploring different cultures' storytelling techniques, and sharing a new story each day for a month.

1118. The Virtual Reality Journey Through the Human Nervous System: Developing an immersive VR experience that navigates through the human nervous system, explaining its complex functions in an accessible manner.

1119. The DIY Convertible Space-Saving Furniture: Designing and constructing furniture that can be easily converted for multiple uses, maximizing space in small living areas and sharing DIY tips.

1120. The 24-Hour Urban Permaculture Challenge: Implementing permaculture principles in an urban setting within 24 hours, documenting the process of creating sustainable and productive green spaces.

1121. The One-Month Culinary Herb Exploration: Dedicating a month to growing, harvesting, and cooking with different culinary herbs, sharing growth tips, health benefits, and recipe ideas.

1122. The Virtual Reality Deep-Sea Exploration Series: Producing a series of VR experiences that take viewers on explorations of deep-sea environments, highlighting marine biodiversity, geology, and conservation issues.

1123. The DIY Bicycle Mobile Library Service: Creating a mobile library on a bicycle, delivering books to communities with limited access to libraries, and documenting the setup and community impact.

1124. The 24-Hour Local Food Security Project: Initiating a project to address local food security within 24 hours, such as setting up a community garden or food-sharing program, emphasizing community resilience.

1125. The One-Week Living with a Historical Diet Challenge: Following the diet of a specific historical period or civilization for a week, exploring historical eating habits, food preparation, and their impacts on health and society.

1126. The Virtual Reality Exploration of the Earth's Core: Offering an educational VR journey to the Earth's core, explaining geological processes, the composition of the inner Earth, and its role in the planet's magnetic field.

1127. The DIY Rainwater Harvesting Art Installation: Creating an art installation that also functions as a rainwater harvesting system, combining aesthetics with environmental sustainability and water conservation.

1128. The 24-Hour Sustainable Fashion Design Sprint: Designing and creating a piece of sustainable fashion from start to finish within 24 hours, focusing on innovative materials and ethical practices.

1129. The One-Month Off-the-Beaten-Path Documentary Series: Creating a documentary series that explores less-known locations, cultures, or communities, uncovering untold stories and showcasing diversity.

1130. The Virtual Reality Prehistoric Ocean Adventure: Developing a VR experience that takes users on a journey through the prehistoric oceans, encountering ancient marine life and exploring extinct underwater worlds.

1131. The DIY Portable and Eco-Friendly Cooking Solutions: Crafting portable cooking solutions that are eco-friendly, such as solar cookers or efficient wood-burning stoves, including design, build, and usage demonstrations.

1132. The 24-Hour Local Renewable Energy Initiatives Showcase: Highlighting local renewable energy projects and initiatives within 24 hours, showcasing community efforts towards sustainability and clean energy.

1133. The One-Week Experiment with Alternative Housing: Experimenting with living in alternative housing options, such as yurts, tiny homes, or treehouses, for a week, documenting the experience, challenges, and benefits.

1134. The Virtual Reality Tour of the World's Sacred Sites: Creating VR tours of sacred sites around the world, exploring their historical, cultural, and spiritual significance in an immersive format.

1135. The DIY Backyard Wildlife Observation Post: Constructing an observation post in the backyard to watch and document local wildlife, sharing the design process, wildlife interactions, and conservation tips.

1136. The 24-Hour Community Skill-Sharing Marathon: Organizing a marathon event where community members share and teach their unique skills to others within 24 hours, fostering learning and community bonds.

1137. The One-Month Journey into Sustainable Crafting: Dedicating a month to creating crafts using sustainable, eco-friendly materials, documenting the crafting process, materials used, and the environmental impact.

1138. The Virtual Reality Simulation of Extreme Sports in Nature: Offering VR simulations that allow users to experience extreme sports in natural settings, combining thrill-seeking with environmental appreciation.

1139. The DIY Solar-Powered Cooling Vest Project: Designing and creating a cooling vest powered by solar energy, detailing the concept, construction, and field testing in hot climates.

1140. The 24-Hour Global Folk Music Celebration: Showcasing folk music from around the world within 24 hours, highlighting the diversity, history, and cultural significance of traditional music.
1141. The One-Week Homemade Natural Remedies and Tonics Making: Crafting a variety of natural remedies and tonics over a week, exploring traditional medicine, ingredients, preparation methods, and uses.
1142. The Virtual Reality Exploration of Hidden Historical Sites: Developing VR content that reveals hidden or lesser-known historical sites, offering an immersive learning experience about history's untold stories.
1143. The DIY Water-Saving Garden Design Challenge: Designing a garden that maximizes water efficiency using drought-resistant plants, mulching, and water-saving irrigation techniques, documenting the design process and results.
1144. The 24-Hour International Virtual Dance Party: Hosting a virtual dance party that connects people from different parts of the world, celebrating global music and dance within 24 hours.
1145. The One-Month Eco-Village Living Experience: Living in an eco-village for a month, sharing insights into sustainable community living, permaculture practices, and the social dynamics of eco-villages.
1146. The Virtual Reality Deep Forest Meditation Experience: Creating a VR meditation experience set in a deep forest, providing users with a tranquil and immersive environment for relaxation and mindfulness.
1147. The DIY Compact Urban Composting Solutions: Developing compact composting solutions suitable for urban dwellers, focusing on balcony or indoor composting systems that are odor-free and efficient.
1148. The 24-Hour Flash Animation Storytelling Project: Creating and sharing a short animated story within 24 hours, using animation to convey a meaningful message or story creatively.
1149. The One-Week Exploration of Natural Building Materials: Investigating and experimenting with natural building materials such as clay, bamboo, or straw bales for a week, documenting the properties, uses, and sustainability aspects.

1150. The Virtual Reality Tour of Future Sustainable Cities: Offering VR tours that imagine the sustainable cities of the future, exploring innovative urban planning, green technologies, and community living concepts.

1151. The One-Day DIY Eco-Friendly Toy Workshop: Crafting toys from recycled materials in a single day, demonstrating the process and the joy it brings to children, fostering creativity and environmental consciousness.

1152. A Month of Forgotten Hobbies Revival: Dedicating each day to reviving a forgotten or old-fashioned hobby, documenting the learning curve, the historical context, and the modern-day relevance.

1153. The 24-Hour Public Space Art Installation Challenge: Collaborating with local artists to design and execute a public art installation in less than 24 hours, focusing on community engagement and beautification.

1154. One Week Living with Smart Home Technologies: Integrating various smart home technologies into daily life for a week, evaluating their impact on efficiency, convenience, and energy consumption.

1155. Virtual Reality Exploration of Ancient Ruins: Creating a VR series that takes viewers on guided tours of ancient ruins worldwide, combining archaeological insights with immersive storytelling.

1156. The DIY Sustainable Kitchenware Project: Designing and crafting sustainable kitchenware items, such as bamboo cutlery or biodegradable dishware, showcasing the process and environmental benefits.

1157. A 24-Hour Challenge to Reduce Carbon Footprint: Attempting to minimize one's carbon footprint to the absolute minimum for 24 hours, sharing strategies, outcomes, and reflections on sustainable living.

1158. The Month-Long Journey into Solar Cooking: Experimenting with various solar cooking methods and devices for a month, documenting recipes, cooking times, and energy savings.

1159. The Virtual Time Travel Series to Historical Events: Producing a series that uses storytelling and animation to transport viewers to pivotal moments in history, offering educational content in an engaging format.

1160. Building a DIY Bicycle-Powered Charging Station: Constructing a station where cyclists can charge their electronic devices using pedal power, documenting the build and community response.

1161. A 24-Hour Immersion in a Language Learning Challenge: Immersing oneself in learning a new language for 24 hours using various methods and documenting the progress, challenges, and techniques.

1162. One Week Creating Art from Upcycled Electronics: Using discarded electronic components to create art for one week, highlighting issues of e-waste and promoting recycling and creativity.

1163. The Virtual Reality Wildlife Conservation Missions: Developing VR experiences that simulate wildlife conservation efforts, allowing users to participate in virtual missions to protect endangered species.

1164. The DIY Hydroponic Garden for Small Spaces: Setting up a hydroponic garden in a small urban space, sharing the step-by-step process, maintenance tips, and the benefits of hydroponic gardening.

1165. A 24-Hour Local Food Challenge: Only consuming food that is produced within a 100-mile radius for 24 hours, exploring local agriculture, food sustainability, and the impact of eating locally.

1166. One Month of Historical Figure Role-Playing: Adopting the persona of a different historical figure each week, exploring their lives, achievements, and the times they lived in through vlogs or reenactments.

1167. Creating a Virtual Reality Ocean Cleanup Game: Designing a game in VR that educates players on ocean pollution and involves them in virtual cleanup efforts, combining fun with environmental education.

1168. The DIY Compostable Packaging Solutions Project: Experimenting with creating compostable packaging solutions at home, testing materials and effectiveness, and advocating for less waste.

1169. A 24-Hour Fitness Challenge Using Nature as the Gym: Completing a series of fitness challenges using only natural elements like rocks, trees, and hills, promoting outdoor activity and connection with nature.

1170. The Month-Long Local Crafts and Artisans Documentary Series: Documenting local crafts and artisans, showcasing their skills, products, and the cultural significance of traditional crafts in daily episodes.

1171. The Virtual Reality Tour of the Human Immune System: Creating an educational VR experience that navigates through the human immune system, explaining its components and how it fights diseases.

1172. Building a DIY Eco-Friendly Water Feature: Constructing a water feature that attracts wildlife and contributes to garden biodiversity, using recycled materials and solar-powered pumps.

1173. A 24-Hour Challenge to Live Without Plastic: Attempting to go a full day without using any plastic products, highlighting the challenges, alternatives, and the importance of reducing plastic consumption.

1174. One Week of Experiments with Plant-Based Dyes: Experimenting with creating and using dyes made from various plants over a week, documenting the processes, color outcomes, and applications.

1175. The Virtual Reality Experience of Extreme Weather Phenomena: Developing VR content that allows users to experience extreme weather conditions firsthand, educating on weather science and safety.

1176. The DIY Vertical Space-Saving Garden for Urban Dwellers: Designing and creating a vertical garden that maximizes space in urban environments, sharing DIY tips, plant selection, and care advice.

1177. A 24-Hour Urban Treasure Hunt for Historical Markers: Organizing a treasure hunt that guides participants to historical markers and sites in a city, combining adventure with educational content.

1178. One Month of Rediscovering Local Libraries: Exploring different local libraries each day for a month, highlighting their resources, programs, and the role of libraries in community enrichment.

1179. Creating a Virtual Reality Mars Colonization Simulation: Designing a VR simulation that allows users to participate in colonizing Mars, addressing challenges and solutions in space colonization.

1180. The DIY Natural Air Purifier Project: Building a natural air purifier using plants and sustainable materials, documenting the effectiveness and improvements in indoor air quality.

1181. A 24-Hour Social Experiment on Digital Detox: Conducting a digital detox for 24 hours and documenting the experience, challenges, and reflections on the impact of digital consumption on daily life.

1182. One Week of Crafting Traditional Musical Instruments: Making traditional musical instruments from scratch over a week, exploring their cultural origins, crafting techniques, and sounds.

1183. The Virtual Reality Deep Dive into Ancient Pyramids: Offering an immersive VR tour inside ancient pyramids, uncovering architectural secrets, historical context, and exploration tales.

1184. Building a DIY Sustainable Birdhouse Community: Creating a series of sustainable birdhouses for local bird species, focusing on eco-friendly materials and designs that support biodiversity.

1185. A 24-Hour Challenge to Capture a City's Hidden Gems: Photographing or filming hidden gems and lesser-known spots in a city within 24 hours, showcasing the beauty and stories behind them.

1186. One Month of Learning and Applying Permaculture Principles: Applying permaculture principles to a garden or community space for a month, documenting the transformation, lessons learned, and ecological impact.

1187. Creating a Virtual Reality Under-the-Earth Minerals Expedition: Developing a VR experience that explores the Earth's crust, teaching about minerals, geology, and the importance of sustainable mining.

1188. The DIY Wind-Powered Sculpture Project: Crafting kinetic sculptures powered by wind, showcasing the intersection of art, engineering, and renewable energy in a creative format.

1189. A 24-Hour Experiment in Urban Soundscaping: Recording and manipulating urban sounds to create a unique soundscape, exploring the acoustic environment of cities and its effects on well-being.

1190. One Week of Solar Cooking Around the World: Using a solar cooker to prepare traditional dishes from different countries each day for a week, focusing on solar cooking techniques and cultural exploration.

1191. The Virtual Reality Journey Through a Beehive: Creating an educational VR experience that takes users inside a beehive, teaching about bee biology, society, and the importance of bees to ecosystems.

1192. Building a DIY Eco-Friendly Skateboard: Constructing a skateboard using sustainable materials and methods, documenting the design, build process, and performance on the streets.

1193. A 24-Hour Challenge to Map Local Biodiversity: Engaging in a citizen science project to map local biodiversity within 24 hours, using apps or platforms to record sightings and contribute to conservation data.

1194. One Month of Exploring Folk Healing Traditions: Investigating and practicing folk healing traditions from around the world for a month, sharing insights into herbal remedies, spiritual practices, and their cultural contexts.

1195. The Virtual Reality Experience of Climbing the World's Tallest Mountains: Offering VR climbs of the world's tallest mountains, providing educational content on mountain ecology, climbing history, and the physical challenges involved.

1196. The DIY Recycled Rainwater Art Installation: Creating an art installation that utilizes recycled rainwater, focusing on environmental messages and the innovative use of water in art.

1197. A 24-Hour Public Speaking and Empowerment Workshop: Hosting a workshop aimed at improving public speaking skills and personal empowerment, documenting participants' journeys and breakthroughs.

1198. One Week of Adventure in Backyard Biodiversity: Spending a week discovering and documenting the biodiversity in a backyard or local park, emphasizing the richness of local ecosystems and the importance of conservation.

1199. Creating a Virtual Reality Experience of Life in Antiquity: Developing a VR experience that immerses users in daily life in ancient civilizations, offering insights into historical lifestyles, architecture, and social structures.

1200. The DIY Energy-Efficient Lighting Solutions Project: Experimenting with creating energy-efficient lighting solutions, including LED adaptations and solar-powered lights, focusing on sustainability and innovation.

1201. The 72-Hour Build Your Own Adventure Playground Challenge: Documenting the design and construction of a community adventure playground using recycled materials and volunteer labor, focusing on play, creativity, and community building.

1202. The One-Month Journey into Zero-Waste Crafting: Embarking on a quest to create zero-waste crafts, from sourcing sustainable materials to the final product, highlighting the importance of reducing waste in the creative process.

1203. The 24-Hour Urban Nature Quest: Exploring and documenting the biodiversity found in an urban setting within 24 hours, encouraging viewers to discover the natural world right in their city.

1204. One Week of Historical Recipe Revival: Cooking and tasting historical recipes from different eras and cultures each day for a week, delving into the history and evolution of culinary arts.

1205. The Virtual Reality Experience of the World's Great Libraries: Offering viewers a virtual tour of the world's most magnificent libraries, exploring their architecture, history, and treasured collections.

1206. The DIY Personalized Rain Gear Project: Designing and creating personalized rain gear, such as umbrellas and raincoats, using waterproofing techniques and custom decorations.

1207. A 24-Hour Challenge to Create a Mini Documentary on Local Heroes: Producing a mini-documentary in 24 hours that highlights the stories of local heroes who make a difference in the community.

1208. The One-Month Edible Landscaping Transformation: Transforming a conventional garden into an edible landscape over a month, documenting the design process, planting edible plants, and the harvest.

1209. The Virtual Reality Exploration of Abandoned Wonders: Creating VR experiences that take viewers on explorations of abandoned wonders around the world, from ancient ruins to modern ghost towns.

1210. The DIY Solar-Powered Night Market: Setting up a night market powered entirely by solar energy, featuring sustainable products and local crafts, highlighting renewable energy in community events.

1211. A 24-Hour Experiment in Sound Healing Techniques: Exploring and documenting various sound healing techniques within 24 hours, including singing bowls, tuning forks, and natural soundscapes.

1212. One Week of Reimagining Public Spaces with Art: Collaborating with artists and the community to reimagine and transform public spaces with art installations for a week, documenting the process and public engagement.

1213. The Virtual Reality Deep Dive into Traditional Crafts: Offering VR workshops that deeply explore traditional crafts, allowing users to learn about the materials, techniques, and cultural significance of crafts like weaving, pottery, and woodcarving.

1214. The DIY Eco-Friendly Insulating Window Treatments Project: Creating and installing eco-friendly insulating window treatments to improve home energy efficiency, documenting the materials, process, and results.

1215. A 24-Hour Urban Cycling Adventure: Documenting a 24-hour cycling adventure through a city, exploring hidden paths, urban art, and cyclist-friendly spots, promoting cycling as a sustainable mode of transport.

1216. The One-Month Challenge to Create an Urban Wildlife Documentary: Spending a month filming and producing a documentary on urban wildlife, showcasing the diversity of species that thrive in city environments.

1217. The Virtual Reality Journey Through Renewable Energy Facilities: Developing VR tours of various renewable energy facilities, such as solar farms, wind turbines, and hydroelectric plants, educating on how renewable energy is harvested.

1218. The DIY Compact Living Solutions Challenge: Designing and implementing compact living solutions in a small space challenge, focusing on multifunctional furniture, smart storage, and minimalist living.

1219. A 24-Hour Flash Challenge to Promote Local Tourism: Creating a series of quick, engaging content pieces in 24 hours that promote local tourism spots, hidden gems, and cultural highlights.

1220. One Week of Learning Traditional Songs on an Instrument: Choosing a musical instrument and spending a week learning to play traditional songs from various cultures, sharing the learning process and performances.

1221. The Virtual Reality Simulation of Ancient Engineering Marvels: Creating VR simulations that allow users to explore and learn about ancient engineering marvels, understanding the science and innovation behind historical structures.

1222. The DIY Backyard Observatory for Amateur Astronomers: Building a simple, effective backyard observatory for stargazing and amateur astronomy, documenting the construction, equipment setup, and celestial observations.

1223. A 24-Hour Challenge to Reduce Household Energy Consumption: Taking on the challenge to significantly reduce household energy consumption in 24 hours, sharing tips, results, and reflections on energy use.

1224. The One-Month Homemade Natural Beauty Products Experiment: Crafting a variety of natural beauty products at home over a month, from skincare to haircare, documenting recipes, the making process, and effectiveness.

1225. The Virtual Reality Escape Room with Historical Puzzles: Designing a VR escape room that incorporates historical puzzles and mysteries, combining fun problem-solving with educational historical content.

1226. The DIY Water Filtration Experiment Using Natural Materials: Testing different natural materials for water filtration, documenting the experiment, results, and implications for sustainable living and emergency preparedness.

1227. A 24-Hour Microa dventure Series in Different Environments: Embarking on micro adventures in various environments (forest, urban, coastal, etc.) within 24 hours, showcasing the accessibility of adventure and nature connection.

1228. One Week of Building a Community Seed Library: Establishing a community seed library in a week, documenting the process of collecting, categorizing, and sharing seeds to promote biodiversity and local gardening.

1229. The Virtual Reality Time Machine to Witness Historical Innovations: Developing a VR "time machine" experience that takes users back to witness key historical innovations as they happened, blending education and immersive storytelling.

1230. The DIY Alternative Energy-Powered Art Installations: Creating art installations powered by alternative energy sources, such as solar or kinetic energy, highlighting the fusion of art, technology, and sustainability.

1231. The 48-Hour Micro-Documentary Marathon: Creating short documentaries on varied subjects within 48 hours, each telling a compelling story or uncovering lesser-known facts.

1232. One Month of Guerrilla Gardening: Transforming neglected urban spaces into green areas by guerrilla gardening each day, documenting the process, plant growth, and community reactions.

1233. The DIY Solar-Powered Music Festival: Organizing a music festival powered entirely by solar energy, showcasing the planning, the technology behind it, and the performances.

1234. A 24-Hour Virtual Reality Cultural Immersion: Spending 24 hours in a VR environment that simulates living in a different culture, highlighting the experiences and learnings about the culture.

1235. The One-Week Portable Shelter Building Challenge: Designing and constructing different portable shelters over a week, focusing on innovative, lightweight, and sustainable designs.

1236. The Virtual Deep-Sea Exploration Series: Creating a series of deep-sea explorations using submersible drones or VR, uncovering the mysteries of the ocean depths and marine life.

1237. The DIY Urban Cooling Projects: Implementing various projects aimed at cooling urban areas, such as reflective surfaces, shade structures, and misting systems, and measuring their impact.

1238. A 24-Hour Historical Reenactment Vlog: Living a day as someone from a historical period, using period-appropriate clothing, tools, and activities, vlogging the experience.

1239. One Month of Inventive Recycling Projects: Tackling different recycling projects each day for a month, finding creative uses for materials that are hard to recycle.

1240. The Virtual Reality Spacewalk Experience for Education: Developing an educational VR experience that simulates a spacewalk, teaching about the physics of space and astronaut tasks.

1241. The DIY Kinetic Art Installations: Creating kinetic art installations that move with wind or human interaction, documenting the design, build, and public interaction.

1242. A 24-Hour Sustainable Living Skills Workshop: Hosting workshops on sustainable living skills like composting, rainwater harvesting, and solar cooking, all within 24 hours.

1243. One Week of Exploring Abandoned Infrastructure: Investigating and documenting abandoned infrastructure like railways, factories, and tunnels each day for a week, exploring their histories and potential for repurposing.

1244. The Virtual Reality Exploration of Ancient Trade Routes: Creating VR experiences that trace ancient trade routes, highlighting historical trade goods, cultural exchanges, and the routes' impacts on civilization.

1245. The DIY Bicycle-Powered Generator for Emergency Use: Building a generator powered by bicycle for emergency situations, including instructions, testing, and practical uses.

1246. A 24-Hour Eco-Friendly Fashion Hackathon: Designing and creating eco-friendly fashion pieces within 24 hours, using sustainable materials and upcycling techniques.

1247. One Month of Backyard Bioblitz Activities: Conducting a different "BioBlitz" activity in the backyard each day for a month, documenting species found and learning about local biodiversity.

1248. The Virtual Reality Ghost Ship Exploration Adventure: Designing a VR adventure that allows users to explore legendary ghost ships, combining historical lore with interactive storytelling.

1249. The DIY Natural Disaster Preparedness Kit: Assembling a comprehensive natural disaster preparedness kit with DIY elements, focusing on sustainability and self-sufficiency.

1250. A 24-Hour Challenge to Create Zero Waste Art: Creating art pieces that produce zero waste within 24 hours, highlighting the creative process and the importance of sustainability in art.

1251. One Week of Crafting with Invasive Species: Using materials from invasive species to craft items each day for a week, discussing the impact of the species and the value of repurposing.

1252. The Virtual Reality Journey Through the Human Heart: Developing an immersive VR experience that navigates through the human heart, explaining its anatomy and function in detail.

1253. The DIY Compact Composting Solutions for Small Spaces: Creating composting solutions that fit in small urban spaces, documenting the setup, use, and composting results.

1254. A 24-Hour Local Language and Dialect Preservation Project: Documenting local languages or dialects at risk of disappearing within 24 hours, including interviews, phrases, and cultural contexts.

1255. One Month of Solar Gadget Inventions: Inventing a new solar-powered gadget each day for a month, focusing on practicality, innovation, and energy efficiency.

1256. The Virtual Reality Deep Jungle Expedition: Taking viewers on a VR expedition through dense jungles, showcasing the ecosystem, wildlife, and challenges of jungle exploration.

1257. The DIY Pedal-Powered Water Filtration System: Building a water filtration system powered by pedal power, including design, construction, and effectiveness tests.

1258. A 24-Hour Pop-Up Recycled Art Gallery: Organizing a pop-up art gallery featuring art made entirely from recycled materials, documenting the setup, artist stories, and visitor reactions.

1259. One Week of Living Like a Nomad Challenge: Adopting a nomadic lifestyle for a week, documenting the experience of mobility, minimalism, and connection to nature.

1260. The Virtual Reality Experience of Climbing Mount Everest: Creating a VR experience that simulates climbing Mount Everest, teaching about the mountain, the climb, and the environmental and physical challenges.

1261. The DIY Backyard Wildlife Pond: Constructing a wildlife pond in the backyard to attract local wildlife, documenting the build, the species it attracts, and maintenance tips.

1262. A 24-Hour Challenge to Make Music with Everyday Objects: Creating music using only everyday objects within 24 hours, showcasing creativity, the musical process, and the final performance.

1263. One Month of Heritage Craft Techniques: Learning and practicing a different heritage craft technique each day for a month, documenting the skills learned and the cultural significance.

1264. The Virtual Reality Time Travel to Witness Scientific Discoveries: Developing VR content that allows users to witness key scientific discoveries throughout history, combining educational content with immersive experiences.

1265. The DIY Energy-Efficient Cooking Challenge: Experimenting with different energy-efficient cooking methods over a month, documenting energy consumption, techniques, and recipes.

1266. A 24-Hour Urban Farming and Gardening Blitz: Setting up and enhancing urban farming and gardening projects within 24 hours, focusing on community participation and sustainable food production.

1267. One Week of DIY Alternative Transportation Builds: Building a different form of alternative transportation each day for a week, from electric skateboards to pedal-powered boats, including design, build, and test rides.

1268. The Virtual Reality Tour of Iconic Movie Locations: Offering VR tours of iconic movie locations, exploring the real-world settings of famous film scenes, and discussing the movies' cultural impact.

1269. The DIY Upcycled Home Insulation Project: Improving home insulation using upcycled materials, documenting the process, techniques, and impact on energy efficiency.

1270. A 24-Hour Challenge to Document Urban Biodiversity: Documenting as many species of plants and animals in an urban area within 24 hours, highlighting urban biodiversity and the importance of green spaces.

1271. One Month of Repurposing Plastic Waste: Finding a new use for different types of plastic waste each day for a month, showcasing innovative ways to repurpose and reduce plastic waste.

1272. The Virtual Reality Exploration of Mars Habitats: Developing VR simulations of potential human habitats on Mars, exploring design challenges, daily life, and sustainability in extraterrestrial environments.

1273. The DIY Bicycle-Powered Smoothie Stand for Charity: Creating a smoothie stand powered by bicycle pedaling, where proceeds go to charity, documenting the setup, operation, and fundraising success.

1274. A 24-Hour Mini Eco-Home Design Challenge: Designing and presenting concepts for mini eco-homes within 24 hours, focusing on sustainability, compact living, and innovative design solutions.

1275. One Week of Exploring Traditional Textile Techniques: Diving into traditional textile techniques like weaving, dyeing, and embroidery, documenting the learning process, techniques mastered, and final creations.

1276. The Virtual Reality Deep Space Exploration Experience: Offering an immersive VR journey through deep space, exploring distant galaxies, nebulae, and astronomical phenomena, combining awe with education.

1277. The DIY Portable Solar Cooking Device: Building a portable solar cooking device, documenting the design, materials used, cooking capabilities, and practicality for outdoor use.

1278. A 24-Hour Adventure in Urban Sketching: Embarking on a 24-hour urban sketching adventure, capturing scenes from city life, and sharing tips on sketching techniques and urban exploration.

1279. One Month of Building a Community Art Mural: Collaborating with local artists and community members to create a large-scale art mural over a month, documenting the design process, community workshops, and the mural's impact.

1280. The Virtual Reality Simulation of Historical Voyages: Creating VR content that simulates historical voyages of exploration, trade, or migration, offering insights into navigation techniques, challenges faced, and historical contexts.

1281. The 48-Hour Tiny Home Build Challenge: Documenting the process of designing and constructing a tiny home within 48 hours, highlighting minimalist living and sustainable construction techniques.

1282. One Month of Urban Exploration Diaries: Exploring a new urban environment each day for a month, uncovering hidden gems, historical sites, and modern urban culture, documenting the adventures and insights.

1283. The DIY Water Filtration Challenge: Creating and testing various DIY water filtration systems using natural and recycled materials, focusing on effectiveness, affordability, and environmental impact.

1284. A 24-Hour International Cuisine Cook-off: Preparing dishes from a different country every hour for 24 hours, exploring global cuisines, cooking techniques, and cultural stories behind each dish.

1285. The Virtual Reality Antarctic Expedition Experience: Developing a VR experience that takes users on an expedition to Antarctica, showcasing the continent's extreme environment, wildlife, and scientific research.

1286. The One-Week Handmade Toy Workshop: Crafting a new handmade toy each day for a week, using sustainable materials and documenting the creative process, play value, and child reactions.

1287. A 24-Hour Public Art Performance Series: Organizing a series of public art performances within 24 hours, including dance, music, and interactive installations, documenting the planning, execution, and public engagement.

1288. One Month of Learning an Endangered Language: Spending a month learning and documenting the process of learning an endangered language, emphasizing the importance of language preservation and cultural heritage.

1289. The Virtual Reality Journey Through the Amazon Rainforest: Creating a VR experience that immerses users in the Amazon rainforest, highlighting biodiversity, conservation efforts, and the challenges facing the rainforest.

1290. The DIY Eco-Friendly Home Office Makeover: Transforming a home office space using eco-friendly and sustainable practices, focusing on recycled materials, energy efficiency, and a healthy workspace environment.

1291. A 24-Hour Sustainable Fashion Design Sprint: Designing and creating a sustainable fashion collection within 24 hours, using upcycled materials and environmentally friendly methods.

1292. One Week of Vintage Camera Photography: Using a different vintage camera each day for a week to capture modern life, exploring the history of photography and the unique qualities of each camera.

1293. The Virtual Reality Space Colony Design Project: Building and exploring a virtual reality space colony, focusing on the challenges of extraterrestrial living, sustainability, and community in space.

1294. The DIY Backyard Observatory for Amateur Astronomers: Constructing a simple backyard observatory, documenting the build process, astronomical observations, and tips for amateur astronomers.

1295. A 24-Hour City Biking Adventure: Exploring a city entirely by bike for 24 hours, showcasing urban cycling routes, cyclist-friendly amenities, and the environmental benefits of biking.

1296. One Month of Crafting with Recyclable Materials: Creating a new craft project each day using recyclable materials, focusing on creativity, sustainability, and reducing waste.

1297. The Virtual Reality Underwater Cities Exploration: Offering an immersive VR experience of exploring hypothetical underwater cities, blending futuristic architecture with marine conservation.

1298. The DIY Solar-Powered Gadget Workshop: Building various solar-powered gadgets, from chargers to small appliances, documenting the design, build process, and functionality.

1299. A 24-Hour Minimalist Lifestyle Experiment: Living with the absolute minimum for 24 hours, documenting the experience, challenges, and reflections on consumerism and minimalism.

1300. One Week of Global Mythology Storytelling: Narrating myths and legends from different cultures each day for a week, exploring the storytelling traditions and moral lessons of each myth.

1301. The Virtual Reality Exploration of Deep Earth Caves: Developing a VR experience that takes users on explorations of deep and uncharted caves, highlighting geological formations and the thrill of spelunking.

1302. The DIY Rainwater Harvesting System Challenge: Designing and installing a rainwater harvesting system, documenting the process, water savings, and impact on garden or home use.

1303. A 24-Hour Interactive Street Art Project: Creating an interactive street art project that invites public participation, documenting the setup, public engagement, and the art's evolution over 24 hours.

1304. One Month of Homemade Musical Instruments: Crafting a new musical instrument from unconventional or recycled materials each day, showcasing the build process, sound quality, and musical performance.

1305. The Virtual Reality Tour of Ghost Towns Around the World: Creating a VR tour that explores ghost towns globally, delving into their history, reasons for abandonment, and current state.

1306. The DIY Portable Eco-Friendly Cooking Stove: Building a portable, eco-friendly cooking stove suitable for camping or emergency situations, focusing on efficiency and sustainability.

1307. A 24-Hour Local Wildlife Conservation Initiative: Launching a wildlife conservation initiative within 24 hours, including habitat restoration, species monitoring, or community education.

1308. One Week of Experimental Gardening Techniques: Trying out innovative gardening techniques each day for a week, documenting the methods, growth results, and sustainability aspects.

1309. The Virtual Reality Reconstruction of Historical Cities: Offering VR experiences that reconstruct historical cities in their prime, allowing users to explore and learn about ancient urban life.

1310. The DIY Wind Energy Project for Home Use: Building a small-scale wind energy project for home use, documenting the construction, energy output, and integration into the home energy system.

1311. A 24-Hour Challenge to Create an Upcycled Fashion Show: Organizing a fashion show featuring upcycled designs created within 24 hours, highlighting sustainability in the fashion industry.

1312. One Month of Adventure Filmmaking: Undertaking a different adventure filmmaking project each day for a month, from planning and shooting to editing, focusing on storytelling and cinematic techniques.

1313. The Virtual Reality Arctic Wildlife Safari: Developing a VR safari that showcases Arctic wildlife, educating users about species adaptation, climate change impacts, and conservation efforts.

1314. The DIY Sustainable Home Cooling Solutions: Implementing sustainable cooling solutions for a home, such as evaporative coolers or green roofs, and documenting the temperature impact and energy savings.

1315. A 24-Hour Global Virtual Cooking Marathon: Hosting a cooking marathon where participants from around the world cook and share their traditional dishes in real-time, celebrating global culinary diversity.

1316. One Week of Rediscovering Lost Arts and Crafts: Exploring and practicing a lost art or craft each day, such as calligraphy, glassblowing, or tapestry weaving, focusing on skill revival and historical context.

1317. The Virtual Reality Experience of Future Transportation Systems: Creating a VR experience that lets users explore future transportation concepts, from hyperloops to flying cars, examining the technology and potential societal impacts.

1318. The DIY Biodegradable Plant Pots Project: Making biodegradable plant pots using various materials and methods, focusing on sustainability, plant health, and reducing plastic use in gardening.

1319. A 24-Hour Challenge to Live on Renewable Energy Only: Attempting to power all daily activities using only renewable energy sources for 24 hours, documenting the preparation, challenges, and insights.

1320. One Month of Building a Miniature Eco-Village: Constructing a miniature eco-village model, complete with sustainable housing, energy solutions, and green spaces, documenting the design principles and construction process.

1321. The 36-Hour Urban Survival Challenge: Navigating a major city with limited resources for 36 hours, showcasing survival tips, urban foraging, and the kindness of strangers.

1322. One Month of Reviving Ancient Sports: Each day, exploring and attempting an ancient sport or game, diving into its history, cultural significance, and trying to play it in the modern era.

1323. The DIY Eco-Friendly Boat Building Project: Constructing a small, eco-friendly boat using sustainable materials and methods, documenting the building process, challenges, and the maiden voyage.

1324. A 24-Hour Pop Culture Time Capsule Creation: Assembling a time capsule that captures the essence of current pop culture, involving community submissions and predictions for the future.

1325. The Virtual Reality Journey into the Human Brain: Developing an immersive VR experience that explores the complexities and wonders of the human brain, highlighting neurological functions and mental health awareness.

1326. One Week of Crafting Art from Ocean Debris: Collecting debris from beaches or waterways each day to create art, emphasizing the environmental impact of pollution on marine ecosystems.

1327. The 48-Hour Back-to-Nature Retreat: Documenting a retreat into nature with no digital devices, focusing on reconnection with the natural world, mindfulness, and personal reflections.

1328. The DIY Urban Air Quality Monitoring Network: Setting up a network of DIY air quality monitors across a city, collecting data, and sharing findings on pollution hotspots and clean air oases.

1329. A 24-Hour Virtual Reality Cultural Festival: Hosting a virtual reality festival showcasing different cultures' music, dance, food, and traditions, fostering global understanding and appreciation.

1330. One Month of Building Sustainable Habitats for Wildlife: Each day, constructing a different type of habitat or shelter for local wildlife, promoting biodiversity and environmental stewardship.

1331. The Virtual Reality Reconstruction of Extinct Ecosystems: Offering VR experiences that bring extinct ecosystems to life, educating on historical biodiversity and the importance of conservation.

1332. The DIY Smart Home Automation Project: Automating a home with DIY smart devices, focusing on sustainability, energy efficiency, and enhancing daily living through technology.

1333. A 24-Hour Challenge to Illuminate a Community: Bringing light to under-illuminated or energy-poor areas using sustainable lighting solutions, documenting the process and community impact.

1334. One Week of Exploring Underground Urban Spaces: Venturing into a city's underground spaces, from subways to catacombs, uncovering their history, mysteries, and urban legends.

1335. The Virtual Reality Space Repair Simulation: Creating a VR simulation where users perform repairs on a spacecraft or space station, combining education on space technology with problem-solving skills.

1336. The DIY Portable Solar Charger Project: Building a portable solar charger for devices, ideal for camping or emergencies, focusing on renewable energy use and practicality.

1337. A 24-Hour Immersive Historical Reenactment: Living as individuals from a specific historical period for 24 hours, from dressing in period attire to following daily routines and diets of the time.

1338. One Month of Miniature Eco-System Builds: Creating a different miniature ecosystem each day, such as terrariums, aquascapes, or insect habitats, focusing on ecological balance and conservation.

1339. The Virtual Reality Deep Ocean Exploration Game: Developing a game in VR that takes players on exploratory missions to the deepest parts of the ocean, teaching marine science and the importance of ocean conservation.

1340. The DIY Upcycled Community Library Box: Constructing a community library box from upcycled materials, encouraging community sharing and reading, and documenting the build and community reactions.

1341. A 24-Hour Flash Mob for Environmental Awareness: Organizing a series of flash mobs in various locations to spread messages about environmental awareness and sustainability.

1342. One Week of Desert Survival Skills: Spending a week in a desert environment, sharing survival techniques, water sourcing, shelter building, and reflections on the harsh conditions.

1343. The Virtual Reality Time Travel Adventure to Ancient Civilizations: Offering a VR adventure that transports users back to ancient civilizations, allowing them to interact with historical figures and environments.

1344. The DIY Recycled Material Playground Project: Building a children's playground using entirely recycled materials, focusing on creativity, safety, and promoting recycling and upcycling.

1345. A 24-Hour Sustainable Cooking and Eating Challenge: Committing to sustainable cooking and eating practices for 24 hours, using locally sourced, organic ingredients and minimal waste cooking methods.

1346. One Month of Bicycle-Powered Innovations: Each day, creating or highlighting a different bicycle-powered device or solution, promoting cycling and renewable energy in daily life.

1347. The Virtual Reality Exploration of Future Earth Scenarios: Developing VR experiences that simulate various future Earth scenarios based on current environmental and social trends, encouraging reflection and action.

1348. The DIY Water Conservation Garden Makeover: Transforming a garden to be water-conservation friendly using drought-resistant plants, mulching, and efficient irrigation systems, documenting the makeover process.

1349. A 24-Hour Experiment in Collective Art Creation: Facilitating a collective art project where participants contribute to a large-scale artwork over 24 hours, showcasing community and collaborative creativity.

1350. One Week of Homemade Natural Health Remedies: Crafting and testing different natural health remedies each day, exploring traditional medicine, effectiveness, and sharing recipes and results.

1351. The 72-Hour Build-a-Bike Workshop: Documenting the process of building bicycles from scratch or recycled parts within 72 hours, focusing on the skills learned, community involvement, and promoting cycling as a sustainable mode of transportation.

1352. One Month of Digital Art Challenges: Each day, taking on a different digital art challenge, exploring various techniques, software, and themes, and sharing the creative process and final artworks with viewers.

1353. The DIY Solar Water Heater Project: Demonstrating how to build and install a solar water heater at home, including materials needed, step-by-step instructions, and analysis of cost-effectiveness and environmental impact.

1354. A 24-Hour Urban Beekeeping Experience: Spending a day with urban beekeepers, learning about the importance of bees in urban ecosystems, challenges of beekeeping in the city, and how viewers can support local bee populations.

1355. The Virtual Reality Exploration of Lost Cities: Creating VR experiences that allow users to explore ancient lost cities, combining archaeological findings with storytelling to bring these places to life.

1356. One Week of Zero-Waste Home Hacks: Sharing a new zero-waste home hack each day for a week, including DIY tutorials on reducing waste in various aspects of daily life, from kitchen practices to personal care.

1357. The DIY Eco-Friendly Insulation Project: Showcasing how to insulate a home using environmentally friendly materials, focusing on the process, benefits, and comparing the effectiveness to traditional insulation methods.

1358. A 24-Hour Flash Filmmaking Challenge on Social Issues: Engaging in a challenge to create short films about pressing social issues within 24 hours, highlighting creativity under time constraints and the power of film to provoke thought and drive change.

1359. One Month of Historical Cooking Techniques: Exploring and practicing a different historical cooking technique each day, documenting the process, the historical context, and the taste tests of dishes prepared using these methods.

1360. The Virtual Reality Journey Through the Solar System: Offering an educational VR journey through the solar system, providing detailed explorations of planets, moons, and other celestial bodies, with scientific commentary and visuals.

1361. The DIY Wind Turbine Project for Home Use: Building a wind turbine capable of generating power for home use, detailing the design, construction, and integration into the home's energy system, alongside lessons on wind energy.

1362. A 24-Hour Local Craftsmanship Tour: Visiting local artisans and craftsmen within 24 hours, showcasing their skills, products, and the significance of preserving traditional craftsmanship in a modern world.

1363. One Week of Smartphone Photography Challenges: Issuing a new photography challenge each day that must be completed using only a smartphone, focusing on different techniques, themes, and editing apps to improve photography skills.

1364. The Virtual Reality Deep-Sea Adventure Series: Creating a series of VR adventures that take viewers on exploratory journeys to the deep sea, showcasing marine life, underwater landscapes, and discussing ocean conservation.

1365. The DIY Natural Swimming Pool Conversion: Transforming a traditional swimming pool into a natural swimming pool, documenting the process, the benefits for biodiversity, and maintenance experiences.

1366. A 24-Hour Sustainable Community Initiative Launch: Launching a new sustainable initiative within a community, such as a recycling program, community garden, or a carpool system, and documenting the process, challenges, and initial outcomes.

1367. One Month of Exploring Physics Through Everyday Objects: Each day, demonstrating a physics concept using everyday objects, making science accessible and engaging, and explaining the principles in an understandable way.

1368. The Virtual Reality Time Travel to Significant Historical Events: Creating VR experiences that transport users to significant historical events, offering immersive learning about historical contexts, figures, and outcomes.

1369. The DIY Furniture Upcycling Series: Taking old or discarded furniture and upcycling it into beautiful, functional pieces, sharing the transformation process, techniques used, and before-and-after results.

1370. A 24-Hour Challenge to Create Art from Nature: Creating art pieces using only materials found in nature within 24 hours, emphasizing creativity, the beauty of natural materials, and environmental consciousness.

1371. One Week of Learning Traditional Folk Dances: Learning and practicing a different traditional folk dance each day, exploring the cultural background, significance, and performing the dances.

1372. The Virtual Reality Exploration of Microscopic Worlds: Offering VR experiences that allow users to explore the world at a microscopic level, from the intricacies of cell structures to the microorganisms in different environments.

1373. The DIY Compost Bin Design Challenge: Designing and building efficient and easy-to-use compost bins for home or community use, focusing on sustainable waste management and soil enrichment.

1374. A 24-Hour Pop-Up Community Repair Workshop: Organizing a community repair workshop where people bring items to be repaired rather than discarded, promoting a culture of repair and sustainability.

1375. One Month of Adventure Vlogging in Remote Locations: Documenting travels to remote locations over a month, focusing on adventure, the natural beauty of untouched places, and personal growth experiences.

1376. The Virtual Reality Reconstruction of Dinosaurs and Their Habitats: Creating VR content that reconstructs dinosaurs and their natural habitats, providing educational insights into paleontology and prehistoric life.

1377. The DIY Bicycle-Powered Home Systems Challenge: Designing and implementing systems powered by bicycle pedaling, such as lighting or small home appliances, documenting the process and effectiveness.

1378. A 24-Hour Urban Gardening Blitz: Transforming unused urban spaces into productive gardens within 24 hours, focusing on community involvement, sustainable food production, and green spaces.

1379. One Week of Silent Film Making: Creating silent films that tell stories through visuals and music, focusing on different genres or themes each day, and exploring the art of visual storytelling.

1380. The Virtual Reality Guide to the Wonders of the World: Developing VR tours of the New and Ancient Wonders of the World, providing historical insights, architectural details, and exploring their significance.

1381. The 30-Day Urban Homesteading Journey: Documenting the process of adopting urban homesteading practices, such as balcony gardening, rainwater harvesting, and composting, and sharing the challenges and successes encountered.

1382. The DIY Wearable Tech Gadgets Series: Creating a series of wearable technology projects, from smart watches to fitness trackers, focusing on the integration of fashion and functionality with step-by-step DIY guides.

1383. A 24-Hour Challenge to Map Hidden Historical Sites: Engaging in a quest to uncover and map out hidden historical sites within a city, revealing untold stories and historical insights through research and exploration.

1384. One Month of International Virtual Language Exchange: Partnering with individuals from different countries to engage in a daily language exchange for a month, documenting the learning process, cultural exchanges, and progress in language skills.

1385. The Virtual Reality Exploration of the Human Genome: Developing an immersive VR experience that takes viewers on a journey through the human genome, explaining genetic science in an accessible and engaging way.

1386. The DIY Sustainable Tiny House on Wheels Build: Documenting the entire process of building a sustainable tiny house on wheels, from design and construction to the challenges of living in a tiny space.

1387. A 24-Hour Global Climate Action Virtual Summit: Hosting a virtual summit that brings together climate activists, scientists, and policymakers from around the world to discuss and share actionable climate solutions within 24 hours.

1388. One Week of Experimental Eco-Art Projects: Each day, creating art that incorporates eco-friendly practices or materials, such as using natural dyes, recycled items, or creating pieces that highlight environmental issues.

1389. The Virtual Reality Time Capsules of Today: Creating VR time capsules that capture life in various places around the world today, preserving the digital experiences for future generations to explore.

1390. The DIY Off-Grid Solar Cooking Solutions: Building and testing various off-grid solar cooking solutions, documenting the construction, recipes tried, and efficiency of each solar cooker design.

1391. A 24-Hour Documentary on the Life of a Tree: Spending 24 hours documenting the life and ecosystem surrounding a single tree, highlighting the biodiversity it supports and its importance to the environment.

1392. One Month of Adventure Sports Photography: Taking on a new adventure sport each day for a month and capturing the action and beauty of each sport through photography, sharing tips and experiences.

1393. The Virtual Reality Journey Through Extinct Volcanoes: Offering an educational VR experience that explores extinct volcanoes around the world, teaching about volcanic activity, geological history, and the ecosystems they support.

1394. The DIY Multi-Use Furniture for Small Spaces Challenge: Designing and building furniture that can be used for multiple purposes in small living spaces, documenting the design process, construction, and functionality.

1395. A 24-Hour Local Folklore and Ghost Stories Tour: Exploring local folklore and ghost stories by visiting reportedly haunted locations or places of historical significance, sharing the stories and personal experiences.

1396. One Week of Smartphone Filmmaking Challenges: Issuing a new filmmaking challenge each day that must be completed using a smartphone, focusing on storytelling, cinematography, and editing techniques.

1397. The Virtual Reality Deep Forest Meditation Sessions: Creating a series of VR meditation sessions set in serene deep forest environments, offering a digital retreat for relaxation and mindfulness.

1398. The DIY Rainwater Collection and Art Installation: Combining rainwater collection with art by creating an installation that is both visually striking and functional for water conservation, documenting the concept, build, and community response.

1399. A 24-Hour Challenge to Create an Urban Oasis: Transforming a neglected urban space into a green oasis within 24 hours, focusing on plant selection, sustainability, and creating a peaceful retreat in the city.

1400. One Month of Rediscovering Traditional Storytelling: Dedicating each day to learning and sharing a traditional story, fairy tale, or legend from around the world, exploring the art of storytelling and cultural heritage.

1401. The 48-Hour Upcycled Community Playground Project: Building a playground from upcycled materials in a local community, documenting the planning, community involvement, and joyful outcomes.

1402. One Month of Ancient Crafts Revival: Each day, exploring and reviving an ancient craft, from pottery making to basket weaving, sharing the historical context and modern application.

1403. The DIY Smart Garden Automation Challenge: Creating an automated garden system using DIY electronics and coding, focusing on water efficiency, plant health monitoring, and sustainable gardening practices.

1404. A 24-Hour International Virtual Dance-Off: Organizing a global virtual dance competition within 24 hours, showcasing diverse dance styles, cultural expressions, and fostering global connections.

1405. The Virtual Reality Experience of the World's Great Rivers: Offering an immersive journey along the world's great rivers in VR, exploring their ecosystems, cultural importance, and conservation issues.

1406. The DIY Bicycle-Powered Community Cinema: Setting up a cinema powered by bicycle generators, documenting the construction, community movie nights, and the joy of pedal-powered entertainment.

1407. A 24-Hour Citywide Kindness Campaign: Initiating acts of kindness across a city within 24 hours, documenting the actions, reactions, and ripple effects of spreading positivity in the community.

1408. One Week of Homemade Wind Instrument Making: Crafting a different wind instrument from scratch each day, exploring the physics of sound, instrument design, and musical performances.

1409. The Virtual Reality Journey Through the Body's Systems: Creating an educational VR journey that navigates through the body's various systems, providing insights into anatomy and physiology in an engaging way.

1410. The DIY Off-Grid Tiny House Build: Documenting the step-by-step build of an off-grid tiny house, focusing on sustainable living, energy independence, and minimalist lifestyle choices.

1411. A 24-Hour Global Street Art Collaboration: Collaborating with street artists around the world to create art pieces within 24 hours, highlighting the power of art to connect and inspire across cultures.

1412. One Month of Eco-Friendly Fashion Innovations: Each day, designing or highlighting an eco-friendly fashion innovation, from sustainable materials to ethical production practices.

1413. The Virtual Reality Exploration of Underwater Coral Reefs: Developing a VR experience that takes users on an exploration of vibrant underwater coral reefs, highlighting marine biodiversity and conservation efforts.

1414. The DIY Solar Oven Cooking Series: Building a solar oven and experimenting with different solar-cooked recipes, documenting the build process, cooking tips, and taste tests.

1415. A 24-Hour Challenge to Produce Zero Waste: Attempting to live a day without producing any waste, sharing strategies for waste reduction, sustainable alternatives, and reflections on the experience.

1416. One Week of Historic Battle Reenactments: Each day, reenacting a historic battle, detailing the historical context, strategies, and outcomes, while exploring the lessons learned and commemorating the past.

1417. The Virtual Reality Space Exploration Series: Producing a VR series that takes viewers on missions to explore space, including detailed tours of the International Space Station, moon landings, and interplanetary exploration.

1418. The DIY Recycled Material Greenhouse Project: Constructing a greenhouse entirely from recycled materials, documenting the creative use of resources, construction challenges, and the greenhouse's impact on plant growth.

1419. A 24-Hour Urban Farm to Table Experience: From harvesting in an urban garden to preparing and sharing a meal, documenting the journey of food from farm to table within a city setting.

1420. One Month of Cultural Immersion Challenges: Immersing in a different culture each week through language learning, cooking, traditions, and customs, sharing insights and promoting cultural appreciation and understanding.

1421. The Virtual Reality Deep-Time Geological Exploration: Offering an immersive VR experience that takes users through Earth's geological history, from the formation of continents to the movement of tectonic plates.

1422. The DIY Portable Water Purification Device Project: Designing and building a portable water purification device suitable for hiking or emergency situations, focusing on simplicity, effectiveness, and sustainability.

1423. A 24-Hour Public Space Transformation Challenge: Transforming a public space with art, landscaping, or furniture within 24 hours, documenting the process, community engagement, and the transformation's impact.

1424. One Week of Building DIY Musical Instruments for Children: Crafting simple musical instruments for children, focusing on using household or recycled materials, and encouraging musical exploration and education.

1425. The Virtual Reality Tour of the Human Mind: Developing a VR experience that explores the complexities of the human mind, including thoughts, emotions, and cognitive processes, in an engaging and understandable format.

1426. The DIY Eco-Friendly Personal Care Products Series: Creating a range of personal care products that are eco-friendly and free from harmful chemicals, documenting recipes, the making process, and user feedback.

1427. A 24-Hour Wildlife Conservation Initiative: Launching and documenting a wildlife conservation initiative within 24 hours, focusing on habitat restoration, species protection, or community education.

1428. One Month of Exploring Microhabitats in Your Backyard: Each day, discovering and documenting a different microhabitat in a backyard, highlighting the diversity of life in small spaces and the importance of all ecosystems.

1429. The Virtual Reality Reconstruction of Extinct Animals: Creating VR experiences that bring extinct animals to life, allowing users to interact with and learn about species that once roamed the Earth.

1430. The DIY Home Energy Efficiency Upgrade Project: Implementing a series of DIY projects to enhance home energy efficiency, documenting the upgrades, energy savings, and tips for homeowners.

1431. A 24-Hour Challenge to Create Sustainable Art: Producing art that focuses on sustainability themes, using eco-friendly materials and practices, and reflecting on environmental issues through creative expression.

1432. One Week of Adventure Travel Vlogs in Hidden Gems: Exploring a hidden gem location each day for a week, showcasing the beauty of lesser-known destinations, adventure activities, and cultural experiences.

1433. The Virtual Reality Architectural Wonders Tour: Offering VR tours of architectural wonders around the world, exploring the design, history, and cultural significance of each structure.

1434. The DIY Bicycle Maintenance and Customization Workshop: Hosting a workshop on bicycle maintenance and customization, sharing knowledge on bike care, repair tips, and ways to personalize bicycles.

1435. A 24-Hour Local Sustainable Development Project: Initiating and documenting a sustainable development project within a local community, focusing on environmental, economic, and social benefits.

1436. One Month of Learning Traditional Healing Practices: Diving into traditional healing practices from various cultures, documenting the learning process, methods, and insights into holistic health approaches.

1437. The Virtual Reality Prehistoric World Exploration: Creating a VR experience that transports users to the prehistoric world, exploring the landscape, flora, and fauna of different geological periods.

1438. The DIY Urban Vertical Farming Project: Setting up a vertical farming system in an urban setting, focusing on sustainable agriculture practices, space efficiency, and the benefits of urban farming.

1439. A 24-Hour Marathon of Random Acts of Music: Organizing a series of impromptu music performances in public spaces over 24 hours, showcasing local talent, community engagement, and the universal language of music.

1440. One Month of Building Eco-Friendly Bird and Insect Houses: Each day, constructing a house or shelter for birds, bees, or beneficial insects, using sustainable materials and practices, and documenting the impact on local wildlife.

1441. The 30-Day Local Language Challenge: Immerse in learning a local or indigenous language for a month, documenting daily progress, interactions with native speakers, and the cultural insights gained.

1442. The DIY Green Roof Installation Series: Showcasing the step-by-step process of installing a green roof on a residential property, including planning, plant selection, and the environmental benefits observed.

1443. A 24-Hour Flash Sculpture Challenge in Public Spaces: Creating temporary sculptures in public spaces using found materials, highlighting the process, public interaction, and the concept of impermanence in art.

1444. One Month of Historical Documentaries on Forgotten Heroes: Each day, releasing a short documentary on a forgotten hero from history, bringing their stories to light and detailing their contributions to society.

1445. The Virtual Reality Deep-Dive into Human Cultures: Developing VR experiences that immerse users in the daily life, traditions, and ceremonies of diverse cultures around the world, fostering empathy and understanding.

1446. The DIY Eco-Friendly Vehicle Conversion Project: Documenting the conversion of a conventional vehicle into an eco-friendly version, whether through electric conversion or biodiesel use, including the challenges and performance results.

1447. A 24-Hour Urban Biodiversity BioBlitz: Conducting a biodiversity "BioBlitz" in an urban area, identifying as many species as possible within 24 hours, and discussing urban ecology and conservation.

1448. One Week of Crafting Instruments from Recycled Materials: Creating musical instruments from recycled materials each day for a week, showcasing the creative process, sound quality, and how to play them.

1449. The Virtual Reality Simulation of Extreme Earth Events: Offering VR simulations of extreme Earth events like earthquakes, tsunamis, and volcanic eruptions, providing educational content on disaster preparedness and Earth sciences.

1450. The DIY Portable Solar Power Station Build: Building a portable solar power station capable of powering small devices or tools, detailing the construction, solar technology, and field testing.

1451. A 24-Hour Challenge to Live Like It's 1900: Spending a day living as people did in 1900, without modern conveniences, documenting the experience, challenges, and insights into past lifestyles.

1452. One Month of Guerrilla Gardening Missions: Undertaking daily guerrilla gardening missions to greenify and beautify neglected urban areas, sharing tips on plant choices, legal considerations, and community responses.

1453. The Virtual Reality Tour of the Universe's Mysteries: Creating a VR series that takes viewers on a journey through the universe's mysteries, from black holes to nebulae, explaining complex astronomical concepts in an engaging way.

1454. The DIY Tiny Home Building for a Sustainable Living: Documenting the entire process of designing and building a tiny home with a focus on sustainable living, from the use of eco-friendly materials to off-grid solutions.

1455. A 24-Hour Street Photography Marathon Across Different Neighborhoods: Capturing the essence of various neighborhoods through street photography over 24 hours, showcasing diversity, culture, and the unique stories of each area.

1456. One Week of Traditional Fishing Techniques Around the World: Each day, exploring and practicing a traditional fishing technique from a different culture, documenting the skills learned and the sustainability of each method.

1457. The Virtual Reality Reconstruction of Ancient Wonders: Developing VR experiences that reconstruct ancient wonders of the world, allowing users to explore and learn about these marvels in their original glory.

1458. The DIY Recycled Art and Furniture Gallery: Curating an art and furniture gallery featuring pieces made entirely from recycled materials, highlighting the artists, the creative process, and the stories behind each piece.

1459. A 24-Hour Mini Renewable Energy Project Challenge: Initiating mini renewable energy projects, such as building a small wind turbine or a solar-powered gadget, within 24 hours, focusing on innovation and sustainability.

1460. One Month of Exploring Microscopic Photography: Diving into the world of microscopic photography, capturing the beauty and details of the micro world each day, and sharing the scientific and artistic insights gained.

1461. The Virtual Reality Exploration of Secret Societies: Offering VR experiences that delve into the history, rituals, and mysteries of secret societies throughout history, blending education with intrigue.

1462. The DIY Urban Cooling Solutions Experiment: Testing and implementing various urban cooling solutions, such as misting stations or reflective pavements, documenting the effectiveness and community feedback.

1463. A 24-Hour Global Folklore and Mythology Podcast Marathon: Hosting a podcast marathon that explores folklore and mythology from around the world, featuring storytellers, historians, and cultural experts.

1464. One Week of Sustainable Fashion Upcycling: Transforming old or discarded clothing into fashionable, wearable art each day for a week, focusing on upcycling techniques and promoting sustainable fashion.

1465. The Virtual Reality Experience of Life as an Astronaut: Creating a VR experience that simulates the daily life of an astronaut, from training to living on the International Space Station, offering insights into space exploration challenges.

1466. The DIY Community Powered Water Filtration System: Building a community-scale water filtration system using locally sourced materials, documenting the build process, community involvement, and impact on local water quality.

1467. A 24-Hour Urban Permaculture Design Challenge: Designing and beginning the implementation of a permaculture project in an urban setting within 24 hours, focusing on sustainable and regenerative design principles.

1468. One Month of Building a Living Roof or Wall: Documenting the process of creating a living roof or wall, from design and plant selection to maintenance, focusing on the benefits for biodiversity, insulation, and aesthetics.

1469. The Virtual Reality Deep Dive into Historical Shipwrecks: Offering VR experiences that explore historical shipwrecks, combining underwater archaeology with storytelling to uncover the stories behind the sunken ships.

1470. The DIY Alternative Energy Experimentation Lab: Setting up a lab to experiment with alternative energy sources, such as biofuels or piezoelectric materials, documenting experiments, results, and potential applications.

1471. A 24-Hour Challenge to Create an Eco-Friendly Art Installation: Creating an art installation that emphasizes eco-friendliness and sustainability within 24 hours, documenting the concept, materials used, and public interaction.

1472. One Week of Exploring Soundscapes in Different Environments: Recording and analyzing soundscapes in various environments each day, from natural settings to urban areas, discussing the impact of sound on well-being and ecology.

1473. The Virtual Reality Adventure Through Fantasy Worlds: Developing VR content that takes users on adventures through fantasy worlds inspired by literature and mythology, blending immersive storytelling with interactive experiences.

1474. The DIY Bicycle Camper Build: Designing and building a lightweight, functional bicycle camper, documenting the planning, construction, and road testing, focusing on minimalist travel and sustainability.

1475. A 24-Hour Local Heritage Craft Fair: Organizing a craft fair that showcases local heritage crafts within 24 hours, promoting traditional skills, local artisans, and community engagement.

1476. The One-Day Urban Accessibility Audit: Documenting the experience of navigating a city with mobility challenges to highlight accessibility issues and advocate for inclusive urban design improvements.

1477. The 30-Day Minimalist Living Experiment: Each day, focusing on a different aspect of minimalist living, documenting the journey of decluttering, simplifying routines, and reflecting on the impact on well-being and environmental footprint.

1478. The DIY Floating Aquaponics System: Building a floating aquaponics system that combines fish farming with hydroponics, sharing the construction process, system management, and the symbiotic relationship between plants and fish.

1479. A 24-Hour Virtual Reality Cultural Heritage Preservation Marathon: Creating VR content that aims to preserve and showcase cultural heritage sites at risk, involving expert insights, historical context, and the significance of preservation efforts.

1480. One Week of Backyard Astrophotography: Capturing the night sky from a backyard each night for a week, focusing on different celestial objects or phenomena, and sharing techniques, equipment used, and the science behind the sights.

1481. The DIY Portable Eco-Friendly Laundry System: Designing and creating a portable, eco-friendly laundry washing system, suitable for small spaces or off-grid living, focusing on water efficiency and minimal environmental impact.

1482. A 24-Hour Challenge to Create a Community Mosaic Mural: Engaging the community to create a large-scale mosaic mural within 24 hours, documenting the collaborative process, the design significance, and the mural's impact on community spirit.

1483. One Month of Historic Recipe Reconstructions: Each day, recreating a historic recipe from different times and cultures, exploring the origins, ingredients, and cooking methods, and reflecting on the historical context and tastes.

1484. The Virtual Reality Under-the-Microscope World: Developing a VR experience that allows users to explore the world under the microscope, from cellular structures to microorganisms, highlighting the beauty and complexity of microscopic life.

1485. The DIY Solar-Powered Water Desalination Project: Building a solar-powered desalination device to convert seawater into drinkable water, documenting the design, construction, and effectiveness of the system.

1486. A 24-Hour Eco-Friendly Fashion Swap Event: Organizing a fashion swap event to promote sustainable fashion, documenting the preparation, the swap process, participant experiences, and the benefits of swapping over buying new.

1487. One Week of Wilderness Survival Skills: Spending a week in the wilderness, each day focusing on a different survival skill, from fire starting to shelter building, sharing tips, challenges, and the value of reconnecting with nature.

1488. The Virtual Reality Time-Lapse Earth Evolution Experience: Creating a VR experience that showcases the evolution of Earth from its formation to the present day through immersive time-lapse visuals, highlighting geological changes, biodiversity evolution, and human impact.

1489. The DIY Bicycle-Powered Community Amenities: Implementing bicycle-powered solutions for community amenities, such as charging stations, small-scale grinders or mills, documenting the community involvement, build process, and usage.

1490. A 24-Hour Local Unsung Environmental Heroes Spotlight: Highlighting local individuals or groups making significant environmental impacts within 24 hours, sharing their stories, projects, and how viewers can support or get involved.

1491. One Month of Exploring Traditional Textiles and Weaving: Diving into the world of traditional textiles and weaving techniques, learning and practicing a different technique each day, and exploring their cultural significance and contemporary applications.

1492. The Virtual Reality Exploration of Future Urban Living: Designing VR simulations that explore concepts of future urban living, including smart cities, vertical farming, and sustainable architecture, focusing on innovation and environmental sustainability.

1493. The DIY Backyard Biome Project: Creating a series of backyard biomes, such as a butterfly garden, a pond ecosystem, or a desert landscape, documenting the creation process, the biodiversity supported, and maintenance tips.

1494. A 24-Hour Challenge to Reduce Digital Footprint: Taking on the challenge to minimize digital footprint and consumption for 24 hours, sharing strategies for digital detox, data privacy, and reflections on the impact of digital consumption on mental health and the environment.

1495. One Week of Crafting with Nature: Using natural materials found in local surroundings to craft different items each day, focusing on the process of gathering materials responsibly, crafting techniques, and the inspiration drawn from nature.

1496. The Virtual Reality Grand Historical Festivals Experience: Bringing historical festivals to life through VR, allowing users to experience the sights, sounds, and activities of festivals from different eras and cultures, enhancing historical education and cultural appreciation.

1497. The DIY Wind-Powered Art Installations: Creating art installations that are powered by or interact with the wind, documenting the conceptualization, design challenges, and the dynamic interaction between art and natural forces.

1498. A 24-Hour Urban Foraging and Wild Food Cooking Challenge: Foraging for edible plants and wild food in an urban setting for 24 hours, followed by cooking and sharing foraged meals, focusing on urban ecology, foraging safety, and sustainability.

1499. One Month of In-Home Science Experiments: Conducting a different simple science experiment at home each day, exploring various scientific principles, documenting the setup, observation, and explanations in an educational and engaging way.

1500. The Virtual Reality Deep-Dive into Art Movements: Creating an immersive VR journey through various art movements, offering interactive galleries that showcase key works, artists, and the historical context of each movement.

1501. The 7-Day Eco-Adventure Challenge: Embarking on a week-long journey to explore eco-friendly adventures, focusing on activities that promote environmental awareness and conservation efforts, and sharing practical tips on sustainable adventure travel.

1502. DIY Urban Space Reclamation Project: Transforming an underutilized urban space into a vibrant community area, such as a pop-up park or community garden, documenting the planning, community involvement, and transformation process.

1503. 24 Hours in a Virtual Reality Historical Event: Immersing in a significant historical event through VR, providing an in-depth look at the event's context, impact, and legacy, and sharing insights into the immersive learning experience.

1504. One Month of Artistic Expression Through Recycled Materials: Creating a new piece of art each day using only recycled or repurposed materials, highlighting creativity in sustainability, and showcasing the artistic process and final creations.

1505. The Ultimate Home Energy Efficiency Makeover: Documenting the process of auditing and upgrading a home for maximum energy efficiency, including the installation of energy-saving devices, insulation improvements, and renewable energy solutions.

1506. A Day in the Life of a Zero-Waste Advocate: Following the daily routine of someone living a zero-waste lifestyle, highlighting the challenges, solutions, and impacts of minimizing waste in everyday life.

1507. Building a Community-Based Renewable Energy Project: Documenting the journey of creating a renewable energy project, such as a community solar garden or a small wind turbine installation, focusing on community engagement, funding, and the project's environmental impact.

1508. 24-Hour Challenge: The Science of Everyday Phenomena: Exploring and explaining the science behind everyday phenomena in a 24-hour challenge, making science accessible and engaging through practical demonstrations and experiments.

1509. One Month to Master a Traditional Craft: Dedicating a month to learning and mastering a traditional craft, from its historical origins to its cultural significance, and documenting the learning process, challenges, and the craft's modern-day relevance.

1510. Virtual Reality Exploration of Endangered Ecosystems: Creating VR experiences that take viewers into endangered ecosystems, aiming to raise awareness about conservation issues, the importance of biodiversity, and efforts to protect these habitats.

1511. The DIY Tiny Eco-Home Challenge: Building a tiny eco-home from sustainable materials, documenting the design choices, construction challenges, and showcasing the benefits of minimalist, eco-friendly living.

1512. A Day of Silence for Mental Health Awareness: Spending a day in silence to promote mental health awareness, reflecting on the experience, its impact on well-being, and sharing insights and resources on mental health.

1513. Cultural Exchange Cooking Series: Partnering with individuals from different cultural backgrounds to create a series of cooking videos, each showcasing a traditional dish from their culture, focusing on the recipe, cooking techniques, and cultural stories behind the dish.

1514. One Week of Wilderness First Aid Lessons: Sharing essential wilderness first aid tips and techniques over a week, covering common outdoor injuries and emergencies, aimed at preparing adventurers for safe exploration.

1515. The Virtual Time Traveler's Guide to Ancient Civilizations: Creating an engaging series that takes viewers on virtual time travels to ancient civilizations, exploring daily life, architectural achievements, and the civilizations' contributions to the modern world.

1516. DIY Sustainable Pet Care Solutions: Crafting eco-friendly pet care solutions, from homemade pet food to sustainable toys and bedding, focusing on reducing the environmental pawprint of pet ownership.

1517. 24 Hours Making Music with Nature: Creating music using only natural elements and sounds found in nature within a 24-hour period, showcasing the process of finding sounds, creating instruments, and composing music.

1518. One Month of Historical Language Learning: Taking on the challenge of learning the basics of a historical language, documenting the study methods, progress, and exploring the language's historical significance and contemporary relevance.

1519. 360-Degree Virtual Reality Street Art Tour: Offering a 360-degree VR tour of iconic street art from around the world, providing background on the artists, the artwork's themes, and the role of street art in urban culture.

1520. The DIY Off-Grid Living Experiment: Documenting the experience of living off-grid for a predetermined period, including the setup of off-grid systems (solar power, water collection, waste management), daily life challenges, and reflections on sustainability and self-sufficiency.

1521. Cross-Cultural Mythology Series: Each episode explores myths from different cultures around the world, highlighting similarities, differences, and the values they reflect in their societies.

1522. The 30-Day Renewable Energy Challenge: Living off different types of renewable energy each week, documenting the setup, the challenges, and the impact on daily life and energy consumption.

1523. DIY Eco-Friendly Product Hacks: Showcasing creative ways to repurpose everyday items into eco-friendly products, from homemade cleaning agents to upcycled decor, encouraging sustainability.

1524. A Week in a Van Life Conversion: Transforming a standard van into a fully functional living space on wheels, focusing on sustainable and space-saving solutions, and documenting the journey and final reveal.

1525. 24-Hour Local Food Challenge: Eating only foods grown or produced within a 100-mile radius for 24 hours, exploring local agriculture, the benefits of eating locally, and the challenge of finding local food sources.

1526. Building a Community Tech Hub from Scratch: Documenting the process of creating a tech hub for a community, including finding a space, sourcing equipment, and hosting educational workshops on technology.

1527. The Art of Silent Film making: Producing a short silent film, focusing on visual storytelling, expression, and the techniques used in the silent film era, followed by a discussion on the film's creation.

1528. One Month of Historical Diets: Experimenting with a different historical diet each week, exploring the foods, cooking methods, and nutritional impacts, and reflecting on how diets have evolved over time.

1529. Virtual Reality Architectural Time Travel: Creating VR experiences that allow users to explore architectural landmarks through different historical periods, highlighting changes in design and function.

1530. The Science Behind Superfoods Series: Investigating the nutritional science behind various superfoods, debunking myths, and providing recipes and tips on incorporating them into a healthy diet.

1531. DIY Urban Soundscapes Project: Recording and creating a soundscape of an urban area, focusing on the diversity of sounds, their sources, and their impact on the urban environment and its inhabitants.

1532. 48-Hour Pop-up Library in Unusual Spaces: Setting up temporary libraries in unexpected locations, such as parks, beaches, or public squares, documenting the setup, visitor interactions, and the promotion of reading.

1533. One Week Living with Artificial Intelligence: Integrating AI tools and assistants into daily life for a week, documenting the benefits, challenges, and insights on how AI can enhance or complicate everyday tasks.

1534. Exploring Abandoned Spaces Series: Visiting and documenting abandoned buildings and spaces, delving into their history, the reasons they were abandoned, and their potential for repurposing.

1535. The Zero-Waste Beauty Routine Challenge: Adopting a zero-waste beauty routine for a month, showcasing DIY beauty products, sustainable beauty tools, and evaluating the overall experience and impact.

1536. 24 Hours Creating Art Underwater: Producing artwork while submerged, focusing on the unique challenges of underwater art creation, the materials and techniques used, and the final artworks.

1537. A Month of Mindfulness and Meditation Techniques: Trying a different mindfulness or meditation technique each day, sharing the experiences, benefits, and challenges of each method.

1538. The Homemade Water Filtration Experiment: Designing and testing homemade water filtration systems using natural and recycled materials, documenting the effectiveness and potential uses.

1539. Creating a Stop Motion Animation Series: Producing a series of stop motion animations, covering the creative process, the challenges of the medium, and the storytelling possibilities it offers.

1540. One Day in the Life of a Historical Figure Reenactment: Spending a day living as a historical figure, from their attire to their daily activities, offering insights into their life and times.

1541. The 72-Hour Urban Regeneration Project: Documenting a rapid community-led initiative to transform a neglected urban area, focusing on sustainable and creative revitalization techniques.

1542. One Month of Forgotten Music Instruments: Each day, exploring a different musical instrument that has fallen out of mainstream use, delving into its history, sound, and playing technique.

1543. DIY Biophilic Home Design Makeover: Implementing biophilic design principles to enhance connection with nature in a home environment, documenting the transformation and its impacts on well-being.

1544. A Week of Crafting With Invasive Plant Species: Using invasive plants to create useful or artistic items, highlighting the environmental impact of these species and creative ways to manage them.

1545. Virtual Reality Tour of Future Mars Colonies: Offering an immersive experience of what living on Mars might look like in the future, based on current plans and scientific speculation.

1546. 24-Hour Challenge: Living With Historical Cooking Methods: Spending a day cooking with techniques and tools from a specific historical period, reflecting on the experience and culinary outcomes.

1547. Building a Community Bicycle Repair Workshop: Documenting the establishment of a free or donation-based bicycle repair workshop, focusing on promoting cycling and community self-reliance.

1548. Exploring Micro histories in a Month: Each day, uncovering and presenting a micro history - a small, overlooked event or element that had a surprising impact on the broader historical context.

1549. The Art of Upcycling Electronic Waste: Transforming electronic waste into functional gadgets, art, or furniture, showcasing the process and the potential for tech waste reduction.

1550. A Day in the Life of a Zero-Emission Commuter: Documenting the challenges and experiences of commuting using only zero-emission modes of transportation, such as electric vehicles, bicycles, or walking.

1551. One Month of Solar Cooking Experiments: Experimenting with different solar cooker designs and recipes, evaluating their efficiency, and promoting solar cooking as a sustainable alternative.

1552. Virtual Reality Exploration of the Ocean's Midnight Zone: Creating a VR experience that takes viewers into the deep ocean's midnight zone, revealing the mysterious life forms and terrain found at these depths.

1553. DIY Natural Dye Making From Local Plants: Harvesting local plants and experimenting with natural dye making, focusing on the process, color outcomes, and sustainable fashion.

1554. 24-Hour International Virtual Poetry Slam: Hosting a global virtual poetry slam, bringing together poets from various countries to share their work and cultural perspectives within 24 hours.

1555. Building a Miniature Ecosystem in a Bottle: Crafting a self-sustaining ecosystem within a sealed bottle, documenting the setup, the ecological balance, and long-term observations.

1556. A Week of Silent Movie Creation: Producing a series of short silent films, focusing on visual storytelling and expression, and exploring the history and technique of silent cinema.

1557. Exploring the World's Sacred Groves: Delving into the cultural and spiritual significance of sacred groves around the world, highlighting their history, ecological importance, and threats.

1558. DIY Water-saving Solutions for the Home Garden: Implementing and testing various water-saving techniques for home gardening, such as drip irrigation, rainwater harvesting, and soil moisture retention hacks.

1559. One Day of Tech Detox in Nature: Documenting a day spent in nature without any digital devices, focusing on the mental and physical benefits of disconnecting from technology.

1560. The Science of Sleep: A 30-Day Experiment: Exploring different sleep science theories and practices each night for a month, documenting the impact on sleep quality, mood, and productivity.

1561. The Zero-Energy Home Challenge: Documenting the transformation of a house to operate on zero energy, focusing on renewable energy installations, energy-saving techniques, and the lifestyle adjustments needed to achieve this goal.

1562. A Month of Global Myth Re-telling: Each day, telling a myth from a different culture, exploring its origins, meanings, and impact on contemporary society, using animation, storytelling, or dramatic reenactments.

1563. DIY Urban Wildlife Sanctuary: Creating a sanctuary for urban wildlife in a small backyard or community space, documenting the design, the types of wildlife attracted, and the ecological benefits over time.

1564. 24 Hours Building a Community Art Installation: Engaging the community to collectively create a large-scale art installation in a public space within 24 hours, showcasing the planning, collaboration, and final unveiling.

1565. Virtual Reality Time Travel to Key Historical Speeches: Offering an immersive VR experience that transports viewers to listen to key historical speeches as if they were there, highlighting the context, the speech's impact, and its relevance today.

1566. The Sustainable Fashion Upcycle Marathon: Spending a week transforming thrift store finds or old clothes into fashionable, modern outfits, focusing on creativity, sewing techniques, and the importance of sustainable fashion.

1567. Building a DIY Solar-Powered Boat: Documenting the process of designing and constructing a boat powered solely by solar energy, including trials, modifications, and the voyage's success.

1568. A Day Without Plastic Challenge: Attempting to go an entire day without using any plastic products, documenting the preparation, challenges, alternatives found, and reflections on plastic dependency.

1569. One Month of Historical DIY Projects: Each day, undertaking a DIY project that people in the past would have done, from making ink and quills to weaving baskets, exploring the history and practicality of each project.

1570. Exploring Abandoned Railways Around the World: Traveling to and documenting abandoned railway lines, delving into their history, why they were abandoned, and the nature or culture that has taken over since.

1571. The Art of Natural Light Photography: Spending a week mastering photography using only natural light, sharing tips, techniques, and the unique aesthetics achieved in various lighting conditions.

1572. 24-Hour Pop-Up Book Exchange Booth: Setting up a book exchange booth in a community for 24 hours, encouraging reading and sharing stories about the books exchanged and the people who visit.

1573. DIY Eco-Friendly Tiny Home on Wheels: Showcasing the step-by-step build of a tiny home on wheels using eco-friendly materials and design principles, including the challenges and solutions found along the way.

1574. Virtual Reality Exploration of Extinct Ecosystems: Creating VR experiences that allow users to explore ecosystems that no longer exist, focusing on what was lost and lessons for conservation.

1575. A Week of Silence in Different Natural Environments: Documenting a week spent in silence, each day in a different natural setting, reflecting on the experience, the sounds of nature, and personal insights gained.

1576. The 30-Day Local Craftsmanship Appreciation Project: Each day, highlighting a local craftsman or artisan, showcasing their work, the skills and dedication involved, and the importance of supporting local crafts.

1577. Urban Foraging and Wild Cooking: Spending a day foraging for edible plants in an urban environment and preparing a meal with the found ingredients, sharing foraging tips and recipes.

1578. The Human-Powered Transportation Experiment: For one month, using only human-powered means of transportation, documenting the experience, benefits, challenges, and impact on lifestyle and health.

1579. Creating a Community Vertical Garden: Building a vertical garden in a community space, documenting the process from design to completion, and discussing the benefits of vertical gardening in urban areas.

1580. A 24-Hour Off-Grid Camping Adventure: Documenting a 24-hour camping trip without any modern conveniences, focusing on survival skills, the connection with nature, and the challenges faced.

1581. The One-Month Minimalist Design Challenge: Transforming a different space or object each day using minimalist design principles, documenting the process, the design choices, and the impact on functionality and aesthetics.

1582. A Week of Solar-Powered Inventions: Each day, creating a new invention that operates solely on solar power, from household gadgets to outdoor tools, showcasing the build process, functionality, and solar efficiency.

1583. 24-Hour Historic Food Marathon: Cooking and tasting historic dishes over 24 hours, exploring recipes from various centuries or civilizations, and delving into the historical context and evolution of each dish.

1584. Building a Community-Powered Rain Garden: Documenting the collaborative effort to design and install a rain garden in a community space, focusing on water conservation, native plant species, and community engagement.

1585. Virtual Reality Dive into Quantum Mechanics: Offering an immersive VR experience that simplifies complex quantum mechanics concepts, making them accessible and engaging through interactive simulations.

1586. The DIY Off-Grid Communication System: Creating a system for off-grid communication, such as a simple radio transmitter or a solar-powered Wi-Fi station, documenting the technical challenges, solutions, and final setup.

1587. A Day in the Life of an Urban Beekeeper: Showcasing the daily routines and responsibilities of an urban beekeeper, highlighting the importance of bees in urban environments and tips for starting urban beekeeping.

1588. One Month of Recycled Art Projects: Each day, tackling a different art project using only recycled or repurposed materials, emphasizing creativity in sustainability and the final artworks.

1589. Exploring the Science of Happiness: A series delving into psychological and neuroscientific research on happiness, including experiments, interviews with experts, and practical happiness-boosting techniques.

1590. 24-Hour Wilderness Survival with Basic Tools: Documenting a survival challenge in the wilderness using only a limited set of basic tools, focusing on survival skills, resourcefulness, and the connection with nature.

1591. The Journey of Restoring a Historic Home: Documenting the restoration process of a historic home, focusing on preserving its heritage while incorporating modern sustainability features.

1592. A Week of Underwater Photography Challenges: Each day, presenting a new challenge related to underwater photography, exploring different aquatic environments, techniques, and the marine life captured.

1593. Virtual Tour of Abandoned Industrial Sites: Creating a series that explores abandoned industrial sites around the world, investigating their history, why they were abandoned, and their current state.

1594. DIY Smart Home Gadgets from Recycled Materials: Designing and building smart home gadgets using recycled materials, showcasing the creative process, functionality, and environmental impact.

1595. 24 Hours Creating Zero Waste Art Supplies: A challenge to create art supplies from scratch without producing waste, documenting the process, the resulting supplies, and their use in creating art.

1596. One Month of Cultural Exchange Dinners: Hosting dinners that each focus on a different culture's cuisine, inviting guests from that culture to share in the meal and discuss their traditions and experiences.

1597. The Science Behind Sports Performance: A series exploring the science of sports performance, including physiology, nutrition, psychology, and technology's role in enhancing athletic ability.

1598. Building a Wind-Powered Water Pump: Documenting the design and construction of a wind-powered water pump for agricultural or community use, focusing on sustainability and engineering challenges.

1599. A Day of Mindful Photography: Spending a day practicing mindfulness through photography, capturing moments that reflect presence, awareness, and the beauty in everyday life.

1600. The One-Week Homemade Musical Challenge: Writing, composing, and performing a musical piece using homemade instruments, documenting the creative process, challenges, and the final performance.

1601. Zero-Waste Cooking Challenge: Spend a week creating meals with the goal of producing zero waste, highlighting creative recipes, waste reduction tips, and reflections on the impact of food waste.

1602. DIY Urban Green Roof Project: Document the process of converting a flat urban roof into a green oasis, focusing on plant selection, the benefits of green roofs, and challenges faced in urban settings.

1603. Historical Fashion Through the Ages: Each episode explores fashion from a different era or decade, including making or sourcing period-accurate clothing and discussing its cultural and social significance.

1604. The 48-Hour Film Project: From scriptwriting to editing, document the creation of a short film within 48 hours, emphasizing creativity under time constraints and the collaborative filmmaking process.

1605. Solar-Powered Tech Gadgets Exploration: Explore and review various solar-powered gadgets, from everyday items to innovative tech, evaluating their performance, practicality, and impact on sustainability.

1606. A Journey Through Local Folktales: Traveling regionally or nationally to collect and narrate local folktales, exploring the storytelling tradition, cultural heritage, and moral lessons of each tale.

1607. Build Your Own Composting System: A step-by-step guide to building a home composting system suitable for different scales, from apartment dwellers to homeowners, focusing on the benefits and challenges of composting.

1608. 24 Hours in a Haunted Location: Spend 24 hours in a location reputed to be haunted, documenting experiences, historical research on the site, and any paranormal activity encountered.

1609. A Week of Living Like a Roman: Adopting the lifestyle, diet, and daily routines of ancient Romans for a week, exploring historical practices, their relevance today, and insights into Roman culture.

1610. The Art of Timelapse Photography: A series teaching the techniques of timelapse photography, showcasing stunning timelapses of different subjects and environments, and sharing tips for beginners.

1611. DIY Pocket Park Creation: Transforming a small, underused urban space into a pocket park, documenting the design process, community involvement, and the park's impact on urban livability.

1612. Around the World in 30 Dances: Each episode explores a traditional dance from a different country, including learning the dance, its cultural background, and performing it in an authentic setting.

1613. Eco-Friendly Pet Care Solutions: Sharing tips and DIY projects for eco-friendly pet care, from homemade pet food to sustainable toys and accessories, emphasizing health and environmental impact.

1614. The Science of Sleep Experiment: Conduct a 30-day experiment exploring different sleep theories and practices, documenting the effects on health, mood, and productivity.

1615. Building a Tiny Library for the Community: Document the creation of a free community book exchange, a tiny library, from construction to installation, and the community's engagement with the project.

1616. One Month of Geocaching Adventures: Embark on daily geocaching adventures, exploring new locations, the thrill of the hunt, and the community aspect of geocaching.

1617. The Ultimate Upcycling Home Decor Challenge: Spend a week transforming discarded items into stylish home decor, showcasing each project's process, creativity, and final reveal.

1618. A Day with Traditional Craftsmen: Spend a day learning from craftsmen who practice traditional arts, from blacksmithing to handloom weaving, documenting their skills, processes, and the importance of preserving these crafts.

1619. The 30-Day Public Speaking Journey: Improve public speaking skills over 30 days, documenting progress through various challenges, workshops, and finally, a public speaking event.

1620. Virtual Reality Exploration of the Human Cell: Create an immersive VR experience that navigates through the structure and functions of a human cell, making complex biological concepts accessible and engaging.

1621. DIY Bicycle-Powered Machines: Showcase the creation of machines powered by bicycle, from simple generators to more complex mechanisms, emphasizing sustainability and human-powered technology.

1622. The History of Board Games Series: Explore the history, evolution, and cultural significance of different board games around the world, including playing these games with experts or enthusiasts.

1623. A Week Off-the-Grid in a Self-Sustaining Cabin: Document the experience of living in a self-sustaining cabin off the grid, focusing on sustainability practices, the challenges of self-sufficiency, and reflections on modern living.

1624. Exploring the World's Most Remote Islands: A series on visiting some of the world's most remote islands, exploring their unique ecosystems, cultures, and the challenges of isolation.

1625. The Art of Handmade Books: Dive into the craft of making books by hand, from binding
to paper making, showcasing the beauty and intricacy of handmade books.

1626. The 30-Day Wild Food Foraging Challenge: Documenting the journey of foraging for wild food every day for a month, learning about edible plants, mushrooms, and their preparation.

1627. DIY Sustainable Water Sports Equipment: Creating eco-friendly water sports equipment, such as surfboards or kayaks, from sustainable materials, showcasing the build process and testing them out.

1628. A Week in the Life of a Medieval Villager: Living as a medieval villager for a week, adopting the lifestyle, crafts, and daily routines of the period, and reflecting on the experience and historical insights.

1629. Exploring the Science of Illusions: A series dedicated to unraveling the science behind various optical and sensory illusions, including creating your own illusions and explaining how they trick the mind.

1630. Building an Eco-Friendly Artist's Retreat: Documenting the design and construction of a sustainable retreat for artists, focusing on eco-friendly materials, renewable energy, and creating an inspiring space.

1631. 24-Hour Challenge: Urban Survival Skills: Navigating a city for 24 hours with limited resources, showcasing urban survival skills, resourcefulness, and tips for emergency preparedness.

1632. One Month of Reviving Ancient Board Games: Rediscovering and playing a different ancient board game each day, exploring their history, rules, and cultural significance.

1633. DIY Vertical Wind Turbine Project: Building a vertical wind turbine for home or community use, documenting the design choices, construction process, and the turbine's efficiency in generating power.

1634. A Day in the Life of a Nomadic Tribe: Spending a day with a nomadic tribe, documenting their traditions, lifestyle, and how they adapt to the modern world while maintaining their cultural identity.

1635. The Ultimate Recycled Fashion Show: Organizing a fashion show where all outfits are made from recycled or upcycled materials, showcasing creativity in sustainable fashion and the final runway event.

1636. Exploring Underwater Caves with Drones: Using underwater drones to explore and document the mysterious world of underwater caves, highlighting the technology, discoveries, and challenges of cave diving.

1637. The 30-Day Local Language Speaking Challenge: Committing to only speak a local or lesser-known language for 30 days, documenting the learning process, daily interactions, and cultural immersion.

1638. Building a Community Outdoor Cinema: Creating an outdoor cinema space for the community, from sourcing equipment to organizing movie nights, focusing on community engagement and shared experiences.

1639. A Week of Crafting Traditional Musical Instruments: Crafting a different traditional musical instrument each day, exploring their cultural origins, construction techniques, and producing sounds.

1640. Virtual Reality Exploration of Ancient Forests: Offering an immersive VR experience of walking through ancient forests around the world, educating viewers on their ecosystems, history, and conservation.

1641. The Art of Making Natural Inks and Pigments: Demonstrating how to make inks and pigments from natural materials, showcasing the process, the variety of colors achievable, and applications in art.

1642. 24 Hours Living Off the Grid: Documenting a day living entirely off-grid, using alternative energy sources, and showcasing the challenges and benefits of a self-sufficient lifestyle.

1643. One Month of Heritage Craft Workshops: Participating in a different heritage craft workshop each day, learning skills like pottery, thatching, blacksmithing, and sharing the educational journey.

1644. DIY Backyard Observatory for Stargazing: Building a simple backyard observatory for stargazing, including selecting the location, constructing the observatory, and sharing tips for amateur astronomers.

1645. Exploring the World's Microclimates: A series visiting areas with unique microclimates, investigating the causes, effects on local ecosystems, and how these climates shape human activities.

1646. 30 Days of Mindful Living Experiments: Each day, experimenting with a different mindfulness practice or technique, documenting the impact on mental health, productivity, and overall well-being.

1647. The Science and Art of Fermentation: Delving into the process of fermentation, exploring various fermented foods and drinks, the science behind fermentation, and recipes to try at home.

1648. Reviving a Derelict Garden into a Permaculture Haven: Transforming a neglected garden into a thriving permaculture garden, documenting the planning, restoration process, and the garden's evolution.

1649. A Week of Silence in Different Natural Settings: Spending each day in silence in a different natural setting, reflecting on the experience, the sounds of nature, and the personal insights gained.

1650. DIY Crafting with Biodegradable Materials: Creating a variety of items using biodegradable materials, focusing on the materials' properties, crafting techniques, and the environmental benefits.

1651. The Zero-Waste Party Planning Guide: Document the process of planning and hosting a completely zero-waste party, focusing on sustainable decor, food, and activities, plus tips on minimizing waste.

1652. Building a Community Maker Space from Scratch: Follow the journey of creating a maker space in the community, from gathering resources and tools to organizing workshops and events that encourage creativity and innovation.

1653. A Month of Experimental Gardening: Try out unconventional gardening methods and experimental plant combinations for a month, documenting the setup, progress, challenges, and results of each experiment.

1654. 24-Hour Urban Nature Challenge: Spend 24 hours finding and documenting nature in an urban environment, showcasing the often-overlooked flora and fauna that thrive in city settings.

1655. The Art of Shadow Puppetry: Dive into the traditional art of shadow puppetry, learning how to create and manipulate puppets, and perform a short story or folklore tale using this ancient technique.

1656. DIY Sustainable Fishing Gear: Design and create eco-friendly fishing gear, focusing on materials that reduce environmental impact, and test their effectiveness in a responsible and sustainable fishing practice.

1657. One Week Living with a Historical Diet: Each day, eat according to the dietary habits of a different historical period or civilization, exploring the nutritional, cultural, and practical aspects of each diet.

1658. Building a Tiny Eco-Friendly Workspace: Document the design and construction of a small, sustainable workspace, using green building materials and techniques, and showcasing the finished, functional space.

1659. The Science of Color Perception: Create a series exploring how humans perceive color, including experiments, the psychological effects of different colors, and how color perception varies across cultures.

1660. A Day in the Life of a Smart City: Explore a day living in a smart city, highlighting the integration of technology in everyday life, from transportation to energy use, and the benefits and challenges of living in such an environment.

1661. Exploring the World of Amateur Radio: Dive into the hobby of amateur radio, including how to get started, the technology involved, and connecting with people from around the world.

1662. The 30-Day Public Art Project: Spend a month creating and installing temporary public art pieces in various locations, documenting the creation process, public reactions, and the impact on community spaces.

1663. DIY Eco-Friendly Personal Hygiene Products: Show how to make your own eco-friendly personal hygiene products, such as toothpaste, deodorant, and shampoo, focusing on natural ingredients and sustainable packaging.

1664. A Week of Wilderness Craftsmanship: Spend a week in the wilderness crafting useful items from natural materials found in the environment, documenting the techniques used and the functionality of the crafted items.

1665. The Virtual Reality Tour of the Solar System's Moons: Develop a VR experience that takes viewers on a tour of the moons in our solar system, highlighting unique features and scientific discoveries of each moon.

1666. 24 Hours Creating Art with AI: Use AI tools to create various forms of art over 24 hours, exploring the intersection of technology and creativity, and discussing the implications of AI in the art world.

1667. One Month of Learning Sign Language: Dedicate a month to learning sign language, sharing daily progress, interactions with the deaf community, and reflecting on the importance of inclusive communication.

1668. Building a Wind-Powered Sculpture Garden: Create a series of wind-powered sculptures for a public or private garden, documenting the design and engineering process, and the kinetic art's interaction with the natural environment.

1669. A Day of Geothermal Exploration: Explore and document geothermal activity in a region, including hot springs, geysers, and volcanic activity, explaining the science behind geothermal energy and its potential uses.

1670. The 30-Day Bike-to-Work Challenge: Challenge yourself to bike to work every day for a month, documenting the experience, benefits, challenges, and the impact on your health and carbon footprint.

1671. The Urban Tree Planting Initiative: Launch a campaign to plant trees in urban areas, documenting the planning process, community involvement, the planting day, and the benefits of urban greening.

1672. A Week of Solar Experimentation: Each day, experiment with a different solar-powered project, from cooking devices to small solar panels for electronic gadgets, showcasing the potential of solar energy in everyday life.

1673. DIY Biodegradable Packaging Solutions: Explore and create various biodegradable packaging solutions, focusing on materials, design, and functionality, and testing their decomposition rates and environmental impact.

1674. The Art of Ice Sculpting: Delve into the world of ice sculpting, from learning basic techniques to creating a detailed sculpture, documenting the ephemeral nature of the art and the sculpting process.

1675. 24 Hours as a Historical Scientist: Spend a day living and working like a scientist from history, using their methods, tools, and working on their theories, highlighting their contributions to science.

1676. Building an Eco-Friendly Playground: Design and construct a playground that incorporates eco-friendly materials and sustainable practices, documenting the community engagement, construction challenges, and the joy it brings to children.

1677. A Month of Foraging and Fermenting: Each day, forage for different wild ingredients and experiment with fermenting them, sharing insights into the foraging locations, fermentation processes, and taste tests of the fermented goods.

1678. DIY Personal Electric Vehicle: Document the process of building a personal electric vehicle, from design and sourcing parts to assembly and road testing, focusing on sustainability and innovation in personal transport.

1679. The Science of Sound Healing: Explore the principles and practices of sound healing, including experiments, interviews with practitioners, and demonstrations of sound healing sessions.

1680. A Week of Living With Historical Tools: Use only tools and technology available from a specific historical period for a week, documenting how daily tasks are accomplished and reflecting on modern conveniences.

1681. Creating a Vertical Aquaponics System: Build a vertical aquaponics system that combines fish farming with hydroponic gardening, showcasing the setup, maintenance, and benefits of aquaponics.

1682. 24-Hour Wilderness Photography Challenge: Spend 24 hours in the wilderness capturing landscapes, wildlife, and natural phenomena, sharing photography tips, challenges faced, and the stories behind the shots.

1683. One Month of Mindfulness in Different Environments: Practice mindfulness each day in a different setting, from busy urban areas to quiet natural spaces, reflecting on the experience and effects on mental health.

1684. DIY Natural Swimming Pond: Transform a traditional pool or create a new pond into a natural swimming pond, documenting the design, construction, and the ecosystem development within the pond.

1685. The Art of Traditional Boat Building: Follow the process of building a boat using traditional methods and materials, focusing on the craftsmanship, cultural significance, and the maiden voyage.

1686. A Day of Zero-Electricity Living: Challenge yourself to go a day without using any electricity, documenting the alternative methods used for lighting, cooking, and entertainment, and reflecting on energy consumption.

1687. Exploring the World of Microgreens: Spend a month growing various types of microgreens, documenting the setup, growth process, nutritional benefits, and creative ways to use them in meals.

1688. Building a Backyard Wildlife Refuge: Create a refuge for wildlife in your backyard, including bird feeders, water sources, and shelters, documenting the attracted wildlife and the habitat's impact on local biodiversity.

1689. 24 Hours Making Music with Homemade Instruments: Craft homemade musical instruments and compose music using them, showcasing the instrument-making process, the sounds they produce, and the final musical piece.

1690. A Week of Reimagined Book Covers: Each day, design a new cover for a classic book, exploring different artistic styles and mediums, and discussing the inspiration and interpretation of the book through the cover design.

1691. The 30-Day Urban Homesteading Challenge: Document transforming a small urban space into a productive homestead, including balcony gardening, composting, and small-scale aquaponics, sharing daily progress, challenges, and successes.

1692. DIY Eco-Friendly Camping Gear: Create a series crafting sustainable camping gear from upcycled materials, including a portable stove, sleeping bag, and tent, focusing on functionality and environmental impact.

1693. A Week of Historical Language Revival: Each day, focus on reviving phrases and words from an almost forgotten language, exploring its history, cultural significance, and potential modern-day use.

1694. Building a Community Art Installation with Recycled Plastics: Engage the community in collecting recycled plastics to create a large-scale art installation, documenting the process, community involvement, and discussions on plastic waste.

1695. 24 Hours Exploring Urban Ecosystems: Spend a day investigating the biodiversity in an urban setting, from parklands to green roofs, highlighting the importance of urban green spaces and biodiversity conservation.

1696. One Month of Global Cooking Challenges: Each day, cook a dish from a different country, focusing on authentic recipes, ingredients, and techniques, while exploring the cultural background and significance of each dish.

1697. The Art of Sand Sculpting: Create a series on sand sculpting, from basic techniques for beginners to advanced sculptures, including time-lapses of creations and tips for sculpting success.

1698. DIY Renewable Energy Experiments for Kids: Design simple renewable energy projects for children, such as a mini wind turbine or solar oven, encouraging interest in science and sustainability from a young age.

1699. A Week of Wilderness Trail Restoration: Document volunteering on wilderness trail restoration projects, showcasing the work involved in maintaining hiking trails, erosion control, and habitat protection.

1700. Exploring the Science of Happiness Through Daily Acts: Engage in a different act each day believed to increase happiness, such as gratitude journaling or random acts of kindness, exploring the psychological science behind each act.

1701. The 24-Hour Minimalist Film Challenge: Produce a short film within 24 hours using minimalist techniques, focusing on simple storytelling, limited locations, and minimal cast, emphasizing creativity over budget.

1702. One Month of Living with Historical Diets: Explore and adopt the diet of a different historical period each week, discussing the nutritional, social, and economic aspects of historical food practices.

1703. Building an Underwater Camera Rig: Document the process of building a DIY underwater camera rig for filming marine life, including design, construction, and testing in various aquatic environments.

1704. A Day in the Life of a Zero-Waste Home: Showcase a day living in a zero-waste home, highlighting waste reduction strategies, sustainable household products, and the challenges and benefits of zero-waste living.

1705. Weekend Warrior Eco-Challenges: Each weekend, tackle a new eco-friendly project or challenge, from installing a rain barrel to conducting a home energy audit, sharing results and encouraging viewers to take on similar projects.

1706. The Science of Coffee from Bean to Cup: Explore the science behind coffee, including the chemistry of brewing, the biology of coffee plants, and the physics of grinding and extraction methods.

1707. DIY Natural Landscaping Techniques: Demonstrate natural landscaping techniques that enhance biodiversity, conserve water, and reduce maintenance, including native plant gardening and creating wildlife habitats.

1708. A Week of Crafting With Kids: Each day, complete a different craft project with children, focusing on educational and eco-friendly crafts, and discussing the benefits of creative activities for child development.

1709. Exploring the World's Ancient Libraries: Create a documentary series exploring ancient libraries around the world, their histories, collections, and the role they played in their societies.

1710. The 30-Day Bike Commute Challenge: Document the experience of commuting by bike every day for a month, discussing the health benefits, environmental impact, and the challenges faced by urban cyclists.

1711. The Art of Glassblowing: Dive into the intricate world of glassblowing, showcasing the process from start to finish, the tools used, and the creation of a beautiful piece of glass art, while exploring its historical significance.

1712. DIY Backyard Biogas Plant: Document the journey of building and operating a small-scale biogas plant in your backyard, showcasing how to convert organic waste into energy and the impact it has on reducing carbon footprint.

1713. A Month of Sustainable Living Innovations: Each day, explore a different sustainable living innovation, from green roofing and living walls to homemade air purifiers, highlighting the science behind them and their environmental benefits.

1714. 24-Hour Flash Fiction Writing Challenge: Challenge yourself to write and publish a piece of flash fiction within 24 hours, sharing the creative process, inspiration, and final story with your audience.

1715. The Science of Sports: Create a series exploring the science behind various sports, examining the physics of a soccer ball's flight, the biology of muscle growth, and the psychology of team dynamics.

1716. One Week of Historical Hairstyling: Each day, attempt to recreate a hairstyle from a different historical period, exploring the tools, techniques, and cultural contexts behind each style.

1717. Urban Foraging Guide: Spend a day urban foraging, identifying edible plants and herbs in the cityscape, discussing their uses, benefits, and how to forage responsibly and safely.

1718. The 30-Day Tiny House Living Experiment: Document the experience of living in a tiny house for 30 days, focusing on the challenges, lifestyle changes, and lessons learned about minimalism and sustainability.

1719. A Day in the Life of a Conservationist: Follow a wildlife conservationist for a day, showcasing their daily tasks, the challenges they face, and the importance of conservation efforts in preserving biodiversity.

1720. DIY Upcycled Musical Instruments: Create musical instruments from upcycled materials, showing the build process, how they're played, and performing a piece of music with the finished instruments.

1721. Exploring Abandoned Theaters Around the World: Venture into abandoned theaters, sharing their history, architectural features, and imagining the performances and stories they once hosted.

1722. A Week of Zero-Waste Beauty Routines: Document adopting a zero-waste beauty routine for a week, exploring alternative products, DIY beauty treatments, and evaluating the effectiveness and environmental impact.

1723. The Ultimate Home Energy Saving Challenge: Over a month, implement various energy-saving tips and hacks in your home, tracking the reduction in energy consumption and sharing practical advice for viewers.

1724. Cooking with Ancient Grains: Focus on recipes featuring ancient grains, discussing their nutritional benefits, historical uses, and providing modern takes on traditional dishes.

1725. Building a Community Free Library: Document the process of setting up a free library in your community, from constructing the library box to stocking it with books and observing community interactions.

1726. The Art of Calligraphy and Hand Lettering: Create a series teaching the basics of calligraphy and hand lettering, including different styles, techniques, and tips for beginners.

1727. 24-Hour Wilderness Survival Challenge with Basic Tools: Take on a survival challenge in the wilderness using only a limited set of basic tools, focusing on essential survival skills, shelter building, and foraging.

1728. Exploring the World's Most Unique Playgrounds: Travel to and showcase unique and innovative playground designs around the world, discussing their creative features, and the importance of play in child development.

1729. DIY Natural Pest Control Solutions: Share natural and eco-friendly pest control solutions for common household pests, focusing on prevention, natural deterrents, and safe removal methods.

1730. One Month of Learning a New Language: Document the journey of learning a new language in 30 days, sharing daily progress, challenges, breakthroughs, and interactions with native speakers.

1731. Crafting with Bioplastics: Explore the process of making bioplastics at home, creating various items from this eco-friendly material, and discussing its potential to replace conventional plastics.

1732. The Physics of Playground Equipment: Delve into the physics behind common playground equipment like swings, slides, and seesaws, explaining the scientific principles in an engaging and accessible way.

1733. A Week of Living According to Different Philosophies: Each day, live according to the principles of a different philosophical school of thought, sharing insights, challenges, and how these philosophies can apply to modern life.

1734. DIY Backyard Obstacle Course for Kids: Show how to build a fun and challenging obstacle course in your backyard using simple materials, focusing on physical activity, creativity, and safe play.

1735. Exploring the Art of Puppetry: Dive into the world of puppetry, showcasing different types of puppets, their construction, and performance techniques, including interviews with puppeteers and behind-the-scenes looks at puppet shows.

1736. 30 Days of Microadventures: Embark on a "microadventure" each day for a month, highlighting small, local adventures that are affordable and accessible, encouraging viewers to explore their surroundings in new ways.

1737. The Science of Baking: Create a series exploring the science behind baking, including the chemistry of different ingredients and techniques, and how they affect the taste, texture, and appearance of baked goods.

1738. One Week of DIY Renewable Energy Projects: Each day, tackle a different DIY project related to renewable energy, such as building a small solar panel or a wind turbine, documenting the process, challenges, and outcomes.

1739. Exploring the History of Cartography: Delve into the fascinating history of map-making, from ancient maps to modern digital cartography, discussing the evolution of techniques, significant maps, and the role of maps in society.

1740. A Day in the Life of a Historical Reenactor: Spend a day with a historical reenactor, exploring the dedication to authenticity, the research involved, and the personal and educational benefits of bringing history to life.

1741. Building a Miniature Greenhouse: Document the process of building a miniature greenhouse, focusing on design considerations, suitable plants, and the benefits of indoor greenhouses for education and relaxation.

1742. The Art and Science of Coffee: From bean to cup, explore the entire coffee-making process, including the science of roasting, grinding, brewing techniques, and the cultural significance of coffee around the world.

1743. DIY Space-Themed Bedroom Makeover for Kids: Transform a child's bedroom into a space-themed adventure, showcasing creative DIY decor ideas, educational space elements, and the makeover process.

1744. Urban Sketching Challenge: Take viewers on a journey through urban sketching, visiting different locations to capture the essence of the scene with sketches, sharing tips and techniques for sketching on the go.

1745. Creating a Sustainable Wardrobe: Spend a month curating a sustainable wardrobe, focusing on ethical fashion choices, thrift store finds, and DIY clothing projects, discussing the impact of fashion on the environment.

1746. The Challenge of Learning a Musical Instrument in 30 Days: Choose an instrument to learn from scratch and document the process over 30 days, sharing practice routines, progress, and performances.

1747. A Week of Exploring Abandoned Railways and Stations: Travel to and document the stories behind abandoned railways and stations, exploring their history, architectural features, and the nostalgia of a bygone era.

1748. DIY Eco-Friendly Soap Making: Show how to make your own soaps using natural, eco-friendly ingredients, including the process, customization options, and the benefits of homemade soap.

1749. The Ultimate Guide to Urban Composting: Create a comprehensive guide to composting in an urban environment, exploring different methods, tips for success, and how to use compost in city gardening.

1750. A Month of Artistic Challenges: Each day, undertake a different artistic challenge, ranging from digital art and painting to sculpture and mixed media, documenting the creative process and the final artworks.

1751. The 30-Day Local History Challenge: Each day, uncover and present a little-known fact or story about your local area's history, including interviews with historians, visits to historical sites, and archival research.

1752. DIY Floating Garden Project: Document the process of creating a floating garden for small spaces or urban areas, showcasing the design, construction, and the variety of plants that thrive in a floating setup.

1753. A Week of Vintage Camera Photography: Use a different vintage camera each day for a week to capture contemporary scenes, discussing the history of each camera, its unique features, and the challenges of using film in a digital age.

1754. The Art of Miniature Bookbinding: Delve into the craft of creating miniature books, from selecting materials and binding techniques to decorating and theming, showcasing the intricate details and patience required.

1755. 24-Hour Public Space Transformation: Transform a public space within 24 hours through art, landscaping, or installation, focusing on community involvement, the transformation process, and the space's impact on the community.

1756. One Month of Homemade Instruments: Create a new musical instrument from scratch or repurposed materials each day, sharing the build process, the sound each instrument makes, and a performance showcasing its musical capabilities.

1757. Exploring the World of Non-Verbal Communication: Spend a week exploring different forms of non-verbal communication across cultures, including body language, gestures, and symbols, highlighting their importance and variations.

1758. DIY Solar-Powered Gadgets for Camping: Design and build a series of solar-powered gadgets useful for camping, such as lights, chargers, and cooking devices, documenting the design choices, build process, and field testing.

1759. The Challenge of Writing a Song a Day: Write and record a new song every day for a month, sharing the inspiration, songwriting process, challenges, and the final recordings.

1760. A Day in the Life of a Restoration Artist: Follow a restoration artist for a day, documenting the intricate work involved in restoring paintings, sculptures, or historical artifacts, and the importance of preserving art for future generations.

1761. Building a Community Rainwater Harvesting System: Document the process of designing and installing a rainwater harvesting system for a community garden or public space, focusing on sustainability, water conservation, and community involvement.

1762. The Science of Play: Create a series exploring the psychological and physiological benefits of play for both children and adults, including interviews with experts and experiments demonstrating play's effects on the brain.

1763. A Week of Eco-Friendly Personal Care Routines: Adopt and showcase a different eco-friendly personal care routine each day, focusing on sustainable products, DIY alternatives, and the impact of conventional products on the environment.

1764. Exploring Ancient Navigation Techniques: Embark on a journey using ancient navigation techniques, such as stellar navigation or reading wind patterns, documenting the learning process, challenges, and the journey itself.

1765. The Art of Stencil Making and Street Art: Dive into the world of stencil art, from designing and cutting stencils to creating street art pieces, discussing the medium's impact and its role in public expression.

1766. DIY Eco-Friendly Insulation Solutions: Explore and implement DIY insulation solutions using sustainable and recycled materials, documenting the process, effectiveness, and tips for insulating homes more eco-consciously.

1767. A Month of Mindful Eating Experiences: Each day, practice and document a different aspect of mindful eating, exploring its benefits on health, well-being, and the relationship with food.

1768. Creating a Wildlife Documentary in Your Backyard: Spend a month filming the wildlife that visits your backyard, creating a documentary that showcases the diversity of urban wildlife and the importance of creating habitats for them.

1769. The 30-Day Upcycling Challenge: Transform discarded items or materials into useful products or art each day, sharing creative upcycling ideas, the transformation process, and the stories behind each item.

1770. A Journey Through Time-Lapse Photography: Create a series capturing time-lapse videos of different subjects and environments, from bustling cityscapes to the growth of a plant, sharing techniques, equipment used, and the stories each time-lapse tells.

1771. The 30-Day Local Wildlife Challenge: Each day, feature a different local wildlife species, exploring their habitats, behaviors, and the conservation efforts required to protect them, using photography, interviews with biologists, and personal observations.

1772. Building an Eco-Friendly Tiny House on Wheels: Document the entire process of designing and constructing a tiny house on wheels, focusing on sustainable materials, energy efficiency, and the challenges and rewards of tiny living.

1773. A Week of Historical Cooking Methods: Experiment with cooking methods from different historical periods each day, such as open-fire cooking, using a hearth, or preparing food in a clay oven, and discuss how these methods influence the taste and preparation of food.

1774. DIY Urban Pollinator Gardens: Show how to transform small urban spaces into pollinator-friendly gardens, documenting the selection of plants, the setup process, and the eventual visitation by bees, butterflies, and other pollinators.

1775. The Science of Everyday Objects: Create a series exploring the science behind everyday objects, explaining the materials, engineering, and physics that make them work, from zippers and ballpoint pens to microwaves and smartphones.

1776. One Month of Rediscovering Lost Arts: Dedicate each day to learning and practicing a lost art or craft, such as calligraphy, tapestry weaving, or traditional woodworking, highlighting the historical significance and potential for modern application.

1777. 24-Hour Wilderness Survival with Minimal Gear: Take on the challenge of surviving in the wilderness for 24 hours with minimal gear, focusing on essential survival skills like shelter building, water sourcing, and fire starting.

1778. Creating Art from Recycled Electronics: Dive into the world of electronic waste art, transforming discarded electronic components into sculptures, installations, or interactive art pieces, discussing the environmental impact of e-waste.

1779. The Ultimate Backyard Biome Project: Transform your backyard into a series of distinct biomes, such as a desert area, a small wetland, and a forested section, documenting the creation process and the biodiversity each biome supports.

1780. A Day in the Life of a Lighthouse Keeper: Explore the historical and modern-day responsibilities of a lighthouse keeper, including maintenance, the operation of the light, and the role of lighthouses in maritime safety.

1781. Weekend DIY Renewable Energy Projects: Tackle a different small-scale renewable energy project each weekend, such as building a homemade solar panel or a small wind turbine, sharing the technical process, challenges, and energy output.

1782. Exploring Ancient Trade Routes by Foot: Embark on a journey to explore segments of ancient trade routes, such as the Silk Road or the Spice Route, on foot, documenting the historical significance, landscapes, and modern remnants of these paths.

1783. The Art of Fermented Foods: Spend a month exploring and creating different fermented foods from around the world, such as kimchi, sauerkraut, kombucha, and kefir, sharing recipes, fermentation techniques, and the health benefits of fermented foods.

1784. Building a Community Art Mural: Document the collaborative process of designing and painting a large-scale mural in a public space, focusing on community involvement, the message behind the mural, and the transformation of the space.

1785. A Week of Underwater Exploration: Using snorkeling or diving gear, explore different underwater environments each day, from coral reefs and kelp forests to freshwater rivers, showcasing the unique ecosystems and discussing conservation issues.

1786. DIY Sustainable Fashion Accessories: Create a series on designing and making sustainable fashion accessories, such as bags, hats, and jewelry, from upcycled or eco-friendly materials, highlighting the creative process and final products.

1787. The Physics of Sports: Produce content exploring the physics behind various sports and athletic movements, demonstrating how understanding physics can improve performance and explaining concepts in an accessible way.

1788. One Month of Mindfulness in Nature: Each day, practice a different mindfulness or meditation technique in a natural setting, sharing the experiences, the impact on mental and emotional well-being, and tips for practicing mindfulness outdoors.

1789. Exploring Microclimates Within a City: Investigate and document the different microclimates found within a single city, explaining the factors that create these microclimates and their effects on local flora, fauna, and human activities.

1790. The Challenge of Creating Zero-Waste Art: Commit to producing art using only zero-waste techniques and materials, discussing the challenges of avoiding waste in the art process and showcasing the finished pieces.

1791. Urban Permaculture Transformation: Document transforming an urban space into a thriving permaculture garden, highlighting principles of permaculture design, community involvement, and the transformation's impact on local ecosystems.

1792. The Art of Silent Communication: Explore the power and art of silent communication through mime, body language, and visual signals, discussing techniques, historical context, and conducting interviews with experts or performers.

1793. DIY Portable Water Filtration Devices: Design and create portable water filtration devices, showcasing the process, materials used, and testing their effectiveness in different conditions, aiming for sustainability and practicality.

1794. A Week of Living Like Inventors: Each day, live and work like a famous inventor, adopting their daily routines, working methods, and attempting to recreate one of their inventions or experiments.

1795. Exploring the Science of Color: Delve into the science behind color perception, how colors affect emotions and behavior, and the role of color in nature and technology, including experiments and demonstrations.

1796. Building a Community Solar Cooker: Document the building of a large-scale solar cooker for community use, focusing on the design, construction process, and the benefits of solar cooking for communal meals and events.

1797. Historical Diets and Their Modern Implications: Explore various historical diets, their nutritional content, and cultural significance, and discuss with nutritionists about their potential benefits and drawbacks in a modern context.

1798. The Journey of Restoring a Vintage Bicycle: Take viewers through the process of finding, restoring, and customizing a vintage bicycle, including the history of the bike, restoration challenges, and the joy of bringing it back to life.

1799. Zero-Waste Gardening Techniques: Share innovative gardening techniques that minimize waste, including composting, mulching, and creating a closed-loop system, highlighting the benefits for the garden and the environment.

1800. A Day in the Life of a Park Ranger: Document the daily duties and experiences of a park ranger, showcasing the work involved in conservation, wildlife protection, and interacting with the public in national parks or protected areas.

1801. Creating Eco-Friendly Art Supplies: Explore the process of making your own eco-friendly art supplies, such as paints, brushes, and canvases, using natural and sustainable materials, and test their effectiveness in art projects.

1802. The Challenge of Photographing Wildlife in the City: Spend a week attempting to photograph urban wildlife, discussing the techniques used, the species encountered, and the importance of biodiversity in urban areas.

1803. Homemade Wind Energy Experiments: Conduct experiments with homemade wind turbines or wind energy devices, documenting the build process, the science behind wind energy, and the potential applications of the devices created.

1804. A Week of Mindful Technology Use: Document a week of consciously reducing and improving technology use, exploring the impact on productivity, mental health, and social relationships, and sharing tips for mindful tech habits.

1805. Exploring the World of Edible Insects: Dive into the practice of entomophagy (eating insects), exploring the nutritional benefits, environmental impact, and cultural significance of edible insects through cooking and taste tests.

1806. DIY Natural Playground for Children: Show how to create a natural playground for children, using elements like logs, stones, and plants, focusing on the benefits of natural play and the creative process.

1807. The Forgotten Art of Letter Writing: Revive the art of letter writing by sending handwritten letters to friends, family, or strangers, discussing the personal touch, thoughtfulness, and anticipation involved in this form of communication.

1808. Underwater Photography Without Scuba Gear: Explore techniques and challenges of underwater photography in shallow waters without the use of scuba gear, showcasing the marine life and environments captured.

1809. Eco-Friendly Van Life Conversion: Document converting a van into an eco-friendly mobile home, focusing on sustainable materials, solar power, and water conservation systems, and the lifestyle changes involved in van life.

1810. The Science and Art of Making Paper: Create a series on the traditional and modern techniques of making paper by hand, including the science of papermaking, creative uses for handmade paper, and the environmental impact of paper production.

1811. Global Street Foods Cooking Challenge: Spend a month cooking and showcasing street foods from around the world, exploring their cultural origins, ingredients, and cooking techniques, with taste tests and reactions.

1812. The Art of Ice Swimming: Document the preparation, safety measures, and exhilarating experience of ice swimming in natural waters, exploring the mental and physical health benefits claimed by enthusiasts.

1813. Building an Eco-Friendly Skatepark: Chronicle the planning, community fundraising, and construction of an environmentally sustainable skatepark, focusing on recycled materials and green design principles.

1814. A Week of Wilderness First Aid Lessons: Deliver essential wilderness first aid tips through a week-long series, covering everything from minor injuries to survival situations, with practical demonstrations and expert advice.

1815. Exploring Ancient Engineering Techniques: Dive into ancient engineering marvels, attempting to replicate small-scale versions of ancient structures or mechanisms using traditional materials and methods.

1816. The Philosophy of Minimalism in Modern Life: Explore the philosophy of minimalism, applying its principles in various aspects of modern life such as digital presence, home decoration, and personal finance, sharing reflections and outcomes.

1817. DIY Recycled Art Installation: Create a public art installation using solely recycled and repurposed materials, documenting the creative process, community engagement, and the message behind the art.

1818. A Month of Silent Film Creation: Each day, create a short silent film, experimenting with different genres, storytelling techniques, and visual effects, culminating in a silent film festival showcasing the work.

1819. Urban Exploration: The City's Forgotten Spaces: Embark on urban exploration adventures to uncover and document the city's abandoned and forgotten spaces, respecting safety and legal boundaries, while uncovering the history and stories behind them.

1820. The Challenge of Vertical Farming at Home: Experiment with setting up a vertical farm in a small space, documenting the setup, plant growth, challenges, and the potential for sustainable urban agriculture.

1821. Rediscovering Traditional Children's Games: Spend a month learning and playing traditional children's games from different cultures, exploring their rules, histories, and the values they impart.

1822. Crafting a Sustainable Wardrobe from Scratch: Challenge yourself to create a sustainable wardrobe by making your own clothes, focusing on sustainable fabrics, minimal waste patterns, and eco-friendly sewing practices.

1823. The Science of Sleep and Dreaming: Delve into the science behind sleep and dreaming, conducting experiments on sleep patterns, dream journaling, and exploring theories behind why we dream.

1824. A Journey Through UNESCO World Heritage Sites: Create a travelogue visiting UNESCO World Heritage sites, delving into their significance, conservation efforts, and the challenges they face in the modern world.

1825. Homemade Musical Instruments Orchestra: Form an orchestra using only homemade musical instruments, documenting the creation of each instrument, rehearsals, and the performance of a piece of music.

1826. DIY Tiny Eco-Habitats for Wildlife: Design and build a series of tiny eco-habitats in your garden or community space to support local wildlife, such as insect hotels, birdhouses, and bat boxes, focusing on biodiversity.

1827. Exploring the Art of Book Scanning: Document the process of digitally scanning rare or personal books, discussing the technology used, copyright considerations, and the importance of preserving written knowledge.

1828. A Week of Zero-Electricity Living Experiment: Live for a week without using electricity, documenting the challenges, creative solutions for daily tasks, and reflections on energy consumption and sustainability.

1829. The Craft of Handmade Paper Toys: Explore the world of handmade paper toys, from traditional designs to modern creations, showcasing the crafting process, stories behind the toys, and their cultural significance.

1830. Creating a Mobile App for Community Service: Document the journey of designing and developing a mobile app aimed at serving the local community, from ideation and coding to user feedback and implementation.

1831. Eco-Friendly Party Planning Guide: Plan and host a completely eco-friendly party or event, showcasing sustainable decor ideas, zero-waste catering options, and engaging eco-conscious activities for guests.

1832. A Day in the Life of a Medieval Monk: Immerse in the daily routines, work, and spiritual practices of a medieval monk, exploring the historical context, the significance of monastic life, and its contributions to culture and knowledge.

1833. The World of DIY Natural Dyes: Experiment with creating natural dyes from various plants, fruits, and minerals, documenting the process, color outcomes, and applications for textiles and art.

1834. Reviving Ancient Board Games: Discover and play board games from ancient civilizations, exploring their rules, historical context, and cultural significance, and attempting to create playable modern versions.

1835. One Month of Living with an Invention a Day: Each day, create and live with a new simple invention designed to solve everyday problems, documenting the ideation process, prototype creation, and testing its effectiveness.

1836. The Art of Traditional Shadow Plays: Explore the ancient art form of shadow plays, documenting the creation of shadow puppets, the storytelling techniques, and performing a traditional narrative, highlighting its cultural significance.

1837. A Week of Cooking with Foraged Foods: Each day, forage for wild foods in different environments and create meals using the gathered ingredients, focusing on the nutritional benefits, foraging ethics, and culinary creativity.

1838. DIY Eco-Friendly Home Gadgets: Showcase the process of creating simple, eco-friendly gadgets that can be used around the home, such as a manual clothes washer or a water-saving device, emphasizing sustainability and practicality.

1839. The Science of Ancient Monuments: Delve into the scientific principles behind the construction of ancient monuments, exploring materials, engineering techniques, and the astronomical or geographical significance of sites like Stonehenge or the Pyramids of Giza.

1840. 30 Days of Minimalist Living Challenges: Each day, take on a new challenge that promotes minimalist living, documenting the process, the impact on daily life, and reflections on consumerism and materialism.

1841. Exploring the World of Artisanal Cheeses: Travel through the process of making artisanal cheeses, from milking to aging, showcasing different cheese-making traditions, techniques, and the science behind cheese production.

1842. A Journey Through Virtual Reality Art Galleries: Create or curate virtual reality art galleries showcasing digital art, historical masterpieces, or student work, exploring the potential of VR in making art accessible and immersive.

1843. Building a Self-Sustaining Aquatic Ecosystem: Document the setup of a self-sustaining aquatic ecosystem in an aquarium, detailing the selection of plants, fish, and the ecological balance required to maintain it.

1844. The Art and Craft of Traditional Bookbinding: Dive into the world of traditional bookbinding, showcasing the tools, materials, and techniques used to bind books by hand, along with the history and significance of different binding styles.

1845. One Month of Upcycled Fashion Design: Each day, redesign or repurpose an existing garment into something new and fashionable, highlighting creativity in sustainable fashion and the process from concept to final piece.

1846. A Day in the Life of a Historical Fiction Writer: Follow the daily routine, research methods, and writing process of a historical fiction writer, exploring how historical facts are woven into engaging narratives.

1847. DIY Biophilic Home Design Elements: Incorporate biophilic design elements into your living space, focusing on projects like indoor vertical gardens, natural lighting enhancements, and using natural materials, to improve well-being through connection with nature.

1848. Exploring Traditional Fishing Techniques: Learn and demonstrate traditional fishing techniques from around the world, focusing on the cultural heritage, sustainability, and the skill involved in these methods.

1849. The Challenge of Building a Paper Bridge: Design and construct a bridge made entirely of paper, capable of supporting weight, showcasing the engineering principles, creativity, and problem-solving involved in the challenge.

1850. A Week of Historical Fitness Routines: Each day, try out a fitness routine or exercise method from different historical periods or cultures, discussing the historical context and comparing their effectiveness to modern workouts.

1851. Creating Art with Natural Materials: Spend a month creating art exclusively with materials found in nature, such as leaves, stones, and wood, focusing on the connection to the environment and the unique challenges of natural media.

1852. The Process of Restoring a Classic Car: Document the detailed process of restoring a classic car from start to finish, including sourcing parts, mechanical repairs, bodywork, and the history of the specific model.

1853. A Year of Living Seasonally: Commit to living in tune with the seasons for a year, adjusting diet, activities, and lifestyle according to seasonal changes, and reflecting on the impact of this practice on well-being and environmental awareness.

1854. The Art of Making Handcrafted Candles: Explore the process of making handcrafted candles, from selecting waxes and scents to molding and decorating, focusing on the craft and creativity involved.

1855. Exploring the World of Microscopic Photography: Delve into microscopic photography, capturing the unseen world of tiny organisms and structures, and discussing the equipment, techniques, and fascinating details revealed at a microscopic level.

1856. A Month of Living with Historical Time-Keeping: Explore and adopt different historical methods of time-keeping each week, from sundials to water clocks, documenting the experience and the impact on daily life and productivity.

1857. The Art of Digital Detoxing: Document a week-long journey of digital detoxing, highlighting strategies for reducing screen time, the challenges faced, and the effects on mental health and social interactions.

1858. DIY Natural Playground Projects: Create a series on building natural playground elements, such as log balance beams, rope swings, and mud kitchens, focusing on child-led play and connection with nature.

1859. Exploring the World through Virtual Geocaching: Engage in virtual geocaching adventures, using online maps and clues to discover historical facts, cultural insights, and hidden gems about different locations around the world.

1860. The Craft of Artisanal Candle Making: Dive into the process of making artisanal candles, exploring various waxes, scents, and molds, and the artistry behind creating unique and decorative candles.

1861. One Week of Zero-Waste Challenges in the Kitchen: Tackle a different zero-waste challenge in the kitchen each day, from eliminating single-use plastics to composting and sustainable cooking practices.

1862. Building a DIY Outdoor Home Cinema: Show the process of creating an outdoor cinema at home, including screen setup, projector choice, and cozy seating, culminating in a family movie night under the stars.

1863. The Science of Sound and Music: Create a series exploring the science behind sound and music, including the physics of sound waves, the psychology of music and emotion, and the technology behind modern sound production.

1864. A Month of Crafting with Recyclables: Each day, take on a new craft project using only recyclable materials, showcasing creative reuse ideas and the potential for upcycling in art and home decor.

1865. Exploring Local Folklore and Legends: Delve into local folklore and legends, sharing stories from your region or exploring myths from around the world, and investigating their origins and meanings.

1866. DIY Personalized Garden Stepping Stones: Guide viewers through making personalized garden stepping stones, incorporating handprints, mosaics, or engraved messages, as a fun and creative outdoor project.

1867. The Art of Latte Making at Home: Share techniques and tips for making artistic latte designs at home, exploring different methods, from simple foam art to more complex designs using syrups and tools.

1868. Weekend Warrior: Home Repair and Improvement Projects: Document tackling different home repair and improvement projects over weekends, providing DIY tips, tricks, and the satisfaction of enhancing your living space.

1869. Exploring the Tradition of Tea Ceremonies: Delve into the cultural and historical significance of tea ceremonies from around the world, attempting to perform them and discussing their philosophical and spiritual aspects.

1870. A Week of Wilderness Photography Challenges: Each day, explore a new wilderness area or natural theme through photography, sharing techniques for capturing landscapes, wildlife, and macro shots in natural light.

1871. Creating a Mindfulness Retreat at Home: Show how to transform a space at home into a mindfulness retreat, focusing on elements that promote relaxation and meditation, including DIY decor, aroma therapy, and soundscapes.

1872. The Journey of Restoring a Vintage Typewriter: Document the process of finding, cleaning, and restoring a vintage typewriter, exploring its history, mechanics, and the charm of analog writing.

1873. DIY Eco-Friendly Pet Toys: Design and create pet toys using eco-friendly and safe materials, showcasing the crafting process and testing the toys with pets for fun and engaging playtime.

1874. Exploring Abandoned Victorian Homes: Venture into abandoned Victorian homes, documenting their architecture, history, and imagining the lives of their former inhabitants, while discussing preservation efforts.

1875. The Challenge of Creating a Vertical Succulent Garden: Build a vertical garden featuring a variety of succulents, sharing the design, plant selection, and care tips, and showcasing the garden's growth over time.

1876. Urban Exploration: Rediscovering Lost Subway Stations: Embark on a journey to explore and document the history and architecture of abandoned subway stations, delving into urban legends and the stories behind their decline.

1877. A Month of International Breakfasts: Each day, prepare and enjoy a traditional breakfast from a different country, exploring the cultural significance of each meal and the ingredients that make them unique.

1878. The Science of Soap Bubbles: Create a series exploring the fascinating science behind soap bubbles, from their iridescent colors to the physics of bubble shapes and sizes, including DIY experiments to do at home.

1879. DIY Sustainable Fashion Accessories: Showcase the process of creating fashion accessories using sustainable, recycled, or upcycled materials, focusing on eco-friendly practices in fashion design.

1880. Exploring Micro-Histories in Your City: Delve into the small, often overlooked historical details and stories in your city, from ancient street corners to forgotten monuments, uncovering the layers of history beneath the urban landscape.

1881. Building a Community Seed Library: Document the creation of a seed library for your community, encouraging local gardeners to share and swap seeds, promoting biodiversity and local food production.

1882. The Art of Nature Journaling: Introduce viewers to the practice of nature journaling, combining art, writing, and observation to document the natural world, offering tips on getting started and the benefits of connecting with nature.

1883. One Week of Living Like a Space Colonist: Simulate living on a space colony for a week, adapting to limited resources, space gardening, and other challenges of extraterrestrial living, inspired by current space habitation research.

1884. DIY Recycled Rainwater Collection System: Show how to design and implement a rainwater collection system using recycled materials, focusing on water conservation and sustainable gardening practices.

1885. Exploring the Evolution of Board Games: Trace the history and evolution of board games from ancient times to the present, highlighting key developments, cultural impacts, and the resurgence of board gaming as a popular hobby.

1886. A Day in the Life of a Zero-Waste Chef: Follow a zero-waste chef for a day, exploring the challenges and creative solutions for cooking sustainably, minimizing food waste, and sourcing ingredients responsibly.

1887. Creating a Wind-Powered Sculpture Garden: Document the process of designing and installing a garden of wind-powered sculptures, focusing on kinetic art, the interplay of art and engineering, and the sculptures' dynamic responses to nature.

1888. The Chemistry of Cooking: Launch a series that delves into the chemistry behind various cooking techniques and food reactions, explaining why certain methods produce specific flavors and textures in dishes.

1889. Eco-Friendly DIY Home Insulation Tips: Share practical DIY tips for improving home insulation in an eco-friendly way, including materials to use, areas to target, and the impact on energy consumption and comfort.

1890. Historical Reenactment of a Famous Expedition: Reenact a famous historical expedition, documenting the preparation, challenges faced, and insights gained from walking in the footsteps of historical figures.

1891. Creating Art from Upcycled Electronics: Explore the process of creating art pieces from upcycled electronic parts, highlighting the transformation of tech waste into visually compelling sculptures or installations.

1892. The World of Competitive Tree Climbing: Delve into the niche sport of competitive tree climbing, showcasing the skills, equipment, and community behind this unique and environmentally conscious sport.

1893. A Month of Mindful Movement Practices: Each day, practice and document a different form of mindful movement, from yoga and tai chi to dance and walking meditations, exploring the physical and mental health benefits.

1894. DIY Portable Eco-Friendly Cooking Stoves: Design and build portable cooking stoves that are eco-friendly, showcasing different models suitable for camping or emergency situations, focusing on sustainability and efficiency.

1895. Exploring the Acoustic Ecology of Different Environments: Record and analyze the unique soundscapes of various environments, from bustling cities to serene forests, discussing the importance of sound in ecological balance and human perception.

1896. Restoring a Historical Garden: Document the journey of restoring a neglected historical garden to its former glory, focusing on research, historical plants, landscape techniques, and the garden's cultural significance.

1897. The Art of Ice Sculpture in Warm Climates: Explore the challenges and techniques of creating ice sculptures in warm climates, including the science of ice preservation and the ephemeral nature of the art form.

1898. DIY Bioluminescent Projects: Experiment with bioluminescent materials to create glowing art or practical items, discussing the science behind bioluminescence and its potential applications in design and safety.

1899. A Week of Wilderness Craftsmanship: Each day, craft a new item using only materials and tools found in the wilderness, showcasing traditional craftsmanship skills and the practical uses of each item in survival situations.

1900. Urban Space Activation Projects: Highlight initiatives to transform underused urban spaces into vibrant community areas, focusing on the planning, community engagement, and the transformative impact of these projects.

1901. The Science of Playground Design: Delve into the science and psychology behind playground design, including how various elements contribute to child development, creativity, and physical fitness.

1902. Exploring Ancient Methods of Water Purification: Investigate and experiment with ancient water purification methods from various cultures, comparing their effectiveness and relevance to modern-day water treatment practices.

1903. One Month of Living by the Lunar Calendar: Document the experience of aligning daily activities, meals, and personal care with the phases of the lunar calendar, reflecting on any impacts on well-being and productivity.

1904. Creating Sustainable Pet Accessories: Design and craft eco-friendly pet accessories, from toys to bedding, using sustainable materials, and share tips on pet care that minimizes environmental impact.

1905. The Forgotten Art of Making Natural Pigments: Explore the process of creating natural pigments from minerals, plants, and other natural sources, showcasing the historical context and applications in art and crafts.

1906. A Day in the Life of a Medieval Artisan: Immerse in the daily life and crafts of a medieval artisan, such as a blacksmith, weaver, or potter, highlighting the skills, tools, and cultural significance of their work.

1907. Building a Community Bird Sanctuary: Show the process of creating a bird sanctuary in a community setting, focusing on attracting various bird species, building birdhouses, and educating the community on bird conservation.

1908. One Week of Zero-Electricity Cooking Challenges: Each day, cook meals without using electricity, exploring alternative cooking methods such as solar cookers, wood fires, and fermentation, and discussing the environmental impact.

1909. The Journey of Restoring an Old Sailboat: Document the restoration of an old sailboat, covering the history of the boat, the restoration process, and the adventures and challenges of taking it back to the water.

1910. Exploring the World of Artisan Bread Making: Dive into artisan bread making, from sourdough starters to traditional baking techniques, showcasing the science of fermentation and the craft behind different types of bread.

1911. A Month of Handmade Musical Instruments: Create a different musical instrument by hand each day, exploring traditional and innovative designs, materials, and the unique sounds each instrument produces.

1912. The Art and Challenges of Aerial Photography: Explore the art of aerial photography using drones, kites, or balloons, focusing on the technical challenges, ethical considerations, and the stunning perspectives it offers.

1913. DIY Eco-Friendly Insulation Techniques for Homes: Demonstrate how to insulate a home using eco-friendly and sustainable materials, discussing the benefits, cost savings, and impact on energy consumption.

1914. Exploring Historical Diets for Modern Health: Investigate and try historical diets to understand their nutritional value and potential benefits or drawbacks for modern health, including expert opinions and historical context.

1915. Creating a Vertical Succulent Wall: Design and build a vertical wall filled with various succulents, sharing the construction process, care tips, and the aesthetic and environmental benefits of vertical gardening.

1916. The Zero-Waste Kitchen Experiment: Spend a month transforming your kitchen to operate under zero-waste principles, documenting the transition, challenges, solutions, and the impact on daily life and waste reduction.

1917. Restoring a Community Landmark: Document the process of restoring a neglected community landmark, from fundraising to the actual restoration work, highlighting the historical significance and community involvement.

1918. A Week of Solar Cooking Around the World: Each day, cook a dish from a different part of the world using a solar cooker, exploring the versatility of solar cooking and the diverse cuisines that can be adapted to it.

1919. DIY Backyard Observatory for Amateur Astronomers: Show how to build a simple backyard observatory, including choosing equipment, construction tips, and your first observations, to inspire amateur astronomers to start observing the night sky.

1920. Exploring the Art of Traditional Tattoos: Delve into the world of traditional tattooing methods across different cultures, their meanings, techniques, and the stories behind the tattoos people carry.

1921. Creating a Home Recycling Center: Design and set up an efficient home recycling center, offering tips on sorting, reducing contamination, and creative ways to repurpose recyclable materials.

1922. The History and Craft of Ancient Pottery: Explore the history, techniques, and cultural significance of ancient pottery, attempting to recreate historical pottery styles using traditional methods.

1923. Urban Wildlife Photography Challenge: Spend a week capturing the often-overlooked wildlife in urban settings, sharing photography tips, the importance of biodiversity in cities, and the stories of urban wildlife.

1924. Building a DIY Eco-Friendly Pond: Create a sustainable pond in your garden, documenting the planning, construction, and the ecosystem development, emphasizing water conservation and habitat creation.

1925. The Art of Hand-Painted Movie Posters: Highlight the disappearing art of hand-painted movie posters, exploring their history, the artists behind them, and creating your own hand-painted poster for a contemporary movie.

1926. A Journey Through Native Plant Landscaping: Transform a section of your garden using native plants, discussing the benefits of native landscaping for the environment, local wildlife, and water conservation.

1927. Exploring the Craft of Artisanal Soap Making: Delve into the process of making artisanal soaps, from sourcing natural ingredients to the chemistry of soap making, and the creative aspects of scent and design.

1928. The Science and Sensation of Spicy Foods: Investigate the science behind why some foods are spicy, the health benefits and risks of consuming spicy foods, and challenge yourself to try some of the world's spiciest dishes.

1929. Reviving Vintage Computers: Document the process of finding, restoring, and operating vintage computers, exploring their history, the evolution of computing technology, and the nostalgia associated with vintage tech.

1930. A Week of Living With Renewable Energy Only: Attempt to power your daily life using only renewable energy sources for a week, sharing the setup, challenges, and insights into the feasibility and impact of renewable energy at the personal level.

1931. The World of Miniature Bookbinding: Create miniature books, focusing on the detailed craft of bookbinding on a tiny scale, the historical context of miniature books, and their uses today.

1932. DIY Sustainable Pet Care: Share tips and projects for sustainable pet care, including making your own pet food, eco-friendly toys, and natural grooming products, emphasizing the health and environmental benefits.

1933. Historical Reenactment of a Day in Ancient Rome: Spend a day living as a citizen of Ancient Rome, adopting their dress, food, activities, and exploring the cultural and historical context of their daily life.

1934. Exploring the Craft of Natural Fiber Textiles: Investigate the process of creating textiles from natural fibers, from plant or animal source to finished fabric, highlighting traditional and sustainable textile crafts.

1935. A Month of DIY Musical Instruments: Challenge yourself to create a different musical instrument from scratch each day for a month, documenting the process, the materials used, and the sound of each instrument.

1936. The Art of Precision in Paper Airplane Making: Dive into the world of competitive paper airplane making, exploring the science of aerodynamics, design variations, and hosting a flight competition.

1937. DIY Off-Grid Solar Lighting Solutions: Showcase the process of creating and installing off-grid solar lighting solutions for different areas of the home or garden, emphasizing sustainability and self-sufficiency.

1938. Exploring the World of Scented Gardens: Create a series on designing and cultivating a scented garden, focusing on plant selection, layout, and the therapeutic benefits of fragrant plants and flowers.

1939. The Challenge of Underwater Basket Weaving: Take on the unique challenge of underwater basket weaving, exploring its origins, techniques, and the added difficulty of working with materials submerged in water.

1940. A Day in the Life of a Museum Curator: Follow a museum curator for a day, exploring the behind-the-scenes work involved in exhibition planning, artifact preservation, and public education.

1941. Building a DIY Pedal-Powered Generator: Document the process of building a pedal-powered generator, from design to construction and testing its effectiveness in powering small devices or lights.

1942. A Week of Historical Language Revival: Each day, focus on reviving phrases and expressions from a nearly forgotten language, exploring its cultural and historical significance, and practical applications today.

1943. Creating Art from Ocean Debris: Highlight the issue of ocean pollution by creating art from debris collected from beaches, showcasing the creative process and the stories behind the collected items.

1944. The Science of Homemade Rockets: Explore the basics of rocket science by designing, building, and launching homemade rockets, discussing the principles of physics involved and safety precautions.

1945. A Month of Mindfulness in Different Environments: Practice and document a different form of mindfulness or meditation each day in various settings, from busy urban areas to serene natural landscapes, reflecting on the experiences.

1946. Exploring the Craft of Artisanal Pencil Making: Delve into the process of making pencils by hand, from selecting the wood and graphite to shaping and branding, highlighting the craftsmanship involved.

1947. The Journey of Planting a Micro-Forest: Document the process of converting a small, barren plot into a dense, biodiverse micro-forest using the Miyawaki method, tracking its growth and ecological impact.

1948. DIY Eco-Friendly Refrigeration Methods: Experiment with building and using non-electric refrigeration methods, such as zeer pots or underground coolers, showcasing their effectiveness and sustainability.

1949. A Week of Experimental Photography Techniques: Each day, experiment with a different unconventional photography technique, such as pinhole cameras, cyanotypes, or light painting, exploring the creative potential of each method.

1950. The Art of Handcrafted Leather Books: Explore the traditional craft of creating handcrafted leather-bound books, from the leather working to the binding process, emphasizing the beauty and durability of handmade books.

1951. Urban Gardening in Small Spaces: Share tips and techniques for creating lush gardens in small urban spaces, including balconies and rooftops, focusing on vertical gardening, container gardening, and sustainable practices.

1952. The Art of Stone Balancing: Dive into the meditative practice of stone balancing, showcasing different techniques, the physics behind the art, and the creative and calming effects of this nature-based activity.

1953. A Day in the Life of a Vintage Restorer: Follow the detailed work of restoring vintage items, from furniture to classic cars, highlighting the restoration process, the history behind the items, and the satisfaction of bringing them back to life.

1954. Building an Underwater ROV: Document the process of building a remotely operated vehicle (ROV) for underwater exploration, including design, construction, and the first dive, exploring marine life or sunken artifacts.

1955. Exploring the World of Edible Flowers: Create a series focusing on different edible flowers, including their culinary uses, health benefits, and how to grow them, culminating in a cooking segment incorporating these blooms.

1956. The Challenge of Writing and Illustrating a Children's Book: Take viewers on the journey of writing and illustrating a children's book, discussing story development, character creation, and the publishing process.

1957. Creating a Community Tool Library: Showcase the establishment of a tool library in your community, from gathering donations and organizing inventory to how the library benefits local DIY enthusiasts and promotes sharing economy principles.

1958. The Science Behind Fermented Drinks: Explore the fermentation process of various traditional and modern drinks, such as kombucha, kefir, and home-brewed beer, including the science, health aspects, and brewing techniques.

1959. A Week of Wilderness Skills Workshops: Host a series of wilderness skills workshops, covering topics like fire-making, foraging, navigation, and shelter building, emphasizing self-reliance and connection with nature.

1960. DIY Biodegradable Planters: Demonstrate how to make planters from biodegradable materials, such as paper pulp, cow dung, or food waste, focusing on sustainability and reducing plastic use in gardening.

1961. The Art of Bread Scoring: Delve into the decorative aspect of bread making by focusing on scoring techniques, showcasing different patterns, their impact on the bread's bake, and tips for beginners.

1962. Exploring Abandoned Amusement Parks: Document visits to abandoned amusement parks around the world, exploring their history, the reasons they were left abandoned, and the eerie beauty of these once joyful places.

1963. A Month of DIY Natural Beauty Treatments: Each day, try a different natural beauty treatment, from homemade face masks to hair treatments, documenting the ingredients, process, and the results on skin and hair health.

1964. The Journey of Crafting a Handmade Quilt: Document the process of making a quilt from start to finish, including design inspiration, fabric selection, piecing, and quilting, emphasizing the storytelling and heritage behind quilting.

1965. Upcycling Electronics into Functional Art: Show how to repurpose old electronics into functional art pieces or new gadgets, focusing on creative reuse, the tinkering process, and the blend of technology and art.

1966. A Day in the Life of an Archaeologist: Give viewers a glimpse into the daily life of an archaeologist, including fieldwork, artifact analysis, and the importance of preserving historical sites and findings.

1967. Building a Solar-Powered Water Feature: Guide viewers through creating a solar-powered water feature for a garden or outdoor space, discussing solar panel selection, water pump installation, and design ideas.

1968. The Tradition of Handmade Musical Instruments: Explore the craftsmanship behind handmade musical instruments, visiting artisans who create instruments like violins, flutes, or guitars, and showcasing the intricate processes involved.

1969. A Week of Eco-Friendly Transportation Challenges: Challenge yourself to use only eco-friendly modes of transportation for a week, such as biking, walking, public transit, or electric vehicles, documenting the experience and environmental impact.

1970. The Art and Science of Natural Dyes: Create a series on making and using natural dyes from plants, minerals, and insects, exploring the history, science, and techniques of dyeing fabrics in an environmentally friendly way.

1971. Reviving Lost Languages: Document the process of learning and reviving a language that is no longer widely spoken, exploring its cultural significance, challenges in learning, and efforts to keep the language alive.

1972. The Art of Kintsugi: Explore the Japanese art of kintsugi, repairing broken pottery with gold, as a metaphor for embracing flaws and imperfections, including a DIY tutorial and philosophical discussion on its meaning.

1973. A Journey Through Virtual Reality History: Create a series exploring historical events and eras through virtual reality experiences, offering immersive insights into different periods and their impact on the present.

1974. The Science of Sustainable Packaging: Investigate sustainable packaging solutions, focusing on the materials science, environmental impact, and innovations that aim to reduce waste and carbon footprint in packaging.

1975. Exploring Micro-Nations: Take viewers on a journey to explore the world's micro-nations, delving into their origins, claims to sovereignty, and what life is like within these unique, self-declared entities.

1976. Creating a Pollinator-Friendly Garden: Document the process of designing and planting a garden that attracts bees, butterflies, and other pollinators, highlighting the importance of pollinators to our ecosystem and food supply.

1977. DIY Water Filtration Systems: Show how to build and test various DIY water filtration systems, comparing their effectiveness, cost, and practicality for use in different scenarios, from camping to emergency preparedness.

1978. A Week of Traditional Storytelling: Each day, feature a different traditional story or folk tale from around the world, told by a skilled storyteller, exploring the cultural values and lessons embedded in these narratives.

1979. Building an Eco-Friendly Mini Golf Course: Document the creative process of designing and building a mini-golf course using recycled materials and eco-friendly designs, focusing on sustainability and fun.

1980. The Art of Time-Lapse Photography: Create a series teaching time-lapse photography, from the basics of capturing stunning time-lapses to advanced techniques and editing, showcasing natural phenomena and bustling cityscapes.

1981. Experimenting with Aquatic Plants in Aquascaping: Dive into the world of aquascaping, focusing on the use of various aquatic plants, their care, and the aesthetic principles behind creating underwater landscapes.

1982. A Day with Art Conservationists: Spend a day with art conservationists, documenting their meticulous work in preserving and restoring artworks, discussing the challenges they face and the importance of their work.

1983. Zero-Waste Event Planning: Plan and execute a zero-waste event, from a small party to a community gathering, sharing tips on minimizing waste, sustainable sourcing, and encouraging participants to engage in eco-friendly practices.

1984. The Craft of Handmade Journals: Show the process of creating handmade journals, including binding techniques, paper selection, and personalized covers, emphasizing the joy of journaling and crafting.

1985. Exploring the World of Citizen Science: Highlight various citizen science projects that viewers can participate in, from bird counting to stargazing, showcasing how ordinary people can contribute to scientific research.

1986. A Month of Mindful Consumption: Document a personal journey of mindful consumption, focusing on making more conscious choices about food, products, and resources, reflecting on the impact on well-being and the environment.

1987. Creating a Living Roof: Guide viewers through the process of creating a living roof or green roof, discussing the benefits for insulation, biodiversity, and reducing runoff, including the technical aspects and plant selection.

1988. The World of Competitive Rock Stacking: Delve into the niche sport of competitive rock stacking, showcasing the balance, patience, and creativity required, and exploring the community and competitions around this unique activity.

1989. DIY Solar Gadgets for Everyday Use: Innovate and build solar-powered gadgets that can be used in everyday life, from solar phone chargers to solar-powered night lights, emphasizing sustainability and practicality.

1990. A Week of Historical Fashion Reconstruction: Each day, reconstruct an outfit from a different historical period, researching the materials, styles, and significance of each garment, and wearing the finished outfits to see how they feel and function.

1991. Exploring Urban Legends Through Animation: Create animated shorts that bring urban legends from around the world to life, exploring their origins, cultural significance, and why they persist in modern society.

1992. The Art of Ice Climbing: Document the challenges and beauty of ice climbing, including preparation, techniques, and safety measures, while exploring stunning icy landscapes and discussing the sport's impact on personal growth.

1993. A Month of Ethical Hacking Challenges: Each day, tackle a new ethical hacking challenge, showcasing the importance of cybersecurity, how vulnerabilities are discovered and patched, and tips for protecting personal data online.

1994. Building a Community Mosaic Project: Lead a community project to create a large mosaic mural, documenting the design process, community involvement, and the final unveiling, highlighting the power of art to bring people together.

1995. The Science of Color in Nature: Explore the science behind the vibrant colors found in nature, from the iridescence of a butterfly's wings to the deep blues of the ocean, discussing the physics and biology of color production.

1996. Creating a Zero-Waste Art Studio: Document the journey of transforming an art studio into a zero-waste environment, focusing on sustainable materials, waste reduction techniques, and the impact on the creative process.

1997. A Week of Living Like a Nomad: Adopt a nomadic lifestyle for a week, exploring different aspects of nomadism, from mobile living solutions to the cultural and historical context of nomadic peoples around the world.

1998. The Tradition of Hand-Carved Wooden Spoons: Delve into the craft of hand-carving wooden spoons, exploring different wood types, carving techniques, and the cultural significance of this humble yet essential tool.

1999. DIY Underwater Habitats for Aquatic Wildlife: Show how to create underwater habitats in ponds or aquariums, enhancing biodiversity and providing refuge for fish, amphibians, and invertebrates, with a focus on ecological balance.

2000. The History and Techniques of Shadow Puppetry: Explore the ancient art of shadow puppetry, including its historical roots in various cultures, how to create and manipulate shadow puppets, and the storytelling potential of this unique performance art.

2001. Innovative Upcycling for Home Decor: Challenge yourself to upcycle found objects into innovative home decor items, showcasing the creative process, the transformation, and tips for viewers to try their own upcycling projects.

2002. Exploring the Microbiomes of Different Environments: Dive into the microscopic world to explore the unique microbiomes of various environments, from rainforests to urban settings, discussing their importance to ecosystem health and human life.

2003. A Journey Through Ancient Board Games: Discover and play ancient board games from around the world, exploring their history, rules, and cultural significance, and attempting to recreate them for modern play.

2004. The Process of Creating a Clay Animation Film: Document the painstaking process of creating a stop-motion clay animation film, from character design and set building to animation and post-production, sharing insights into this unique art form.

2005. Restoring a Historic Ship: Follow the restoration of a historic ship, detailing the craftsmanship involved in woodworking, metalworking, and rigging, and the historical research guiding the restoration.

2006. Designing a Sustainable Tiny Home on Wheels: Take viewers through the design and construction process of a sustainable tiny home on wheels, focusing on eco-friendly materials, energy efficiency, and the challenges of compact living.

2007. The Art and Science of Natural Landscapes Photography: Share tips and techniques for capturing the beauty of natural landscapes, discussing the artistry behind composition and lighting, and the scientific phenomena that create breathtaking scenes.

2008. A Week of Exploring Folk Music Instruments: Each day, introduce a different folk music instrument from around the world, discussing its history, how it's played, and its cultural significance, including performances to demonstrate its sound.

2009. Creating an Edible Forest Garden: Document the process of designing and planting an edible forest garden, emphasizing permaculture principles, plant selection for biodiversity, and the benefits of edible landscaping.

2010. The Challenge of Building a Bicycle from Scratch: Take on the challenge of building a bicycle entirely from scratch, detailing the selection of materials, the engineering and assembly process, and the final test ride.

2011. A Day with Art Restorers: Spend a day with professionals dedicated to art restoration, documenting their meticulous techniques, the science behind preservation, and the ethical considerations in restoring historical artworks.

2012. The Challenge of a Plastic-Free Week: Embark on a week-long challenge to live without using any plastic products, sharing daily experiences, the difficulties encountered, and sustainable alternatives discovered.

2013. Exploring the World of Invisible Art: Dive into art forms that exist on the edge of perception or are meant to be invisible, such as UV paintings, anamorphic installations, or art that's only visible under specific conditions, discussing the philosophy behind invisible art.

2014. Building a Community Food Forest: Document the process of transforming a communal space into a food forest, focusing on permaculture design principles, community involvement, and the journey from planting to harvest.

2015. A Week of Experimental Musical Instruments: Each day, create and play an experimental musical instrument, exploring unconventional sound production methods, materials, and the musical possibilities of these unique creations.

2016. The Science of Sandcastles: Delve into the physics and engineering principles behind building the perfect sandcastle, including the role of water content, sand grain size, and structural techniques, with a competitive building challenge.

2017. DIY Off-Grid Living Solutions: Showcase a series of DIY projects aimed at supporting off-grid living, such as water collection systems, solar dehydrators, and compost toilets, emphasizing sustainability and self-sufficiency.

2018. Exploring Historical Diets for a Month: Each week, adopt a different historical diet, from ancient Roman fare to medieval European cuisine, discussing nutritional content, historical context, and how these diets would fare by modern health standards.

2019. The Art of Bonsai for Beginners: Introduce the basics of bonsai, including selecting trees, pruning techniques, and care, weaving in the philosophical and aesthetic principles that guide bonsai cultivation.

2020. One Month of Living Like Different Historical Figures: Each week, live according to the daily routines, diets, and personal habits of a famous historical figure, reflecting on the insights and challenges of walking in their shoes.

2021. Creating a Wildlife Documentary in Your Backyard: Spend a month capturing the diversity of wildlife that visits your backyard, from birds to insects, creating a documentary that highlights the importance of urban biodiversity.

2022. A Journey Through Textile Arts: Explore various textile arts from around the world, including weaving, dyeing, and embroidery, showcasing traditional techniques, cultural significance, and modern adaptations.

2023. The Process of Making Artisanal Chocolate: Document the journey of making chocolate from bean to bar, focusing on the selection of beans, roasting, grinding, and molding, including the science and art behind creating fine chocolates.

2024. Urban Beekeeping Essentials: Introduce viewers to the basics of urban beekeeping, from setting up hives to maintaining healthy bee colonies, and the role of bees in urban ecosystems and food production.

2025. A Week of Solar-Powered Inventions: Each day, invent and test a new solar-powered device, showcasing the creativity and potential of solar energy to power everyday objects and solutions.

2026. The Lost Art of Handwritten Letters: Spend a month reconnecting through the art of handwritten letters, exploring the history, personal touch, and impact of taking the time to write by hand in a digital age.

2027. Eco-Friendly DIY Home Cleaning Products: Demonstrate how to make your own home cleaning products using natural and non-toxic ingredients, highlighting the benefits for health, the environment, and savings.

2028. A Day in the Life of a Historical Reenactor: Follow a historical reenactor through preparations and a day of living as a person from a specific historical period, exploring the research, costume creation, and immersion in historical lifestyle.

2029. The Challenge of Making Wearable Tech: Design and create a piece of wearable technology, from conceptualization to the technical build, focusing on the integration of fashion and functionality.

2030. Documenting the Revival of an Endangered Craft: Choose a craft that's at risk of disappearing, document the skills and knowledge required to practice it, and highlight efforts to preserve and revive the craft for future generations.

2031. The Art of Dry Stone Walling: Explore the ancient craft of building stone walls without mortar, highlighting its history, techniques, and the beauty and durability of these structures in landscapes around the world.

2032. A Month of Microadventures in the City: Each day, embark on a new "microadventure" within your city, encouraging viewers to see their urban environment through a lens of exploration and discovery, from secret gardens to rooftop sunrises.

2033. Creating a Living Art Installation: Document the creation of a living art installation that evolves over time, such as a mural with growing plants or an interactive sculpture, emphasizing the fusion of art, nature, and community engagement.

2034. The Science of Perfect Coffee: Delve into the chemistry and physics behind brewing the perfect cup of coffee, exploring different brewing methods, the impact of water quality, and the science of taste.

2035. Restoring a Vintage Arcade Machine: Take viewers through the process of restoring a vintage arcade machine, from sourcing parts to troubleshooting electronics, highlighting the nostalgia and craftsmanship involved.

2036. A Week of Wearable Art Projects: Each day, create and showcase a piece of wearable art, from jewelry made of unconventional materials to clothing with integrated digital technology, discussing the concept and creation process.

2037. The Journey of a Seed to a Tree: Document the growth of a tree from seed, capturing milestones in its development, and weaving in educational content about plant biology, the importance of trees in ecosystems, and conservation efforts.

2038. DIY Eco-Friendly Boat Building: Showcase the process of building an environmentally friendly boat, focusing on sustainable materials, low-impact construction methods, and the adventure of its maiden voyage.

2039. Exploring the World of Invisible Inks: Dive into the history and science of invisible inks, from lemon juice to more sophisticated chemical solutions, demonstrating how to make and reveal messages, and their uses throughout history.

2040. A Day in the Life of a Luthier: Follow a luthier (a maker of stringed instruments) for a day, exploring the artistry and precision involved in crafting instruments, the selection of materials, and the music they ultimately produce.

2041. Urban Homesteading Challenges: Take on a series of challenges related to urban homesteading, such as balcony composting, indoor herb gardening, or rainwater harvesting, sharing successes, failures, and lessons learned.

2042. The Magic of Time-Lapse Photography in Nature: Create a series of time-lapse videos capturing natural phenomena, such as the opening of a flower, cloud patterns, or the night sky, discussing the technology and patience required.

2043. Building a Wind-Powered Art Installation: Document the design and construction of an outdoor art installation powered by the wind, exploring the intersection of art, engineering, and environmental awareness.

2044. A Month of Historical Costume Making: Each week, choose a different historical period and create a costume using authentic materials and methods, exploring the history, fashion, and cultural context of each era.

2045. DIY Backyard Wildlife Pond: Show how to create a wildlife pond in a backyard, documenting the digging, planting, and establishment of a mini ecosystem that attracts frogs, birds, and insects.

2046. The Challenge of Living on a Capsule Wardrobe: Commit to living with a capsule wardrobe for a month, documenting the selection process, the combinations created, and reflections on consumerism and personal style.

2047. Exploring the Art of Stencil Graffiti: Dive into the world of stencil graffiti, from creating intricate stencils to executing a piece of street art, discussing its origins, cultural significance, and legal considerations.

2048. A Week of Sustainable Travel Challenges: While traveling, adopt sustainable practices each day, such as zero-waste packing, using public transportation, and supporting local economies, sharing tips and reflections on the impact.

2049. The Process of Making Handcrafted Guitars: Document the detailed process of making handcrafted guitars, from wood selection and shaping to finishing and stringing, showcasing the craftsmanship and sound quality.

2050. Exploring Bioluminescence in Nature: Create a documentary exploring the phenomenon of bioluminescence, visiting locations where it occurs naturally, from glowing plankton to fireflies, and explaining the science behind this magical glow.

2051. The Art of Making Traditional Handmade Toys: Dive into the world of traditional toy-making, showcasing how to create classic toys from different cultures using age-old techniques and natural materials.

2052. A Journey Through Astro-Photography: Share the adventure of capturing the night sky, from planning and setup to the stunning reveal of galaxies, stars, and planets through the lens, including tips for beginners.

2053. The Challenge of a Tech-Free Weekend: Document the experience of spending a weekend without modern technology, exploring alternative ways to entertain, communicate, and navigate, reflecting on the impact on mindfulness and social connections.

2054. Creating a Mini Documentary on Local Artisans: Profile local artisans in your community, from potters to blacksmiths, telling their stories, showcasing their craft, and exploring the importance of preserving traditional skills.

2055. Eco-Friendly Wedding Planning Tips: Offer guidance on planning a sustainable wedding, covering eco-friendly venue choices, decorations, catering options, and attire, encouraging couples to celebrate without compromising on environmental values.

2056. The Science and Craft of Homemade Preserves: Explore the science behind making jams, pickles, and other preserves at home, including the chemistry of preservation, health benefits, and creative flavor combinations.

2057. Reviving Your City's Forgotten Histories: Uncover and share stories of forgotten historical events, locations, or figures in your city, using archival research, interviews, and on-location visits to bring these hidden histories to light.

2058. Building a DIY Outdoor Adventure Course: Show how to design and construct an outdoor adventure course in your backyard or community space, including obstacles, zip lines, and climbing elements, focusing on safety and fun.

2059. A Month of Global Meditation Practices: Each day, explore and practice a different meditation technique from around the world, discussing its origins, benefits, and how to incorporate it into daily life for mental and emotional well-being.

2060. The Art of Puppet Making and Performance: Delve into puppet making, from simple sock puppets to complex marionettes, culminating in a puppet show that tells a compelling story or educates on a particular theme.

2061. Converting a Van into a Mobile Workshop: Document the transformation of a standard van into a fully equipped mobile workshop, detailing the design, tools needed, and the projects you can tackle on the go.

2062. Exploring the World of Natural Swimming Pools: Investigate the design, construction, and maintenance of natural swimming pools, highlighting their eco-friendly benefits and how they seamlessly integrate into landscapes.

2063. The Tradition of Oral Storytelling: Embark on a journey to preserve the tradition of oral storytelling, recording and sharing stories from elders in various communities, exploring the themes, morals, and cultural significance of these tales.

2064. DIY Sustainable Fashion Show: Organize a fashion show featuring outfits made from recycled or upcycled materials, highlighting the creativity in sustainable fashion and encouraging a dialogue on reducing textile waste.

2065. A Week of Wilderness Living Skills: Each day, focus on a different wilderness living skill, such as fire-building, shelter construction, or natural navigation, sharing practical tips and the importance of being prepared in the wild.

2066. The Process of Restoring a Historic Garden: Take on the project of restoring a historic garden, documenting the research into its original design, the restoration work, and the challenges and rewards of bringing history back to life.

2067. Creating a Comic Strip Series: Develop and share a comic strip series, detailing the process from concept and character design to storytelling and digital or hand-drawn execution, offering insights into the world of comic art.

2068. The Craft of Artisanal Cheese Making at Home: Guide viewers through the process of making artisanal cheese at home, covering the science of cheese making, different types of cheese, and tips for aging and flavoring.

2069. Exploring the Potential of Urban Vertical Farms: Investigate the concept and execution of vertical farming in urban environments, discussing the technology, benefits, and challenges of growing food in vertically stacked layers.

2070. A Day in the Life of a Historical Novelist: Follow the daily routine, research process, and writing discipline of a historical novelist, exploring how historical facts are woven into fictional narratives to bring the past to life.

2071. Reviving Ancient Sports and Games: Explore and participate in ancient sports and games that have fallen out of mainstream practice, detailing their historical significance, rules, and the experience of playing them today.

2072. The Art of Glassblowing in Modern Designs: Document the intricate process of glassblowing, focusing on how contemporary artists incorporate modern designs and techniques into this age-old craft.

2073. Building a Sustainable Treehouse: Take viewers on the journey of designing and constructing an eco-friendly treehouse, emphasizing the use of sustainable materials, minimal environmental impact, and integration with the surrounding ecosystem.

2074. A Month of Minimalist Living Experiments: Each week, adopt a different aspect of minimalist living, such as decluttering, digital detox, and simple living, sharing insights on the challenges and benefits of a minimalist lifestyle.

2075. Crafting Traditional Musical Instruments: Showcase the process of making traditional musical instruments from around the world, from woodwinds to stringed instruments, highlighting the cultural heritage and musicality of each piece.

2076. Urban Exploration: Rediscovering Abandoned Spaces: Delve into the exploration of abandoned buildings and spaces within cities, uncovering their history, the reasons for their abandonment, and capturing the beauty in decay.

2077. Creating a Personal Meditation Garden: Guide viewers through the process of designing and creating a meditation garden in a personal space, focusing on elements that promote peace, mindfulness, and connection with nature.

2078. The Challenge of Photographing Wildlife at Night: Share techniques and experiences of capturing nocturnal wildlife through photography, discussing the equipment used, challenges faced, and the behavior of animals at night.

2079. Eco-Friendly Printmaking Techniques: Explore various environmentally friendly printmaking techniques, from non-toxic etching to vegetable-based inks, highlighting how artists can create beautiful prints while minimizing their ecological footprint.

2080. A Week of Historical Diets Challenge: Each day, try a different historical diet, from ancient Roman feasts to Victorian meals, exploring the historical context, nutritional value, and preparing meals based on historical recipes.

2081. The Science of Sustainable Landscaping: Delve into the principles of sustainable landscaping, covering topics like water conservation, native plant gardening, and creating habitats for local wildlife, with practical advice for viewers.

2082. DIY Recycled Metal Sculptures: Demonstrate the process of creating sculptures from recycled metal pieces, including sourcing materials, welding techniques, and the inspiration behind each piece.

2083. Restoring a Community's Historical Murals: Document the restoration of historical murals in a community, focusing on the significance of the murals, the restoration techniques used, and the community's involvement in preserving their local history.

2084. A Journey Through the World of Spices: Explore the history, cultivation, and culinary uses of various spices from around the world, including visits to spice farms, markets, and incorporating them into traditional and modern recipes.

2085. The Art of Natural Light Photography: Share tips and techniques for mastering photography using only natural light, discussing the challenges and advantages of different lighting conditions throughout the day.

2086. Building an Eco-Friendly Surfboard: Document the process of designing and crafting a surfboard using sustainable materials, focusing on the environmental impact of surfboard production and alternative green technologies.

2087. Exploring the Craft of Handmade Paper Flowers: Create a series on crafting realistic paper flowers, covering various techniques and materials, and the potential uses of paper flowers in decor, art, and celebrations.

2088. The Tradition of Oral Histories: Embark on a project to collect and preserve oral histories from elders in various communities, discussing the importance of storytelling in preserving culture and personal histories.

2089. Sustainable Cooking Techniques: Highlight sustainable cooking practices, such as using seasonal and locally sourced ingredients, minimizing energy consumption, and reducing food waste, with recipes and tips for eco-conscious cooking.

2090. Creating Art with Augmented Reality: Dive into the world of augmented reality art, showcasing how artists can use AR to create interactive pieces that blend the digital and physical worlds, including tutorials on getting started with AR in art.

2091. The Art of Digital Detoxing: Embark on a series exploring the benefits and challenges of digital detoxing. Document a week-long journey of significantly reducing screen time, highlighting alternative activities and the impact on mental health and social connections.

2092. DIY Rainwater Harvesting System: Create a step-by-step guide to designing and installing a simple rainwater harvesting system suitable for urban homes, focusing on sustainability, water conservation, and practical uses for the collected water.

2093. Exploring the World of Eco-Art: Dive into the genre of eco-art, showcasing artists who use recycled materials or nature-themed projects to raise awareness about environmental issues. Highlight the creative process and the messages behind their works.

2094. A Journey Through the Stars: Amateur Astronomy: Share the basics of getting started with amateur astronomy, including choosing the right telescope, navigating the night sky, and capturing celestial events through astrophotography.

2095. Building a Community Garden from Scratch: Document the transformation of an unused plot of land into a thriving community garden. Focus on planning, volunteer recruitment, sustainable gardening practices, and the garden's role in fostering community spirit.

2096. The Craft of Artisanal Bread Making: Explore the art and science of making artisanal bread at home. Cover different types of bread, fermentation processes, and how to achieve the perfect crust and crumb, along with tips for beginners.

2097. Urban Cycling Adventures: Create a series on urban cycling, featuring different routes, safety tips, and the benefits of biking in the city. Highlight unique cycling paths, local laws, and how to navigate traffic safely.

2098. Reviving Traditional Folk Dances: Showcase the beauty and cultural significance of traditional folk dances from around the world. Document learning these dances, their historical contexts, and efforts to keep them alive in modern times.

2099. Eco-Friendly Fashion Hacks: Offer viewers creative ways to upcycle their existing wardrobe, focusing on sewing and customization techniques that breathe new life into old garments, promoting sustainable fashion choices.

2100. The World of Miniature Cooking: Delve into the fascinating hobby of miniature cooking, creating tiny, edible dishes in a fully functional miniature kitchen. Explore the appeal and challenges of cooking at such a small scale.

2101. Creating a Wildlife Corridor in Suburbia: Document the process of creating a wildlife corridor in a suburban area, focusing on native plant species, attracting local wildlife, and the importance of biodiversity in urban planning.

2102. A Week of Historical Reenactments: Each day, reenact a different historical event or day in the life of a historical figure, using authentic costumes, tools, and settings to bring history to life for viewers.

2103. DIY Home Energy Efficiency Audit: Guide viewers through conducting a home energy efficiency audit. Cover how to identify leaks, inefficient appliances, and ways to conserve energy, including simple fixes and upgrades.

2104. Exploring Abandoned Railway Lines: Take viewers on an exploration of abandoned railway lines, delving into their history, the reasons for their closure, and the natural landscapes they traverse now.

2105. The Process of Making Natural Cosmetics: Create a series on crafting natural cosmetics at home, from lip balms and lotions to homemade makeup, focusing on natural ingredients, benefits, and customizing products for different skin types.

2106. A Month of Zero-Waste Challenges: Each day, tackle a new challenge to reduce waste in different areas of life, from food and shopping to personal care and cleaning, sharing successes, obstacles, and tips for a zero-waste lifestyle.

2107. Exploring the Art of Shadow Art: Investigate the unique art form of creating images and scenes from shadows using objects, hands, or bodies. Highlight the creative process, techniques, and the transient beauty of shadow art.

2108. Sustainable Living on a Budget: Offer practical advice for adopting sustainable living practices without breaking the bank. Cover topics like thrifting, reducing energy consumption, and low-cost, eco-friendly home improvements.

2109. A Beginner's Guide to Fermentation: Introduce viewers to the world of fermentation, covering the basics of fermenting vegetables, dairy, and beverages at home. Discuss the health benefits and share simple starter recipes.

2110. The Renaissance of Analog Photography: Explore the resurgence of interest in analog photography. Discuss the appeal of film in a digital age, tips for beginners, and how to develop film at home or in a darkroom.

2111. The Art of Urban Foraging: Embark on urban foraging adventures, identifying edible plants and fruits in city environments. Discuss safety, ethics, and the nutritional benefits of foraged food, including preparation tips for urban-gathered meals.

2112. Creating an Upcycled Art Installation: Document the journey of creating a large-scale art installation using entirely upcycled materials. Highlight the conceptualization, community involvement, and the message behind promoting sustainability through art.

2113. A Week of Living with AI Assistants: Experiment with integrating various AI assistants into daily life for a week, exploring their capabilities, limitations, and the impact on efficiency, privacy, and human interaction.

2114. The Craft of Homemade Musical Instruments: Delve into the creation of musical instruments from recycled or everyday materials. Showcase the build process, the science of sound production, and performances using the crafted instruments.

2115. Exploring Historical Cooking Techniques: Investigate and demonstrate cooking techniques from different historical periods and cultures, such as cooking over an open fire, using a clay oven, or preparing meals without modern conveniences.

2116. The World Through Macro Photography: Reveal the unseen world through macro photography, capturing the intricate details of insects, plants, and everyday objects. Share tips on macro photography techniques and the stories behind the shots.

2117. Designing a Sustainable Tiny Home Interior: Focus on the interior design of a tiny home, emphasizing sustainability, multifunctional spaces, and minimalism. Discuss choices in materials, space-saving solutions, and the philosophy behind tiny living.

2118. Rediscovering Lost Crafting Techniques: Unearth and revive crafting techniques that are nearly forgotten, such as basket weaving, lacemaking, or traditional woodworking, highlighting their cultural significance and potential for modern application.

2119. A Series on Space Colonization: Explore the concept of space colonization through a series, discussing the challenges, proposed solutions, and the science behind living on other planets, including interviews with experts in the field.

2120. DIY Eco-Friendly Air Conditioning Alternatives: Investigate and build alternative cooling systems that are environmentally friendly, such as using evaporative coolers or creating passive cooling designs, detailing the process and effectiveness.

2121. The Adventure of Geocaching: Take viewers on geocaching adventures, exploring the blend of technology and treasure hunting in nature and urban environments, sharing tips for beginners and the excitement of the find.

2122. Restoring a Community Playground: Document the process of restoring and upgrading a community playground, focusing on volunteer efforts, safety improvements, and adding inclusive play equipment for all children.

2123. The Science of Composting: Create an educational series on the science behind composting, covering different methods, the biology of decomposition, and how to successfully compost in various environments.

2124. A Journey Through Indigenous Art Forms: Explore indigenous art forms from around the world, delving into their cultural backgrounds, techniques, and contemporary applications, possibly collaborating with indigenous artists.

2125. The Challenge of Building with Natural Materials: Document the process of constructing a structure using only natural materials, such as cob, bamboo, or straw bales, focusing on traditional techniques and sustainable building practices.

2126. Urban Wildlife Documentaries: Produce mini-documentaries on wildlife in urban settings, highlighting the adaptability of various species, their interactions with human environments, and conservation efforts within cities.

2127. The Art of Herbal Tea Blending: Share the process of blending herbal teas, discussing the properties of different herbs, blending techniques for flavor and health benefits, and tips for growing your own tea garden.

2128. Reviving Vintage Electronics: Take on projects to restore and repurpose vintage electronics, such as radios, turntables, or early computers, discussing the history, technical challenges, and the nostalgia factor.

2129. Sustainable Fashion Through Thrifting and Upcycling: Showcase the potential of thrifting and upcycling in creating a sustainable wardrobe, including thrift hauls, upcycling projects, and styling tips for second-hand clothes.

2130. A Guide to Backyard Astronomical Observations: Offer a beginner's guide to observing celestial bodies from your backyard, covering basic stargazing equipment, what to look for in the night sky, and how to record observations.

2131. The Art of Living Walls: Dive into the creation and maintenance of living walls, both indoors and outdoors. Highlight the benefits for air quality, aesthetics, and biodiversity, and guide viewers through building their own.

2132. Rediscovering Ancient Astronomy: Explore ancient methods of astronomy, including how ancient civilizations understood the cosmos. Re-create ancient astronomical instruments and compare their accuracy with modern tools.

2133. A Month of Mindful Photography: Challenge yourself to capture one photo a day that reflects a mindful observation of your surroundings. Share the stories behind the photos and the impact of this practice on mindfulness and creativity.

2134. Sculpting with Recyclable Materials: Showcase the process of creating sculptures using only recyclable materials, emphasizing the importance of recycling and how art can be made sustainably.

2135. Historical Reenactment of Maritime Explorers: Embark on a journey reenacting the voyages of famous maritime explorers. Use historical ships, navigational tools, and techniques to understand the challenges they faced.

2136. DIY Eco-Friendly Personal Care Products: Create a series on making your own personal care products, such as shampoo, deodorant, and toothpaste, using natural and eco-friendly ingredients, highlighting the health and environmental benefits.

2137. A Week of Silence: Document the experience of spending a week in silence, exploring the effects on mental health, creativity, and personal reflection, and sharing insights and challenges encountered.

2138. The Process of Making Handcrafted Shoes: Explore the traditional craft of shoemaking, from selecting materials to the final stitching. Highlight the skill, artistry, and customization involved in creating handmade footwear.

2139. Urban Gardening in Unconventional Spaces: Show how to start gardens in unconventional urban spaces, like rooftops, balconies, or alleyways. Discuss container gardening, vertical farming, and space-efficient crops.

2140. Reviving the Art of Handwritten Maps: Create and showcase beautifully detailed, handwritten maps of local areas or fictional worlds, discussing the historical significance of cartography and techniques for beginners.

2141. Sustainable Cooking Methods: Explore and demonstrate sustainable cooking methods that minimize energy use, such as solar ovens, pressure cooking, and raw food recipes, focusing on the environmental impact of cooking.

2142. A Series on Ocean Conservation: Dive into the issues facing the world's oceans, from pollution to overfishing. Highlight conservation efforts, marine biodiversity, and what individuals can do to help.

2143. Exploring the World of Textile Dyeing: Experiment with different natural and synthetic dyeing techniques for textiles. Share the history, cultural significance, and science behind the colors used in fabric dyeing.

2144. The Craft of Handmade Papermaking: Document the process of making paper by hand, from pulping recycled materials to pressing and drying, including creative uses for the finished paper in art and everyday life.

2145. Building a Community Free Library: Follow the journey of building and stocking a free library in your community. Highlight the importance of access to literature, community engagement, and the joy of sharing books.

2146. A Beginner's Guide to Composting: Offer a comprehensive guide to starting a composting system at home, covering different methods, what can be composted, and the environmental impact of reducing food waste.

2147. The Art of Stop Motion Animation: Create a series on producing stop motion animation, from crafting characters and sets to the frame-by-frame shooting process, sharing tips and tricks for beginners.

2148. A Journey Through Native Plant Landscaping: Transform a garden space using native plants, discussing the benefits for local ecosystems, attracting wildlife, and maintaining a garden that thrives naturally.

2149. Creating a Portable Solar Power Station: Show viewers how to build a portable solar power station for camping or emergency use, covering the components needed, assembly, and practical applications.

2150. The History and Technique of Mosaic Art: Explore the ancient art form of mosaic, from its historical roots in Mesopotamia and Rome to contemporary applications. Demonstrate techniques for creating your own mosaic art pieces.

2151. Crafting With Bioplastics: Experiment with making bioplastics at home from natural ingredients. Document the process, test the durability of the bioplastics in various applications, and discuss the environmental benefits.

2152. The Physics of Play: Create a series exploring the physics behind common playground equipment like swings, slides, and seesaws. Use experiments to explain concepts like momentum, gravity, and friction in an accessible way.

2153. A Deep Dive into Coral Reefs: Produce a documentary-style series on coral reefs, covering their ecological importance, the threats they face from climate change and pollution, and ongoing conservation efforts.

2154. Zero-Waste Crafting: Challenge yourself to a month of crafting projects using only scrap materials or waste products. Focus on repurposing items creatively, reducing waste, and sharing tips for sourcing materials.

2155. The Art of Fermentation: Explore the world of fermentation, from vegetables and dairy to beverages. Share historical context, health benefits, and step-by-step guides for fermenting at home.

2156. DIY Natural Landscaping: Show how to design a landscape using native plants and sustainable practices. Highlight the benefits of natural landscaping, such as attracting wildlife, conserving water, and reducing maintenance.

2157. Exploring Ancient Navigation Techniques: Recreate ancient navigation techniques used by sailors and explorers before the advent of modern technology. Document attempts to navigate using the stars, sun, and natural landmarks.

2158. Building a Miniature Book Library: Craft a collection of miniature books, from classics to personal journals. Share the process of miniaturization, bookbinding techniques, and creative uses for your tiny tomes.

2159. Urban Beekeeping for Beginners: Document the journey of starting an urban beekeeping project, covering the basics of bee biology, hive management, and the benefits of bees for urban environments.

2160. Eco-Friendly Event Planning: Plan and execute an event following eco-friendly principles. Share insights on minimizing waste, choosing sustainable materials, and ensuring the event is accessible and inclusive.

2161. The Science of Sleep: Create content exploring the science behind sleep, including sleep cycles, the benefits of a good night's sleep, and tips for improving sleep quality based on the latest research.

2162. Handcrafting Customized Stationery: Dive into the craft of making personalized stationery. Show techniques for paper making, printing designs, and adding personal touches like wax seals or hand-drawn elements.

2163. The Journey of Restoring a Historic Landmark: Document the restoration of a local historic landmark. Share the history of the place, the restoration process, challenges faced, and the community's role in preservation.

2164. Creating a Permaculture Balcony Garden: Design a permaculture garden on a balcony or small space. Discuss the principles of permaculture design, plant selection, and how to create a self-sustaining ecosystem in a limited area.

2165. The Art and Mechanics of Clockmaking: Delve into the world of clockmaking, exploring the intricate mechanics behind clocks and watches. Share the process of designing and assembling a working clock from scratch.

2166. Adventures in Sourdough Baking: Chronicle the journey of starting a sourdough culture and experimenting with different sourdough bread recipes. Share successes, failures, and the science of sourdough fermentation.

2167. Sustainable Travel Vlogging: Share experiences of traveling sustainably, focusing on eco-friendly accommodations, transportation, and activities. Highlight the impact of travel on the environment and local communities.

2168. The Renaissance of Traditional Crafts: Explore the revival of traditional crafts such as weaving, pottery, and blacksmithing. Interview artisans, participate in workshops, and discuss the significance of keeping these crafts alive.

2169. A Guide to Ethical Wildlife Photography: Offer tips for capturing wildlife through photography in an ethical manner. Discuss the importance of respecting wildlife, minimizing disturbance, and promoting conservation through photography.

2170. Designing a Self-Cleaning Ecosystem Aquarium: Show how to create an aquarium that mimics a natural ecosystem, requiring minimal intervention. Explain the balance of plants, fish, and microorganisms needed for a self-sustaining system.

2171. The Art of Silent Filmmaking: Create a series of short silent films, focusing on storytelling through visual cues, expressions, and body language. Discuss the history of silent cinema and its influence on modern filmmaking techniques.

2172. Urban Survival Skills Series: Share urban survival tips, from navigating without a smartphone to finding edible plants in city parks. Include practical advice for dealing with power outages, water shortages, and urban foraging.

2173. Creating Art from Upcycled Tech: Dive into the world of tech art by upcycling old electronics into interactive art pieces. Showcase the creative process, from conceptualization to the technical build, and the final interactive experience.

2174. A Journey Through Microscopic Worlds: Utilize a microscope to explore and document the unseen worlds around us, from pond water ecosystems to the intricate structures of plants and insects, discussing the science behind what's observed.

2175. Building a Portable Tiny House: Document the challenges and triumphs of designing and constructing a portable tiny house, focusing on innovative space-saving solutions, sustainable materials, and the freedom of a mobile lifestyle.

2176. The Renaissance of Letterpress Printing: Explore the traditional craft of letterpress printing, from setting type by hand to operating vintage presses. Highlight the tactile beauty of letterpress and its resurgence in the digital age.

2177. DIY Backyard Observatory for Stargazing: Guide viewers through building a simple backyard observatory, discussing the selection of telescopes, construction of a viewing platform, and tips for amateur astronomers.

2178. Exploring the Culture of Coffee Around the World: Delve into the diverse ways coffee is enjoyed around the world, from Italian espressos to Turkish coffee. Discuss the cultural significance and rituals associated with coffee consumption.

2179. Sustainable Living on a Boat: Share the experience of living sustainably on a boat, focusing on challenges like energy consumption, waste management, and minimizing the ecological footprint while exploring the seas.

2180. The Art of Natural Perfumery: Create a series on crafting perfumes using natural ingredients. Cover the basics of scent composition, extraction methods, and blending your own unique fragrances.

2181. Revitalizing Community Spaces with Murals: Document the process of transforming bland community spaces with vibrant murals, from planning and design to the collaborative painting process and the mural's impact on the community.

2182. A Week of Experimental Fashion: Challenge yourself to create and wear experimental fashion pieces for a week, documenting the design process, public reactions, and reflections on fashion as a form of self-expression and art.

2183. The Science of Renewable Energy at Home: Explore the science behind home-based renewable energy solutions, such as solar panels, wind turbines, and bioenergy. Share DIY projects, efficiency tips, and the impact on household energy consumption.

2184. Documenting the Night Sky Through the Seasons: Capture and document the changes in the night sky over the course of a year, discussing celestial events, constellations, and the science behind seasonal changes in the stars.

2185. Crafting with Natural Fibers: Show how to craft items using natural fibers like wool, cotton, and bamboo. Include spinning, dyeing with natural dyes, and creating textiles or art pieces, emphasizing sustainability and skill.

2186. Exploring Abandoned Historical Sites: Take viewers on explorations of abandoned historical sites, uncovering their stories, the reasons for their abandonment, and the beauty found in decay, while respecting the sites and safety guidelines.

2187. The Tradition of Hand-Crafted Paper: Dive into the craft of making paper by hand, from sourcing sustainable materials to the final pressing and drying process. Explore traditional and modern uses for handcrafted paper.

2188. Zero-Waste Home Makeover: Transform a room or home into a zero-waste space, sharing tips for reducing waste in home decor, furniture selection, and everyday living, promoting sustainability and minimal environmental impact.

2189. The Art of Historical Battle Reenactments: Delve into the world of historical battle reenactments, covering the preparation, costumes, tactics, and the educational value of bringing history to life through detailed recreations.

2190. Designing a Sustainable Wardrobe: Offer guidance on building a sustainable wardrobe, from selecting eco-friendly fabrics and ethical brands to tips for caring for garments to extend their life and reduce fashion waste.

2191. Homemade Natural Insect Repellents: Demonstrate how to make effective, natural insect repellents using herbs and essential oils, discussing the science behind the ingredients and their environmental impact compared to commercial products.

2192. The Science of Color in Everyday Life: Explore the science behind color perception, how colors influence mood and behavior, and the role of color in nature and technology, including experiments that viewers can try at home.

2193. A Guide to Building Cob Structures: Document the process of building small cob structures, from mixing natural materials to construction techniques, highlighting the sustainability and efficiency of cob in modern green building.

2194. Exploring the World of Honey: Dive into the different types of honey, exploring their unique flavors, health benefits, and the process of honey production from beehive to table, including visits to local beekeepers.

2195. Eco-Friendly Pet Care Solutions: Offer tips and DIY solutions for eco-friendly pet care, covering everything from homemade pet food and treats to sustainable pet toys and bedding, emphasizing a low environmental impact.

2196. The Art of Sand Sculpture: Showcase the process of creating intricate sand sculptures, from planning and sculpting techniques to the temporary nature of the art form, including tips for beginners interested in sand art.

2197. Zero-Waste Gardening Techniques: Share strategies for achieving a zero-waste garden, including composting, natural pest control, and recycling household waste as garden resources, aiming for sustainability in home gardening.

2198. The History and Craft of Quilting: Explore the rich history of quilting, including its cultural significance, traditional patterns, and modern interpretations, culminating in a project that walks viewers through creating their own quilt.

2199. Urban Exploration: Revitalizing Lost Spaces: Highlight efforts to revitalize and repurpose abandoned urban spaces, from graffiti art projects to community gardens, discussing the challenges and impacts of these transformations.

2200. A Culinary Tour of Medieval Recipes: Recreate medieval recipes, exploring the history, ingredients, and cooking methods of the time. Discuss how these dishes reflect the culture and societal norms of the medieval period.

2201. Creating a Mindful Morning Routine: Share a series of mindful morning routines that incorporate meditation, journaling, gentle exercise, and healthy eating, discussing the benefits of starting the day with intention.

2202. DIY Solar Water Heating Systems: Guide viewers through the process of building and installing a basic solar water heating system, discussing the principles of solar thermal energy and potential cost savings.

2203. The Journey of Restoring an Old Sailboat: Document the restoration of an old sailboat, covering the carpentry, painting, and rigging work involved, and the eventual launch and maiden voyage.

2204. The Tradition of Handwritten Illuminated Manuscripts: Explore the art of creating illuminated manuscripts by hand, including calligraphy, gold leaf application, and miniature painting, highlighting historical techniques and their modern applications.

2205. Sustainable Travel Packing Tips: Offer tips and hacks for packing light and sustainably for travel, focusing on eco-friendly products, minimizing waste, and choosing versatile clothing and gear.

2206. Homesteading Skills for Urban Dwellers: Teach basic homesteading skills that can be applied in an urban setting, such as balcony gardening, basic woodworking, and preserving food, emphasizing self-sufficiency and sustainability.

2207. The Art of Japanese Woodblock Printing: Introduce the traditional art of Japanese woodblock printing (ukiyo-e), from carving the blocks to mixing and applying the ink, showcasing the process of creating a print from start to finish.

2208. Reviving the Lost Art of Soap Box Derbies: Document the building of a soap box racer and participating in a local soap box derby, exploring the history of the derby, construction techniques, and the community aspect of the event.

2209. Mindfulness in Motion: The Art of Tai Chi: Share the principles and basic movements of Tai Chi, discussing its benefits for health and mindfulness, and guiding viewers through a simple Tai Chi routine suitable for beginners.

2210. Exploring the Impact of Urban Green Spaces: Investigate the importance of green spaces in urban environments, including parks, rooftop gardens, and green walls, discussing their benefits for mental health, biodiversity, and combating climate change.

2211. DIY Bicycle Repair and Maintenance Workshop: Launch a series teaching basic bicycle repair and maintenance skills, covering everything from fixing a flat tire to adjusting brakes and gears, aiming to empower cyclists to care for their bikes.

2212. The Art of Bonsai for Urban Dwellers: Explore the practice of bonsai, making it accessible for those living in urban environments. Discuss selecting suitable species, shaping techniques, and the meditative aspects of bonsai care.

2213. A Deep Dive into the World of Spices: Travel through the history, cultivation, and culinary uses of various spices. Include visits to spice farms, tutorials on making spice blends, and their health benefits.

2214. Revitalizing Public Spaces with Guerrilla Gardening: Document guerrilla gardening efforts to beautify neglected urban spaces with flowers and plants. Discuss the movement's origins, legal aspects, and tips for aspiring guerrilla gardeners.

2215. The Tradition of Shadow Theatre: Delve into the ancient art of shadow theatre, exploring its history, cultural significance, and storytelling techniques. Offer a tutorial on creating shadow puppets and setting up a simple home theatre.

2216. Sustainable Fashion: Thrift Store Transformations: Showcase the transformation of thrift store finds into fashionable pieces, highlighting the creativity and environmental benefits of repurposing and upcycling clothing.

2217. Building a DIY Backyard Retreat: Guide viewers through creating a peaceful retreat space in their backyard, focusing on DIY projects like building a small pond, a meditation corner, or a reading nook using sustainable materials.

2218. Exploring the Science of Fermentation: Create a series on the fermentation process, from sauerkraut and kimchi to homemade yogurt and beer. Discuss the microbiology involved, health benefits, and step-by-step guides for beginners.

2219. The Craft of Handmade Pottery: Take viewers on a journey through the process of creating pottery by hand, from kneading the clay to the final glaze. Share the therapeutic aspects of pottery and the satisfaction of creating functional art.

2220. Eco-Friendly Pet Ownership: Offer advice on sustainable pet ownership, covering eco-friendly pet products, homemade pet food recipes, and tips for reducing your pet's environmental pawprint.

2221. A Guide to Historical Costume Creation: Document the process of researching, designing, and sewing historical costumes, emphasizing accuracy, techniques, and the stories behind different garments.

2222. Upcycling Furniture with Unique Finishes: Show how to give old furniture new life with creative finishes, including decoupage, faux marbling, and distressing techniques, focusing on the transformation process and tips for beginners.

2223. The Joy of Homemade Pasta: Share the art of making pasta from scratch, covering various types of pasta, shaping techniques, and pairing with homemade sauces, highlighting the simplicity and satisfaction of homemade Italian cuisine.

2224. Creating a Pollinator Paradise: Educate on designing a garden that attracts bees, butterflies, and other pollinators. Discuss plant selection, the importance of biodiversity, and how to create habitats for pollinators in urban and rural settings.

2225. The Basics of Solar Cooking: Introduce solar cooking by building a DIY solar cooker and experimenting with different recipes. Highlight the benefits of solar cooking, including energy conservation and the ability to cook during power outages.

2226. Art Therapy Projects for Mental Well-being: Launch a series on art therapy projects that individuals can do at home to improve mental health, discussing the therapeutic benefits of art and guiding viewers through various creative exercises.

2227. A Travel Vlog Series on UNESCO World Heritage Sites: Explore and document UNESCO World Heritage Sites, delving into their historical, cultural, and natural significance, and offering tips for responsible and sustainable tourism.

2228. The World of Indoor Vertical Farming: Dive into the technology and techniques behind indoor vertical farming. Discuss its potential to revolutionize urban agriculture, sustainability aspects, and how viewers can start their own small-scale vertical farm.

2229. Restoring a Classic Car on a Budget: Document the journey of restoring a classic car with a limited budget, focusing on DIY repairs, sourcing affordable parts, and the challenges and triumphs of the restoration process.

2230. Adventures in Wild Edible Foraging: Take viewers on foraging trips to identify and harvest wild edibles in various environments. Share safety tips, nutritional information, and recipes using foraged ingredients.

2231. Zero-Waste Home Makeovers: Document the transformation of different areas in a home to fully embrace zero-waste principles. Highlight practical swaps, DIY solutions, and the impact on waste reduction and sustainability.

2232. The Chemistry of Cooking: Create a series that explores the fascinating chemistry behind everyday cooking processes, such as caramelization, emulsification, and fermentation, including experiments and recipes that illustrate these concepts.

2233. Historical Documentaries on Lost Civilizations: Produce a series of documentaries exploring lost civilizations around the world. Delve into their history, culture, achievements, and the mysteries surrounding their decline or disappearance.

2234. DIY Backyard Biomes: Show how to create different biomes in your backyard, such as a desert area, a mini rainforest, or a pond ecosystem, discussing the plants and animals that can thrive in each and the ecological balance.

2235. Adaptive Clothing Design: Highlight the importance and creativity behind designing adaptive clothing for individuals with disabilities. Showcase the design process, the challenges addressed, and the impact on users' lives.

2236. The Science of Sleep: Launch an educational series on the science of sleep, covering topics like sleep cycles, the effects of sleep deprivation, and tips for improving sleep quality, including interviews with sleep experts.

2237. Exploring Micro-Housing Communities: Document visits to micro-housing and tiny home communities around the world. Explore their design, community living aspects, sustainability features, and the lifestyle of residents.

2238. A Culinary Journey Through Fermented Foods: Take viewers on a global culinary journey to explore fermented foods from various cultures. Discuss their traditional significance, preparation methods, and health benefits.

2239. Crafting Historical Instruments: Delve into the craft of making historical musical instruments, such as lutes, harpsichords, or traditional flutes. Share the historical context, craftsmanship involved, and the music they produce.

2240. Eco-Friendly DIY Cleaning Products: Demonstrate how to make your own eco-friendly cleaning products. Share recipes, the science behind the ingredients, and comparisons of their effectiveness against commercial products.

2241. Mindfulness in Digital Spaces: Discuss strategies for practicing mindfulness and promoting mental health in digital spaces. Cover topics like managing screen time, mindful social media use, and digital detoxing.

2242. Recreating Ancient Engineering Marvels: Attempt to recreate small-scale versions of ancient engineering marvels using period-accurate materials and techniques, discussing the historical significance and challenges faced by ancient engineers.

2243. The Art of Ice and Snow Sculptures: Document the process and challenges of creating sculptures from ice and snow, including tools, techniques, and the ephemeral nature of working with these materials.

2244. Urban Permaculture Designs: Showcase urban permaculture projects, discussing design principles, implementation challenges, and the benefits of permaculture in city environments for sustainability and food security.

2245. Journey Through the World's Great Libraries: Create a travelogue visiting some of the world's most iconic libraries. Explore their history, architecture, and the unique collections they house, emphasizing the importance of libraries in preserving human knowledge.

2246. DIY Renewable Energy Projects: Share projects that demonstrate how to harness renewable energy sources at home, such as building a small wind turbine, a solar oven, or a hydroelectric generator.

2247. The Tradition of Oral Histories: Highlight the importance of oral histories by recording and sharing stories from elders in various communities, exploring the role of storytelling in preserving cultural heritage.

2248. Restoring and Repurposing Vintage Furniture: Document the process of restoring vintage furniture pieces, focusing on techniques, materials, and the transformation from worn to cherished items, along with ideas for repurposing.

2249. A Guide to Ethical Wildlife Encounters: Offer advice for ethically interacting with wildlife, whether in the wild or at sanctuaries and rescue centers. Discuss how to respect animal welfare and promote conservation.

2250. Creating a Capsule Art Supply Kit: Show how to curate a minimalist art supply kit that maximizes creativity with minimal materials. Discuss choosing versatile tools and supplies, and demonstrate a range of projects using the kit.

2251. A Series on Urban Acoustic Ecology: Explore the sounds of the city by delving into urban acoustic ecology. Record and analyze the unique soundscapes of different neighborhoods, discussing the impact of urban sounds on well-being and the environment.

2252. The Art of Precision Paper Cutting: Showcase the meticulous craft of precision paper cutting. Share techniques for creating intricate designs, the history behind this art form, and its applications in contemporary art and decoration.

2253. Building a Community Maker Space: Document the process of creating a maker space in your community, from gathering resources and tools to organizing workshops and events that encourage creativity and innovation among participants.

2254. The Science Behind Athletic Performance: Create content exploring the science of sports and athletic performance, including nutrition, psychology, and biomechanics, featuring insights from experts and tips for amateur athletes.

2255. Eco-Friendly Wedding Planning: Offer guidance on planning a sustainable wedding, covering eco-friendly venue choices, decorations, catering options, and attire, encouraging couples to celebrate without compromising environmental values.

2256. Restoring a Classic Arcade Machine: Take viewers through the process of restoring a classic arcade machine, from sourcing parts to troubleshooting electronics, highlighting the nostalgia and craftsmanship involved.

2257. A Culinary Tour of Ancient Recipes: Recreate ancient recipes, exploring the historical context, ingredients, and cooking methods of the time. Discuss how these dishes reflect the culture and societal norms of the ancient world.

2258. Exploring the Impact of Color on Mood: Delve into the psychology of color, creating experiments and visual content to explore how different colors can influence mood, behavior, and perceptions in various settings.

2259. The Journey of Learning a Traditional Dance: Document the process of learning a traditional dance from a specific culture, including the history, techniques, and significance of the dance, culminating in a performance.

2260. DIY Vertical Farming at Home: Show how to set up a vertical farm in a small space, discussing the benefits of vertical farming, suitable plants for vertical growth, and tips for maximizing yield in limited spaces.

2261. A Week of Living Like a Victorian: Immerse yourself in Victorian life for a week, adopting the lifestyle, crafts, and daily routines of the period. Reflect on the experience, historical insights, and the relevance of Victorian innovations today.

2262. Creating Sustainable Art Supplies: Explore alternatives to traditional art supplies by creating eco-friendly, sustainable options. Share recipes and techniques for making paints, inks, and other materials from natural sources.

2263. The Challenge of Writing a Novel in a Month: Document the personal challenge of writing a novel in a month, sharing the ups and downs, creative processes, time management strategies, and the journey from concept to completion.

2264. Designing a Self-Sustaining Ecosystem in an Aquarium: Showcase the creation of a self-sustaining aquatic ecosystem within an aquarium. Discuss the balance of plant life, aquatic animals, and microorganisms required for a self-maintaining environment.

2265. Exploring Traditional Textile Techniques: Delve into the world of traditional textile techniques from various cultures, such as weaving, dyeing, and embroidery. Share the history, process, and modern applications of these age-old crafts.

2266. The Art of Underwater Sculpture Gardens: Highlight the creation and significance of underwater sculpture gardens, discussing the intersection of art, environmental conservation, and the creation of artificial reefs to support marine life.

2267. A Journey Through the Coffee Bean Lifecycle: From farm to cup, explore the entire lifecycle of coffee, including cultivation, harvesting, processing, roasting, and brewing, highlighting sustainable practices and the global coffee culture.

2268. Reviving Historical Board Games: Rediscover and play historical board games, exploring their rules, cultural background, and significance. Attempt to modernize these games or create replicas for contemporary play.

2269. Eco-Friendly Transportation Solutions: Explore and test various eco-friendly transportation options, from electric vehicles and bicycles to public transit and carpooling, discussing their environmental impact and practicality for daily life.

2270. The Process of Making Handcrafted Candles: Dive into the craft of candle making, covering different waxes, scents, and molds. Share the therapeutic aspects of candle making and tips for beginners to create their own candles at home.

2271. The Art of Crafting Custom Board Games: Dive into the process of designing and creating custom board games, from brainstorming themes and mechanics to prototyping and playtesting, highlighting creativity in game design.

2272. Exploring the World of Vintage Cameras: Showcase a collection of vintage cameras, discussing their history, unique features, and the art of film photography in the digital age, including tips for beginners interested in analog photography.

2273. DIY Eco-Friendly Home Insulation: Demonstrate how to improve home insulation using sustainable, eco-friendly materials. Discuss the benefits of proper insulation for energy conservation and provide step-by-step guides for homeowners.

2274. A Culinary Journey Through Forgotten Fruits and Vegetables: Rediscover and cook with fruits and vegetables that have fallen out of common use. Explore their history, nutritional value, and how to incorporate them into modern recipes.

2275. The Renaissance of Mechanical Typewriters: Delve into the resurgence of interest in mechanical typewriters, exploring their appeal, the tactile experience of typing, and the community of enthusiasts preserving these machines.

2276. Creating a Wildlife Oasis in Suburban Backyards: Share tips and projects for transforming a suburban backyard into a haven for local wildlife, including birdhouses, native plant gardens, and water features to attract various species.

2277. The Craft of Artisanal Chocolate Making: Take viewers behind the scenes of artisanal chocolate making, from bean to bar. Highlight the process of selecting beans, roasting, grinding, and shaping chocolates, emphasizing the craft and creativity involved.

2278. Restoration of Vintage Toys: Document the process of restoring vintage toys to their former glory. Share restoration techniques, the historical significance of different toys, and the joy of bringing nostalgia back to life.

2279. Building a Community Solar Project: Chronicle the development of a community solar power project, from planning and funding to implementation. Discuss the benefits of solar energy and how communities can come together to achieve sustainable goals.

2280. A Week of Zero-Waste Cooking Challenges: Each day, create meals that produce zero waste, highlighting creative uses for leftovers, composting, and minimizing packaging. Share tips for planning, shopping, and cooking sustainably.

2281. The Tradition of Herbal Medicine: Explore the world of herbal medicine, covering the cultivation of medicinal plants, the preparation of remedies, and the historical and cultural significance of herbalism across different cultures.

2282. Adventures in Urban Exploration: Take viewers on urban exploration adventures to discover hidden, abandoned sites within cities. Discuss the history and stories behind these places while emphasizing safety and respect for property.

2283. Sustainable Aquaculture at Home: Introduce viewers to the basics of setting up a sustainable home aquaculture system, combining fish farming with hydroponics to create a symbiotic environment for growing food.

2284. The Process of Creating Handmade Journals: Share the detailed process of crafting handmade journals, from selecting paper and covers to binding techniques. Discuss the personal significance and uses of keeping a journal.

2285. Exploring Historic Railways and Trains: Embark on a journey to explore historic railways and trains, sharing their history, the evolution of rail travel, and the experience of riding on vintage trains in the modern era.

2286. A Guide to Ethical Foraging: Offer a comprehensive guide to ethical foraging, including how to identify edible plants, mushrooms, and herbs safely, the importance of sustainable harvesting practices, and legal considerations.

2287. The Art of Calligraphy and Hand Lettering: Create a series teaching the basics of calligraphy and hand lettering, including different styles, tools, and techniques, and how to incorporate beautiful lettering into everyday life.

2288. Reviving Traditional Sailing Skills: Share the experience of learning traditional sailing skills on classic boats, discussing navigation, rope work, and the art of sailing without modern electronic aids.

2289. A Month of Creative Upcycling Projects: Each day, tackle a different upcycling project, turning discarded items into useful or decorative pieces. Highlight the transformation process, environmental impact, and creativity involved.

2290. Exploring the Wonders of Bioluminescence: Delve into the natural phenomenon of bioluminescence, visiting locations where it can be observed, and explaining the science behind glowing organisms in nature.

2291. DIY Tiny Home on Wheels Series: Chronicle the entire process of designing, building, and living in a tiny home on wheels. Cover zoning laws, space-saving hacks, and the joys and challenges of tiny living.

2292. Historical Cooking Show: Each episode, recreate a meal from a different historical era or civilization, discussing the cultural context, ingredients used at the time, and how these dishes would have been prepared and served.

2293. The Physics of Everyday Objects: Create a series that explains the physics behind everyday phenomena and objects, making complex concepts accessible and engaging through experiments and visual demonstrations.

2294. Eco-Friendly Urban Transportation Solutions: Explore innovative urban transportation solutions that are eco-friendly, such as electric scooters, bikes, car-sharing programs, and public transit enhancements, discussing their impact on city life and the environment.

2295. Reviving Endangered Crafts: Document efforts to revive and preserve endangered crafts and techniques from around the world, interviewing artisans, showcasing the crafting process, and discussing the importance of preserving these traditions.

2296. Creating a Sustainable Wardrobe from Scratch: Share the journey of creating a sustainable wardrobe, focusing on ethical fashion choices, DIY projects, and how to repurpose existing clothing, emphasizing minimalism and responsible consumption.

2297. Art from Recycled Materials: Showcase artists who create stunning artworks from recycled and upcycled materials. Discuss the creative process, the message behind the art, and tips for viewers to start their own recycled art projects.

2298. The Science of Plant Communication: Delve into the fascinating world of plant communication and intelligence, exploring how plants communicate with each other and with other organisms, and what humans can learn from them.

2299. Adventure in Learning New Languages: Document the challenge of learning a new language, including the methods used, progress updates, and the cultural insights gained along the way, encouraging viewers to embark on their own language learning journey.

2300. Building an Off-Grid Cabin in the Wilderness: Follow the journey of building a cabin in the wilderness, entirely off-grid. Cover the planning, challenges, sustainable practices, and the peaceful retreat created away from modern life.

2301. A Guide to Mindful Technology Use: Offer practical advice for using technology mindfully, aiming to reduce digital overload and promote digital wellness. Include tips for detoxes, mindful app use, and balancing online and offline life.

2302. Historical Diaries Series: Narrate episodes based on historical diaries from different periods and cultures, bringing to life the personal experiences, historical events, and daily life of people from the past.

2303. Sustainable Living in Different Environments: Explore sustainable living practices in various environments, from urban apartments to rural homesteads. Discuss how sustainability challenges and solutions vary by location.

2304. The Art of Custom Bicycle Making: Dive into the world of custom bicycle making, from designing unique frames to choosing components and custom paint jobs. Highlight the craftsmanship and personalized approach to cycling.

2305. Reviving the Lost Art of Letter Writing: Encourage a revival of letter writing by showcasing the beauty and intimacy of handwritten correspondence. Share tips for crafting meaningful letters, choosing stationery, and starting pen pal exchanges.

2306. Global Street Art and Murals: Explore street art and murals from cities around the world. Discuss the artists, the stories behind the artworks, and how street art transforms public spaces and communicates social messages.

2307. Astronomy for Beginners: Start an astronomy series for beginners, covering how to start stargazing, understanding celestial events, and using telescopes and apps to explore the night sky.

2308. Exploring Underwater Caves: Take viewers on thrilling explorations of underwater caves, sharing the beauty, dangers, and scientific importance of these hidden ecosystems, along with the specialized gear and training required.

2309. Zero-Waste Beauty Routines: Demonstrate how to achieve a zero-waste beauty routine, reviewing sustainable beauty products, DIY skincare recipes, and tips for reducing plastic waste in beauty regimes.

2310. The Craft of Artisanal Coffee Making: Explore the craft behind artisanal coffee, from bean selection and roasting to various brewing methods, highlighting the subtleties that make for a perfect cup of coffee.

2311. The Art of Natural Light Photography: Create a series that teaches viewers how to harness natural light for photography. Cover different times of day, weather conditions, and environments to showcase how natural light can transform images.

2312. Exploring Traditional Pottery Techniques Around the World: Travel virtually or in reality to different cultures to explore their unique pottery techniques. Document the process of making pottery with local artisans, highlighting the cultural significance behind each style.

2313. A Journey Through Quantum Computing: Demystify the complex world of quantum computing for viewers. Explain its principles, potential applications, and how it differs from classical computing, including interviews with experts in the field.

2314. Crafting Eco-Friendly Jewelry: Share the process of creating jewelry from eco-friendly, sustainable materials. Include tutorials on sourcing materials, design inspiration, and techniques for making wearable art that's kind to the planet.

2315. The Science of Colorful Autumn Leaves: Produce a video explaining why leaves change color in autumn. Delve into the science behind it, including the role of chlorophyll, carotenoids, and anthocyanins, and how weather affects the color display.

2316. Building a Community Composting Initiative: Document the creation of a community composting program, from planning and setup to managing contributions and using the compost. Highlight the environmental impact and how communities can replicate the project.

2317. Rediscovering Ancient Board Games: Explore ancient board games from various cultures, their rules, and historical context. Craft replicas and demonstrate how to play, emphasizing the continuity of play and strategy across centuries.

2318. DIY Tiny Greenhouses: Show viewers how to build their own tiny greenhouses using upcycled materials. Discuss plant selection, climate considerations, and the joy of growing your own food or flowers in small spaces.

2319. Mental Health and the Great Outdoors: Create content that explores the benefits of spending time in nature on mental health. Include scientific research, personal anecdotes, and tips for integrating nature into daily life for wellness.

2320. The Evolution of Animation Techniques: Take viewers on a journey through the history of animation, from traditional hand-drawn techniques to CGI and virtual reality animations, highlighting key innovations and iconic works.

2321. Eco-Friendly Travel Vlogs: Share experiences of traveling in an environmentally friendly manner. Focus on sustainable accommodations, transportation methods, and activities that minimize the ecological footprint while exploring new places.

2322. Urban Gardening Success Stories: Feature successful urban gardening projects, from rooftop gardens to window farms. Share the stories of individuals or communities who have transformed their spaces into green oases.

2323. Creating Art with AI: Dive into the intersection of art and artificial intelligence. Show how AI can be used as a tool for creating unique artworks, discussing the creative process, ethical considerations, and the future of AI in art.

2324. The World of Ethical Hacking: Introduce viewers to ethical hacking, including its importance in cybersecurity, common techniques, and how it's used to protect against cyber threats, possibly with demos in a controlled environment.

2325. Homemade Natural Dyes for Textiles: Experiment with creating natural dyes from plants, fruits, and vegetables. Document the dyeing process, showcasing how different materials and mordants affect the color and longevity of the dye.

2326. The Cultural Significance of Masks: Explore the cultural, historical, and artistic significance of masks from around the world. Discuss their use in ceremonies, festivals, theater, and as art, including making a mask inspired by traditional techniques.

2327. Reviving Vintage Audio Equipment: Share the process of finding, restoring, and enjoying vintage audio equipment like turntables, tube amplifiers, and speakers. Highlight the warmth and richness of analog sound that enthusiasts cherish.

2328. Sustainable Fishing Practices: Educate on sustainable fishing practices, including catch and release, selecting sustainable seafood, and the impact of overfishing on marine ecosystems, aiming to promote responsible fishing habits.

2329. The Chemistry of Baking: Delve into the chemistry involved in baking, explaining the science behind leavening agents, gluten formation, and the Maillard reaction, making complex concepts accessible through baking demonstrations.

2330. Exploring the Night Sky in Different Cultures: Examine how various cultures have interpreted the night sky, their constellations, and astronomical myths. Discuss the importance of these celestial stories in their cultural heritage and knowledge of the universe.

2331. Restoring a Historical Garden: Document the restoration of a neglected historical garden to its former glory, focusing on historical research, plant selection based on original designs, and the community's involvement in bringing the garden back to life.

2332. The Art and Science of Sound Healing: Explore the practice of sound healing, including the history, different instruments used (like singing bowls, gongs, and tuning forks), and the scientific basis behind how sound frequencies can promote healing and well-being.

2333. DIY Off-the-Grid Living Solutions: Share innovative DIY projects for living off the grid, such as solar-powered systems, rainwater harvesting, and waste composting. Highlight the challenges, solutions, and daily life adjustments needed for off-the-grid living.

2334. A Journey Through Ancient Textiles: Delve into the history and techniques of ancient textiles from around the world, exploring traditional weaving, dyeing, and embroidery methods. Attempt to recreate ancient textiles using historically accurate techniques.

2335. Exploring the Philosophy of Minimalism: Create a series that explores the philosophy of minimalism in various aspects of life, including possessions, digital presence, and relationships. Discuss the benefits, challenges, and how to start adopting a minimalist lifestyle.

2336. Sustainable Urban Architecture: Showcase innovative examples of sustainable urban architecture, focusing on green buildings, eco-friendly materials, and designs that minimize environmental impact while enhancing urban living spaces.

2337. The Evolution of Board Games: Trace the evolution of board games from ancient times to the present, highlighting how games reflect cultural, social, and technological changes. Include interviews with game designers and historians.

2338. Crafting with Invasive Species: Tackle the problem of invasive species by turning them into craft materials or products. Explore the environmental impact of specific invasive species and how responsibly harvesting them for crafts can contribute to ecosystem management.

2339. Reviving Traditional Folk Songs: Discover and revive traditional folk songs from various cultures, exploring their origins, lyrical significance, and musical structures. Collaborate with musicians to bring these songs to a contemporary audience.

2340. The Science of Sustainable Agriculture: Dive into the science behind sustainable agriculture practices, including crop rotation, organic farming, and permaculture. Highlight innovative technologies and methods that are making farming more sustainable and efficient.

2341. Building a Solar-Powered Workshop: Document the process of creating a fully solar-powered workshop, covering the installation of solar panels, energy storage solutions, and the adaptations needed to run power tools and machinery on solar power.

2342. Mindfulness in Nature Series: Create a series that combines mindfulness practices with the beauty of nature. Guide viewers through mindfulness exercises in various natural settings, emphasizing the connection between mental health and the natural world.

2343. Zero-Waste Art Projects: Showcase art projects that adhere to zero-waste principles, using recycled or natural materials. Discuss the inspiration behind each project and the importance of sustainability in the art world.

2344. A Guide to Urban Beekeeping: Offer a comprehensive guide to starting an urban beekeeping project, including choosing a location, setting up hives, caring for bees, and harvesting honey, all within the context of urban environments.

2345. Exploring the World of Zines: Dive into the culture and creation of zines, showcasing the process of making a zine from concept to distribution. Highlight the role of zines in grassroots communication, art, and activism.

2346. The Lost Art of Shadow Play: Revive the ancient art of shadow play by crafting traditional shadow puppets and staging performances. Explore the cultural history of shadow play in various countries and its storytelling potential.

2347. Eco-Friendly Event Planning: Share tips and ideas for planning events, from small gatherings to large celebrations, that are eco-friendly. Cover aspects like sustainable decorations, waste reduction, and choosing green vendors and venues.

2348. Journey into the World of Microgreens: Guide viewers through the process of growing microgreens at home, discussing the nutritional benefits, different varieties, and how to incorporate microgreens into daily meals.

2349. The Craft of Handmade Instruments: Document the craftsmanship involved in making musical instruments by hand, from traditional stringed instruments to unique creations. Share the maker's journey, the musical quality of the instruments, and their cultural significance.

2350. A Year of Living Historically: Embark on a challenge to live each month following the lifestyle, customs, and technologies of a different historical period. Document the experience, insights gained, and the impact on modern-day perspectives.

2351. The Art of Sustainable Cooking: Share recipes and techniques for sustainable cooking, focusing on minimizing waste, using local and seasonal ingredients, and energy-efficient cooking methods. Highlight the importance of sustainable eating habits for the environment.

2352. Exploring the World of Bookbinding: Dive into the craft of bookbinding, showcasing various techniques from simple stitching to more complex binding methods. Include tutorials for beginners and discuss the importance of preserving the art of handmade books.

2353. Urban Wildlife Documentaries: Create mini-documentaries on wildlife in urban settings, highlighting how various species adapt to city life. Discuss biodiversity in cities and how urban planning can support wildlife habitats.

2354. DIY Recycled Art Supplies: Demonstrate how to make art supplies from recycled materials, such as homemade paper, natural inks, and eco-friendly glues. Discuss the environmental impact of traditional art supplies and the benefits of making your own.

2355. A Journey Through Virtual Museums: Take viewers on virtual tours of museums around the world, exploring their collections and the stories behind key exhibits. Discuss the role of museums in preserving culture and history in the digital age.

2356. The Science of Homebrewing: Explore the science behind homebrewing beer, wine, or cider, covering the fermentation process, flavor development, and tips for beginners. Include experiments to illustrate scientific concepts.

2357. Reviving Historical Hairstyles: Recreate and showcase historical hairstyles, exploring their cultural significance, the techniques used to achieve them, and their evolution over time. Offer tutorials for viewers interested in historical fashion.

2358. Eco-Friendly Home Decor Projects: Share ideas and tutorials for eco-friendly home decor, focusing on upcycling, using sustainable materials, and DIY projects that enhance the home without harming the environment.

2359. A Guide to Birdwatching in Urban Areas: Introduce viewers to the joys of birdwatching in urban environments. Share tips for spotting and identifying birds, creating bird-friendly spaces, and the importance of urban biodiversity.

2360. The Art of Ice Dyeing: Showcase the technique of ice dyeing fabrics, offering a step-by-step guide and exploring the unpredictable and unique patterns created by this method. Discuss how to use natural dyes for an eco-friendly approach.

2361. Zero-Waste Beauty Routine: Create content focusing on building a zero-waste beauty routine, from skincare to makeup. Share recipes for homemade beauty products, tips for reducing packaging waste, and sustainable beauty brands.

2362. The World of Autonomous Vehicles: Delve into the technology behind autonomous vehicles, exploring the current state of self-driving cars, the potential impact on society and the environment, and ethical considerations.

2363. Historical Fiction Writing Process: Document the process of writing a historical fiction novel, from researching historical periods and events to developing characters and plots that bring the past to life.

2364. Creating a Capsule Kitchen: Introduce the concept of a capsule kitchen, focusing on minimalism and sustainability in cooking. Discuss how to choose versatile ingredients and kitchen tools to simplify meals and reduce waste.

2365. The Evolution of Dance Music: Explore the history and evolution of dance music across different cultures and eras. Include discussions with musicians, dancers, and historians, and showcase how dance music has influenced society.

2366. DIY Sustainable Aquaponics System: Guide viewers through setting up a small-scale aquaponics system at home, combining fish farming with hydroponic gardening. Discuss the benefits for sustainability and self-sufficiency.

2367. Exploring the Benefits of Forest Bathing: Create content around the concept of forest bathing (Shinrin-yoku), including its origins, health benefits, and how viewers can practice mindful walks in nature to improve well-being.

2368. The Craft of Distilling Essential Oils: Share the process of distilling essential oils from plants and herbs. Cover the equipment needed, the distillation process, and the uses of homemade essential oils for health and wellness.

2369. Revitalizing Traditional Games and Sports: Highlight efforts to revitalize traditional games and sports that are at risk of being forgotten. Share the cultural significance, rules, and attempts to modernize them for wider participation.

2370. The Journey of Minimalist Living: Document the personal journey towards minimalist living, discussing the decision-making process, the challenges and benefits of decluttering, and how minimalism can lead to a more focused and fulfilling life.

2371. The Art of Upcycled Fashion Design: Showcase the process of transforming discarded textiles and clothing into fashionable, contemporary pieces. Highlight the importance of sustainability in fashion and provide DIY upcycling tips.

2372. Building a Community Herb Garden: Document the creation of a community herb garden, from planning and planting to maintenance and harvesting. Share the benefits of communal gardening and how to use herbs in cooking, teas, and natural remedies.

2373. A Deep Dive into the World of Board Game Design: Explore the process of designing a board game from concept to completion. Discuss game mechanics, theme development, playtesting, and the journey to publication.

2374. Exploring the Science of Happiness: Delve into psychological research on happiness, including studies on gratitude, social connections, and mindfulness. Offer practical advice for incorporating happiness-boosting habits into daily life.

2375. Sustainable Seafood Cooking Series: Create a cooking series focused on sustainable seafood, covering how to source ethically caught fish, seafood preparation techniques, and recipes that highlight the natural flavors of the ocean.

2376. The Challenge of Living Plastic-Free for a Month: Document the personal challenge of avoiding single-use plastics for an entire month. Share insights, struggles, alternatives found, and the overall impact on waste reduction.

2377. Restoration of a Vintage Typewriter: Take viewers through the meticulous process of restoring a vintage typewriter, discussing the history of typewriting, mechanical repair techniques, and the joy of tactile writing in a digital age.

2378. Journey Through Indigenous Mythology: Explore indigenous mythologies from around the world, sharing stories, their cultural significance, and how these ancient beliefs reflect and inform contemporary indigenous identities.

2379. DIY Backyard Wildlife Sanctuary: Show how to convert a backyard into a sanctuary for local wildlife, including bird feeders, water features, and native plantings. Discuss the benefits of encouraging biodiversity in residential areas.

2380. The Art of Analog Photography in a Digital World: Explore the resurgence of interest in analog photography. Share tips on using film cameras, developing film, and the unique aesthetic qualities that film brings to photography.

2381. Eco-Friendly Tiny House Solutions: Focus on innovative eco-friendly solutions for tiny house living, including composting toilets, solar power setups, and rainwater harvesting systems. Highlight the sustainability aspect of downsizing.

2382. A Beginner's Guide to Astrophotography: Offer a comprehensive guide for beginners interested in astrophotography. Cover equipment basics, shooting techniques, and how to capture celestial events and deep-sky objects.

2383. Reviving Local Folklore Through Animation: Use animation to bring local folklore and legends to life. Discuss the process of adapting these stories for animation, the research involved, and the importance of preserving folklore.

2384. Zero-Waste Kitchen Hacks: Share practical tips and hacks for achieving a zero-waste kitchen, including food storage solutions, minimizing food waste, and sustainable cooking practices.

2385. The Journey of a Handmade Book: Document the process of creating a handmade book, from paper making and binding to cover design. Highlight the craftsmanship and personal touch involved in book arts.

2386. Cycling Across [Your Country]: A Sustainability Journey: Document a long-distance cycling journey across your country, focusing on sustainable travel, encounters with diverse communities, and the environmental observations made along the way.

2387. The Lost Art of Making Natural Remedies: Explore traditional and lost art of making natural remedies from herbs, plants, and other natural ingredients. Discuss historical uses, preparation methods, and modern applications of these remedies.

2388. Urban Exploration: Historical Sites in Your City: Take viewers on an urban exploration adventure to discover and learn about historical sites and hidden gems in your city, discussing the history and significance of each location.

2389. A Seasonal Guide to Foraging: Create a seasonal guide for foraging wild edibles in your region. Include safety tips, ethical foraging practices, and how to prepare and use foraged items in recipes.

2390. Creating a Meditation Garden: Show viewers how to design and create a meditation garden, a tranquil space for reflection and mindfulness. Discuss plant selection, layout, and elements that contribute to a peaceful environment.

2391. The Art of Time-Lapse Photography: Guide viewers through the process of creating stunning time-lapse videos, from selecting the right equipment and settings to choosing compelling subjects and editing the final footage.

2392. Revitalizing Community Spaces with Guerrilla Gardening: Showcase the transformative power of guerrilla gardening by taking neglected public spaces and turning them into vibrant, plant-filled areas. Discuss the impact on the community and the environment.

2393. The Science of Coffee: Dive into the chemistry and biology behind the perfect cup of coffee. Explore different brewing methods, the effect of roasting on flavor, and how to taste coffee like a professional.

2394. Eco-Friendly Pet Ownership: Offer tips for raising pets in an environmentally sustainable way. Cover topics like eco-friendly pet products, homemade pet food, and reducing your pet's carbon pawprint.

2395. A Journey Through Art History: Create a series that takes viewers on a journey through art history, exploring different periods, styles, and artists. Include DIY projects inspired by each era to engage viewers creatively.

2396. Sustainable Fashion Through the Ages: Explore the evolution of sustainable fashion practices from past to present. Highlight historical methods of clothing production and how they can inspire more sustainable fashion choices today.

2397. Building a Solar-Powered Workshop: Document the process of creating a workshop powered entirely by solar energy. Discuss the setup, the benefits and challenges of solar power, and the range of projects that can be powered by renewable energy.

2398. The Psychology of Color in Design: Delve into how colors influence mood, behavior, and design choices. Explore the use of color in various contexts, such as interior design, branding, and art.

2399. Creating Wildlife Habitats in Urban Gardens: Show how to design urban gardens that attract and support local wildlife. Discuss plant selection, water features, and creating shelter to encourage biodiversity in city settings.

2400. A Global Tour of Street Food: Take viewers on a culinary journey exploring street food from around the world. Highlight the cultural significance of street food, the stories of the people who prepare it, and how to make some of these dishes at home.

2401. The Tradition of Oral Storytelling: Revive the tradition of oral storytelling by sharing stories from various cultures, accompanied by analysis and discussion about the art form's significance in preserving history and culture.

2402. Adapting to Climate Change in the Garden: Offer advice for gardeners on adapting their practices to deal with the effects of climate change. Include tips on selecting resilient plant species, conserving water, and improving soil health.

2403. The Basics of Sailboat Navigation: Teach the fundamentals of navigating a sailboat using traditional methods like reading charts, understanding tides, and using a compass, as well as modern GPS technology.

2404. A Week Without Single-Use Plastics: Challenge yourself to live a week without using single-use plastics, documenting the experience, the challenges faced, and sustainable alternatives discovered.

2405. Restoring a Piece of Local History: Document the restoration of a historic landmark or artifact in your community, covering the history, the restoration process, and the significance of preserving local heritage.

2406. The Art of Glass Etching: Introduce viewers to the techniques and tools required for glass etching. Showcase projects from simple designs to more complex artworks, and discuss the applications of glass etching in home decor and art.

2407. Cycling Cities of the World: Explore how different cities accommodate and encourage cycling. Highlight bike-friendly infrastructure, community cycling events, and tips for urban cycling safety and enjoyment.

2408. The Science of Mindful Eating: Discuss the principles of mindful eating, including the psychological and physiological benefits. Offer tips for practicing mindful eating and how it can enhance the relationship with food.

2409. DIY Vertical Wind Turbine for Urban Homes: Guide viewers through building a vertical wind turbine suitable for urban settings. Discuss the design, materials needed, and the potential energy savings.

2410. Rediscovering Ancient Footpaths and Trails: Take viewers on a journey along ancient footpaths and trails, exploring their historical significance, natural beauty, and what they can teach us about the landscape and history of an area.

2411. Zero-Waste Cooking Show: Create a series focusing on zero-waste cooking techniques, showcasing how to use every part of an ingredient, minimize food waste, and prepare delicious, sustainable meals.

2412. The Art of Origami and Mathematics: Explore the fascinating intersection between origami and mathematics. Demonstrate complex folding techniques that illustrate mathematical principles, and discuss origami's applications in engineering and design.

2413. Historical Landmark Restoration Vlog: Document the restoration process of a historical landmark, highlighting the challenges, the craftsmanship involved, and the importance of preserving history through architecture.

2414. A Guide to Ethical Travel: Produce a series offering tips for traveling ethically and sustainably. Cover how to respect local cultures, minimize environmental impact, and support local economies while exploring new destinations.

2415. DIY Natural Swimming Pools: Show viewers how to create a natural swimming pool in their backyard, discussing the ecological benefits, the filtration system that uses plants instead of chemicals, and maintenance tips.

2416. Exploring the World of Wearable Tech: Delve into the latest advancements in wearable technology, from fitness trackers to smart fabrics. Discuss the tech's potential impacts on health, privacy, and fashion.

2417. The Art of Soap Making: Share the process of making soap from scratch, including cold process and melt and pour methods. Highlight natural ingredients, the science of saponification, and customizing soaps with colors, scents, and shapes.

2418. Urban Farming Innovations: Explore innovative urban farming techniques and technologies, such as rooftop gardens, hydroponics, and vertical farming. Discuss the potential of urban farming to address food security and sustainability in cities.

2419. The Craft of Custom Leatherwork: Introduce viewers to the art of crafting custom leather goods, from wallets and belts to bags and shoes. Share techniques, tools, and tips for beginners interested in leather crafting.

2420. Revitalizing Abandoned Spaces Through Art: Highlight projects that transform abandoned urban spaces into vibrant art installations or community gardens. Discuss the impact on the community and the process of revitalizing neglected areas.

2421. Astronomy for Kids: Create content that introduces children to the basics of astronomy. Use engaging visuals and simple explanations to cover topics like the solar system, constellations, and simple stargazing tips.

2422. Sustainable Living in Cold Climates: Offer tips and strategies for maintaining a sustainable lifestyle in cold climates. Cover energy-efficient heating, winter gardening, and eco-friendly insulation options.

2423. The Philosophy of Minimalist Design: Delve into the principles of minimalist design in various fields, such as architecture, interior design, and digital products. Discuss the emphasis on functionality, simplicity, and the aesthetic of less is more.

2424. The Science of Natural Disasters: Produce a series explaining the science behind natural disasters, such as earthquakes, hurricanes, and volcanic eruptions. Discuss prevention, preparedness, and the impact on affected communities.

2425. Building a DIY Electric Bike: Guide viewers through converting a standard bicycle into an electric bike. Discuss the components needed, the assembly process, and the benefits of electric biking for commuting and recreation.

2426. A Beginner's Guide to Composting: Create a comprehensive guide to starting a compost pile at home. Cover the basics of what can and cannot be composted, troubleshooting common issues, and how to use compost in gardening.

2427. Exploring Traditional Textiles Around the World: Travel virtually to different countries to explore their traditional textiles, weaving techniques, and the cultural stories behind them. Include DIY projects inspired by each tradition.

2428. The Impact of Light Pollution: Investigate the effects of light pollution on the environment, wildlife, and human health. Discuss ways to reduce light pollution and the importance of dark sky initiatives.

2429. Journey Into the World of Rare Books: Explore the fascinating world of rare and antique books. Share insights into collecting, preserving, and the historical significance of some of the world's most sought-after volumes.

2430. Eco-Friendly DIY Home Projects: Showcase a series of DIY home improvement projects focused on sustainability. Include upcycling furniture, creating energy-saving solutions, and using environmentally friendly materials.

2431. The Art of Digital Detoxing: Create a challenge series that encourages viewers to reduce their digital footprint for a week, sharing tips on mindfulness, alternative activities, and the benefits experienced from disconnecting.

2432. Reviving the Tradition of Handwritten Letters: Showcase the beauty and personal touch of handwritten letters. Include tutorials on calligraphy, choosing stationery, and the joy of receiving physical mail in an increasingly digital world.

2433. Sustainable Urban Design Innovations: Explore cutting-edge sustainable urban design projects around the world, highlighting green buildings, eco-friendly transportation solutions, and public spaces that prioritize sustainability and community.

2434. A Culinary Exploration of Ancient Grains: Dive into the history and benefits of ancient grains like quinoa, amaranth, and farro. Share recipes that modernize these traditional ingredients for contemporary palates.

2435. The World of Miniature Gardening: Introduce viewers to the enchanting world of miniature gardening, including fairy gardens and terrariums. Offer DIY projects, maintenance tips, and ideas for incorporating miniature gardens into home decor.

2436. DIY Renewable Energy Experiments: Conduct and share experiments with small-scale renewable energy projects, such as building a simple wind turbine or solar panel, to teach viewers about the principles of renewable energy.

2437. The Journey of Restoring a Classic Boat: Document the detailed restoration of a classic or vintage boat, covering the history of the vessel, the restoration process, and the challenges and rewards of bringing it back to its former glory.

2438. Historical Costume Recreation: Take on the challenge of recreating historical costumes using authentic materials and techniques. Share research findings, sewing tutorials, and the final reveal in a historical setting.

2439. Exploring the Benefits of Cold Water Swimming: Investigate the physical and mental health benefits of cold water swimming. Include personal experiences, safety tips, and interviews with health experts and seasoned swimmers.

2440. The Science of Plant-Based Dyes: Explore the process of making dyes from plants, discussing the types of plants used, the chemistry of dyeing, and techniques for applying natural dyes to fabrics.

2441. A Guide to Building Cob Ovens: Provide a step-by-step guide to building a cob oven from natural materials. Discuss the benefits of cob ovens for baking and how they can be incorporated into sustainable living practices.

2442. The Art of Silent Film Making Today: Challenge viewers to create their own silent films, discussing the history of silent cinema, storytelling techniques without dialogue, and the creative process behind visual storytelling.

2443. Urban Foraging for Edible Plants: Teach viewers how to safely identify and forage for edible plants in urban environments. Discuss the rules of ethical foraging, safety considerations, and how to prepare foraged finds.

2444. Creating an Off-Grid Homestead from Scratch: Document the journey of creating an off-grid homestead, including choosing a location, planning and building structures, and establishing self-sufficient systems for water, power, and food.

2445. The World of Competitive Tabletop Gaming: Delve into the world of competitive tabletop gaming, covering strategies, game mechanics, and the community and culture around board games and role-playing games.

2446. Mindfulness Through Pottery: Share the therapeutic benefits of pottery, focusing on the mindfulness aspects of working with clay. Include beginner tutorials, tips for setting up a home studio, and ideas for pottery projects.

2447. Eco-Friendly DIY Pest Control Solutions: Offer natural and eco-friendly solutions for common household pests. Discuss the importance of humane and environmentally conscious methods and how to implement them effectively.

2448. The Lost Art of Map Reading and Navigation: Revive traditional map reading and navigation skills in an age of GPS and digital maps. Include practical exercises, the science of navigation, and the joy of exploring with a physical map.

2449 A Series on Treehouses Around the World: Showcase unique and innovative treehouses from around the globe, discussing their design, construction, and how they harmonize with their natural surroundings.

2450. Zero-Waste Home Office Setup: Share ideas and tips for creating a sustainable and eco-friendly home office. Discuss choosing sustainable office supplies, reducing energy consumption, and organizing a clutter-free and productive workspace.

2451. Urban Survival Skills Series: Share essential urban survival skills for modern city dwellers, covering topics from navigating public transportation systems efficiently to finding hidden green spaces for relaxation and mindfulness.

2452. The Craft of Homemade Musical Instruments: Dive into the world of creating musical instruments from everyday items or recycled materials. Showcase the building process, the science of sound, and performances using the homemade instruments.

2453. Exploring the World Through Geocaching: Create a series on geocaching, an outdoor recreational activity that uses GPS to hide and seek containers. Highlight the adventure, the places discovered, and the community aspect of geocaching.

2454. A Beginner's Guide to Astronomy: Introduce the basics of astronomy to beginners, covering how to start stargazing, understanding constellations, and using telescopes. Include tips for urban astronomers dealing with light pollution.

2455. Sustainable Living on a Boat: Document the lifestyle of living sustainably on a boat. Discuss the challenges and solutions for energy, waste, and water management while showcasing the beauty and freedom of life at sea.

2456. The Art of Traditional Tea Making: Explore the traditional methods of tea making across different cultures. Cover the history, rituals, and techniques for preparing the perfect cup of tea, including visits to tea plantations.

2457. Eco-Friendly Home Renovation Tips: Share tips and projects for renovating homes in an eco-friendly manner. Focus on sustainable materials, energy efficiency improvements, and minimizing the environmental impact of renovations.

2458. Journey Into the World of Rare Plants: Take viewers on a journey to discover rare and exotic plants. Discuss their unique characteristics, habitats, and the importance of conserving biodiversity.

2459. The Philosophy Behind Minimalist Lifestyle: Delve into the philosophy and practice of minimalism beyond just decluttering. Explore how adopting a minimalist lifestyle can lead to greater focus, freedom, and fulfillment.

2460. Historical Cooking Series: Medieval Cuisine: Recreate dishes from the medieval period, exploring the ingredients, cooking methods, and cultural context of medieval cuisine. Share insights into the dietary habits of different social classes.

2461. DIY Eco-Friendly Beauty Products: Demonstrate how to make your own beauty products using natural and eco-friendly ingredients. Share recipes for skincare, haircare, and makeup products, highlighting the benefits of homemade alternatives.

2462. The Art and Science of Color: Create a series exploring the fascinating world of color – its physics, psychology, and application in art and design. Include experiments, DIY projects, and discussions on color theory.

2463. Building a Tiny Eco-House from Scratch: Document the process of building a tiny house that's eco-friendly, from planning and material selection to construction and living in a reduced space while minimizing environmental impact.

2464. Cultural Traditions Series: Wedding Customs Around the World: Explore wedding customs and traditions from various cultures around the world. Discuss the symbolism, rituals, and celebrations that make each culture's approach to weddings unique.

2465. Restoring Vintage Bicycles: Share the process of finding, restoring, and customizing vintage bicycles. Highlight the history of different models, restoration tips, and the joy of bringing old bikes back to life.

2466. A Deep Dive Into Urban Farming Technologies: Explore the latest technologies in urban farming, such as hydroponics, aquaponics, and vertical farming. Discuss their potential to transform food production in urban environments.

2467. Adventures in Sourdough Baking: Chronicle the journey of mastering sourdough bread from starter to loaf. Share the science of sourdough fermentation, baking tips, and the satisfaction of baking artisan bread at home.

2468. Exploring Abandoned Railways: Take viewers on explorations along abandoned railway lines, uncovering their history, the nature reclaiming the tracks, and the communities they once connected.

2469. The World of Ethical Fashion: Investigate the ethical fashion movement, including sustainable sourcing, fair labor practices, and eco-friendly production methods. Highlight brands and designers making a positive impact.

2470. Creating a Wildlife-Friendly Garden: Show how to design and plant a garden that attracts and supports local wildlife. Discuss plant selection, creating habitats, and the importance of urban green spaces for biodiversity.

2471. The Science of Silence: Explore the concept of silence, its psychological effects, and the search for the quietest places on Earth. Discuss the importance of silence in an increasingly noisy world and how people can find and appreciate moments of quiet.

2472. DIY Solar Gadgets for Everyday Use: Demonstrate how to create simple solar-powered gadgets that can be used in daily life, such as chargers, garden lights, and small appliances. Highlight the benefits of using solar energy and tips for beginners.

2473. Journey Through Historical Diets: Embark on a culinary exploration of diets from different historical periods and cultures. Experiment with creating meals based on these diets, discussing their nutritional content, societal roles, and what they reveal about past lifestyles.

2474. The Art of Pinstriping Vehicles: Dive into the world of automotive pinstriping, showcasing the skills and creativity involved in this decorative art form. Share techniques, tools, and the history behind pinstriping's role in car culture.

2475. Exploring Ancient Navigation Techniques: Create a series that explores how ancient civilizations navigated the world without modern technology. Attempt to replicate methods used by Viking, Polynesian, and Arab navigators using the stars, winds, and currents.

2476. Urban Beekeeping Guide: Offer a comprehensive guide to keeping bees in urban environments. Cover the basics of bee biology, hive management, and the benefits of urban beekeeping for pollination and biodiversity.

2477. Eco-Friendly Party Planning: Share ideas and tips for hosting parties and events in an eco-friendly manner. Focus on sustainable decorations, waste reduction, and creative, environmentally friendly party favors.

2478. The Healing Power of Plant-Based Diets: Explore the health benefits and healing potential of plant-based diets. Include expert interviews, nutritional advice, and simple plant-based recipes for viewers to try.

2479. Restoring a Community Park: Document the transformation of a neglected community park into a vibrant public space. Highlight volunteer efforts, landscaping changes, and the positive impact on the community's well-being.

2480. A Guide to Astrophotography on a Budget: Show viewers how to capture stunning images of the night sky without expensive equipment. Share tips on using smartphones, basic DSLRs, and simple techniques to photograph stars, planets, and meteor showers.

2481. Sustainable Water Use in the Home Garden: Educate viewers on techniques for sustainable water use in gardening, such as rainwater harvesting, drip irrigation, and choosing drought-resistant plants.

2482. The World of Competitive Robotics: Take viewers inside the world of competitive robotics, from high school tournaments to professional leagues. Highlight the design and engineering challenges, teamwork, and the excitement of competition.

2483. Crafting Artisanal Spirits at Home: Introduce the craft of distilling artisanal spirits at home, covering the legal aspects, the distillation process, and how to infuse flavors to create unique liquors.

2484. Mindful Consumption in the Digital Age: Discuss strategies for mindful consumption of digital content, emphasizing the importance of quality over quantity, setting boundaries, and the impact of digital consumption on mental health.

2485. Reviving the Lost Art of Storytelling: Showcase the power and importance of oral storytelling. Feature stories from various cultures, tips for effective storytelling, and how storytelling can foster community and connection.

2486. Eco-Friendly Fashion Upcycling: Highlight creative ways to upcycle old or thrifted clothes into fashionable, eco-friendly outfits. Share sewing and customization techniques that viewers can use to give their wardrobes a sustainable makeover.

2487. Building a Community Library Box: Guide viewers through the process of building and setting up a community library box, a "take a book, leave a book" exchange. Discuss its impact on literacy and community bonding.

2488. A Year of Learning New Skills: Challenge yourself to learn a new skill each month for a year, documenting the learning process, the challenges faced, and how these skills have enriched your life or changed your perspective.

2489. The Art of Ferrofluid Sculptures: Delve into the science and art behind creating ferrofluid sculptures. Explain what ferrofluid is, how to safely handle and manipulate it, and showcase the mesmerizing movements and patterns it can create.

2490. Sustainable Living Through Community Co-Ops: Explore the benefits and workings of community co-operatives for food, housing, and services. Highlight how co-ops promote sustainability, economic fairness, and community resilience.

2491. The Psychology of Space: Explore how physical spaces influence our mood, productivity, and well-being. Delve into the design principles behind creating harmonious living and working environments and how to apply these ideas in your own space.

2492. Eco-Friendly Textile Innovations: Highlight innovations in sustainable textiles, such as fabrics made from recycled materials or organic fibers. Discuss the environmental impact of traditional textiles and the future of eco-friendly fashion.

2493. Urban Exploration: Hidden Histories in Your City: Take viewers on an urban exploration adventure to uncover hidden historical sites and stories in your city. Discuss the history behind abandoned buildings, underground tunnels, and forgotten landmarks.

2494. The Art of Bento Boxes: Dive into the Japanese tradition of bento boxes, showcasing how to prepare and pack aesthetically pleasing and balanced meals. Discuss the cultural significance and the artistry behind creating bento.

2495. Renewable Energy DIY Projects for Teens: Engage younger viewers with simple renewable energy projects they can do at home or school, such as building a mini solar-powered car or a simple wind turbine. Discuss the science behind each project.

2496. Backyard Bioblitz Challenge: Encourage viewers to conduct a bioblitz in their own backyards, identifying and cataloging as many species as possible. Discuss biodiversity, the importance of local ecosystems, and how to participate in citizen science.

2497. The Lost Art of Darning and Mending Clothes: Teach viewers the traditional skills of darning and mending clothes. Highlight the sustainability aspect of extending the life of garments and the satisfaction of repairing beloved items.

2498. Exploring the World of Microgreens: Guide viewers through the process of growing microgreens at home. Cover the health benefits, various methods of cultivation, and creative ways to include microgreens in daily meals.

2499. A Travel Series on UNESCO Intangible Cultural Heritage: Create a series exploring UNESCO's Intangible Cultural Heritage list, showcasing traditional arts, crafts, festivals, and culinary traditions from around the world.

2500. The Science of Composting: Provide an in-depth look at the science behind composting, including the different types of composting methods, the role of microorganisms, and tips for successful composting at home.

2501. Homemade Natural Cleaning Products: Show viewers how to make effective, eco-friendly cleaning products at home using simple, natural ingredients. Discuss the benefits of ditching chemical cleaners for health and the environment.

2502. Creating a Zero-Waste Kitchen: Offer practical advice for achieving a zero-waste kitchen, from bulk shopping to composting and everything in between. Share personal experiences and the impact on waste reduction.

2503. Historical Battle Reenactments: Delve into the world of historical battle reenactments, exploring the dedication to historical accuracy, the camaraderie among participants, and the educational value of bringing history to life.

2504. DIY Solar Water Features for Gardens: Teach viewers how to create solar-powered water features for their gardens. Discuss the benefits of adding water elements to outdoor spaces and the basics of solar power systems.

2505. The Art of Slow Travel: Share insights and experiences from practicing slow travel, emphasizing deeper cultural immersion, environmental sustainability, and the benefits of taking time to truly explore a destination.

2506. Mindfulness and Creativity Workshops: Host virtual workshops that combine mindfulness practices with creative activities, such as painting, writing, or music, discussing how mindfulness can enhance creativity and vice versa.

2507. A Series on Living with Less: Document the journey of minimizing possessions to live a more focused, intentional life. Discuss the challenges and rewards of decluttering, downsizing, and choosing experiences over things.

2508. The Renaissance of Analog Audio: Explore the resurgence of interest in analog audio, from vinyl records to reel-to-reel tapes. Discuss the appeal of analog sound, the community of collectors, and how to start your own analog audio setup.

2509. Eco-Friendly Pet Care: Share tips for raising pets sustainably, covering eco-friendly pet products, homemade pet food recipes, and reducing your pet's environmental pawprint.

2510. Urban Sketching Adventures: Take viewers on urban sketching adventures, exploring different locations and sharing tips for capturing the essence of urban landscapes and architecture through sketching.

2511. The Art of Natural Perfumery: Guide viewers through the process of creating their own natural perfumes using essential oils and botanical extracts. Discuss the basics of scent composition and how to blend notes for personalized fragrances.

2512. Exploring Urban Green Roofs: Highlight the benefits and beauty of green roofs in urban environments. Showcase various green roof projects, discuss their impact on biodiversity, insulation, and reducing urban heat islands, and offer tips for starting a green roof project.

2513. Reviving Classic Board Games: Dive into the history and revival of classic board games. Share how to play these games with a modern twist, their strategic depth, and the cultural significance behind some of the world's oldest games.

2514. Sustainable Travel Destinations: Feature eco-friendly travel destinations that prioritize sustainability and conservation. Share insights on how these places manage tourism responsibly and how travelers can support sustainable tourism practices.

2515. The Craft of Handmade Paper: Delve into the process of making paper by hand, from pulping to pressing and drying. Explore the artistic possibilities of handmade paper, such as embedding flowers or incorporating different textures.

2516. A Year in an Eco-Village: Document life in an eco-village over the course of a year, highlighting the community's practices in sustainable living, organic farming, renewable energy use, and their approach to building a sustainable society.

2517. The Science of Psychedelic Plants: Explore the science, history, and cultural significance of psychedelic plants. Discuss their use in traditional medicine, recent research into their therapeutic potential, and the ethical considerations of their use.

2518. DIY Tiny Off-Grid Systems: Show viewers how to create off-grid systems for tiny living spaces, such as solar power setups, rainwater collection systems, and composting toilets. Emphasize the simplicity and sustainability of off-grid living.

2519. A Guide to Eco-Friendly Crafting: Share ideas for eco-friendly crafting projects that use recycled or sustainable materials. Offer tutorials on creating art, home decor, or fashion items that minimize environmental impact.

2520. Exploring the Art of Shadow Play: Showcase the traditional art form of shadow play, including how to create shadow puppets and perform stories. Discuss its historical roots and how it can be used as an educational tool today.

2521. The Philosophy of Permaculture: Dive into the principles of permaculture design and its philosophy of working with, rather than against, nature. Share examples of permaculture in practice in gardens, farms, and urban spaces.

2522. Zero-Waste Meal Prep Series: Create a series dedicated to meal prepping with zero waste. Share recipes, storage tips, and how to use every part of the food to minimize waste while preparing healthy and delicious meals.

2523. Reviving Forgotten Music Instruments: Highlight musical instruments that have fallen out of mainstream use. Share their history, how they're played, and their unique sounds, perhaps even collaborating with musicians to bring these sounds to a modern audience.

2524. The Art of Book Sculptures: Introduce viewers to the world of book sculptures, where old books are transformed into stunning pieces of art. Share techniques, inspiration, and the thought process behind selecting books and themes.

2525. Wildlife Gardening for Beginners: Guide viewers on how to create a garden that attracts and supports local wildlife. Discuss plant selection, water features, and creating shelters to encourage biodiversity in even the smallest of spaces.

2526. The History and Culture of Tea: Take viewers on a journey through the history and culture of tea around the world. Explore different types of tea, brewing methods, and the cultural practices associated with tea drinking.

2527. Upcycling Electronics into Art: Showcase creative projects that repurpose old electronics into art or functional items. Share the process, tools needed, and the importance of recycling electronics responsibly.

2528. A Deep Dive into Coral Reef Ecosystems: Educate viewers on the complexity and beauty of coral reef ecosystems. Discuss the importance of reefs, threats to their survival, and conservation efforts to protect these underwater worlds.

2529. The Renaissance of Handwritten Zines: Highlight the resurgence of zines as a form of personal and political expression. Discuss how to create a zine, from content creation to distribution, and the role of zines in community building.

2530. Building a Community Art Project: Document the process of creating a community art project, from brainstorming ideas with community members to the execution and unveiling of the project. Highlight the power of art to bring communities together.

2531. The Art of Upcycling Furniture: Show viewers how to breathe new life into old furniture through upcycling techniques. Discuss selecting pieces, preparation work, and creative ways to refurbish and repurpose furniture for a modern look.

2532. Beginner's Guide to Astronomy: Create a series that introduces beginners to astronomy. Cover topics like identifying constellations, using telescopes, understanding celestial events, and tips for backyard stargazing.

2533. Creating a Wildlife Pond in Your Garden: Document the process of creating a pond that attracts wildlife, from planning and digging to planting and maintenance. Highlight the benefits for biodiversity and enjoyment.

2534. Eco-Friendly Travel Hacks: Share tips and tricks for eco-friendly traveling, covering everything from packing light and choosing sustainable accommodations to minimizing your carbon footprint while exploring new destinations.

2535. The Science of Sustainable Farming: Explore innovative techniques and practices in sustainable farming. Discuss topics such as crop rotation, organic farming, integrated pest management, and the use of technology in reducing environmental impact.

2536. DIY Natural Cosmetics: Teach viewers how to make their own natural cosmetics, such as lip balm, face masks, and moisturizers. Share recipes that use organic and non-toxic ingredients for healthy, eco-friendly beauty products.

2537. Historical Documentaries on Lost Civilizations: Produce a series of documentaries exploring lost civilizations around the world. Cover their histories, cultures, achievements, and the mysteries surrounding their decline.

2538. The Art of Making Traditional Instruments: Showcase the craftsmanship involved in making traditional musical instruments from various cultures. Discuss the materials used, the construction process, and the instrument's cultural significance.

2539. Urban Homesteading Essentials: Offer guidance on how to start an urban homestead, covering topics like container gardening, raising chickens in the city, and creating a mini aquaponics system for sustainable living in small spaces.

2540. The Journey of Artisan Coffee: From bean to cup, explore the process of making artisan coffee. Visit local roasteries, discuss the roasting process, brewing methods, and how to taste and appreciate the subtle flavors of specialty coffee.

2541. Restoring Vintage Cameras: Document the process of restoring vintage cameras, from cleaning and repairing to testing them out with film. Share the history of different camera models and tips for photography enthusiasts interested in vintage gear.

2542. Mindful Eating Practices: Create content around the concept of mindful eating, discussing its benefits for physical and mental health. Offer practical tips for implementing mindful eating habits and simple exercises to enhance the dining experience.

2543. The Craft of Bookbinding: Dive into the world of bookbinding, showing different techniques and styles. Teach viewers how to bind their own books, journals, or sketchbooks, discussing the tools and materials needed.

2544. Sustainable Living in Cold Climates: Focus on challenges and solutions for sustainable living in colder regions. Discuss energy-efficient heating, winter-proofing homes, and growing food in cold climates using greenhouses and indoor gardens.

2545. Exploring the Benefits of Forest Bathing: Highlight the Japanese practice of Shinrin-yoku, or forest bathing. Discuss its mental and physical health benefits, and offer tips for practicing forest bathing in different types of natural settings.

2546. The History and Culture of Street Art: Explore the evolution of street art, from graffiti to large-scale murals. Discuss the cultural significance, legal aspects, and how street art has been used as a tool for social commentary and urban beautification.

2547. Guide to Ethical Animal Encounters: Share advice on how to have ethical wildlife encounters, emphasizing the importance of respecting animals' natural habitats and behaviors. Cover safaris, marine life tours, and ethical sanctuaries.

2548. DIY Eco-Friendly Home Decor: Teach viewers how to create home decor items using sustainable, recycled, or upcycled materials. Share projects that add a personal touch to the home while being mindful of the environment.

2549. A Series on Forgotten Sports: Bring attention to traditional and forgotten sports from around the world. Explore their histories, rules, and the cultural significance behind each sport, including attempts to revive interest in them.

2550. Building a Community Food Forest: Document the process of creating a food forest in a community setting. Discuss planning, plant selection, the benefits of permaculture, and how community members can work together to maintain and enjoy the space.

2551. The Art of Zero-Waste Gift Giving: Showcase creative and thoughtful gift ideas that minimize waste, including homemade gifts, experiences over material items, and eco-friendly wrapping techniques.

2552. Exploring the History and Science of Clocks: Delve into the fascinating world of clocks, covering their evolution from sundials to atomic clocks. Discuss the science of timekeeping and its impact on society throughout history.

2553. Sustainable Cooking with Seasonal Produce: Create a cooking series focused on using seasonal and locally sourced produce. Highlight the environmental benefits and offer recipes that showcase the flavors of each season.

2554. The Craft of Stained Glass Making: Introduce viewers to the art of stained glass making, from design and cutting glass to soldering and assembling. Share the history of stained glass and its use in modern decor and art.

2555. Exploring Underground Cities and Tunnels: Take viewers on a journey through the world's underground cities and tunnel systems. Discuss their historical significance, engineering marvels, and the mysteries they hold.

2556. A Beginner's Guide to Sustainable Fishing: Educate viewers on sustainable fishing practices, including catch and release, selecting sustainable seafood, and the impact of fishing on marine ecosystems.

2557. DIY Vertical Gardening for Small Spaces: Show how to create vertical gardens in small urban spaces, such as balconies or patios. Discuss the benefits of vertical gardening, plant selection, and care tips.

2558. The Science Behind Natural Disasters: Produce a series explaining the science behind natural disasters, such as earthquakes, hurricanes, and volcanic eruptions. Discuss ways communities can prepare for and mitigate the impacts of these events.

2559. Rediscovering Ancient Board Games: Explore ancient board games from various cultures, their rules, and historical significance. Attempt to recreate these games and play them, offering viewers a glimpse into the pastimes of ancient civilizations.

2560. Eco-Friendly Pet Care Solutions: Share tips for raising pets in an environmentally friendly manner, including homemade pet food recipes, sustainable pet toys, and eco-friendly waste management practices.

2561. The Art and Benefits of Journaling: Create content around the benefits of journaling for mental health, creativity, and self-improvement. Offer tips on starting a journaling habit, different journaling techniques, and ideas for journal prompts.

2562. Homemade Natural Insect Repellents: Demonstrate how to make effective, natural insect repellents using essential oils and other safe, non-toxic ingredients. Discuss the benefits of natural over commercial repellents.

2563. The Tradition of Tea Ceremonies Around the World: Explore the cultural significance and rituals of tea ceremonies in different countries. Share the history, types of tea used, and the mindfulness aspect of tea preparation and consumption.

2564. Building a Cob House: Document the process of building a house using cob, a natural building material made from earth, water, and straw. Highlight the sustainability aspects, challenges, and the warmth and beauty of cob construction.

2565. A Series on Iconic Trees Around the World: Explore the stories and significance of iconic and historic trees around the world. Discuss their importance in various cultures, historical events they've witnessed, and conservation efforts.

2566. The Art of Making Handcrafted Soap: Guide viewers through the process of making handcrafted soap, covering different methods, natural ingredients, and customization options for creating unique soaps.

2567. Restoring a Historic Garden: Share the journey of restoring a historic or neglected garden to its former beauty. Discuss the research involved, plant selection based on historical accuracy, and the challenges faced during the restoration process.

2568. Urban Cycling Tips and Routes: Offer tips for safe and enjoyable urban cycling, including navigating city traffic, bike maintenance, and showcasing scenic and bike-friendly routes in various cities.

2569. The World of Miniature Books: Delve into the charming world of miniature books, discussing their history, how they are made, and their appeal to collectors. Show viewers how to create their own miniature books.

2570. Sustainable Living Through Tech Innovations: Highlight technological innovations that promote sustainable living, such as smart home devices for energy efficiency, apps for reducing food waste, and platforms for sharing resources within communities.

2571. The Magic of Bioluminescence: Explore the natural phenomenon of bioluminescence, from glowing marine life to fireflies. Share the science behind it, where to witness it in the natural world, and its applications in biotechnology.

2572. Building an Eco-Friendly Tiny House Community: Document the journey of creating a tiny house community focused on sustainability. Discuss the planning, collaboration, and challenges of living in and maintaining an eco-conscious community.

2573. A Deep Dive into Urban Legends: Explore and debunk popular urban legends from around the world. Delve into their origins, cultural significance, and the truth (or lack thereof) behind these compelling tales.

2574. Creating Art from Recycled Plastic: Highlight artists who use recycled plastic to create stunning pieces of art. Discuss the process of collecting, preparing, and transforming plastic waste into art, and the message behind their work.

2575. The History of Cartography: Take viewers on a journey through the history of map-making. Explore the evolution of maps, significant cartographic breakthroughs, and how maps have shaped our understanding of the world.

2576. Back to Basics: Living Without Modern Conveniences: Challenge yourself to live without certain modern conveniences for a period. Document the experience, the adjustments made, and reflections on the role of technology in daily life.

2577. Exploring the World of Edible Flowers: Introduce viewers to the beauty and taste of edible flowers. Share information on identification, harvesting, culinary uses, and recipes to incorporate flowers into dishes.

2578. The Art of Traditional Archery: Delve into the world of traditional archery. Cover its history, the craftsmanship of bows and arrows, techniques, and the mental and physical benefits of practicing archery.

2579. Sustainable Fashion: From Concept to Closet: Follow the journey of creating sustainable fashion, from the design concept and choosing eco-friendly materials to the production process and final product. Highlight the importance of ethical fashion choices.

2580. The Craft of Handmade Musical Instruments: Showcase the process of crafting musical instruments by hand, from traditional string instruments to unique, innovative creations. Discuss the artistry, skill, and acoustic science involved.

2581. Exploring Ancient Methods of Timekeeping: Investigate ancient and traditional methods of timekeeping, from sundials to water clocks. Explore their design, mechanics, and how they influenced the development of modern timekeeping devices.

2582. Zero-Waste Home Office Setup: Offer tips for creating a sustainable and zero-waste home office. Discuss choosing eco-friendly office supplies, minimizing digital clutter, and incorporating plants for a greener workspace.

2583. The Journey of a Seed Saving Gardener: Document the process of saving seeds from your garden, covering why seed saving is important for biodiversity, how to harvest and store seeds, and tips for successful germination in the next season.

2584. A Culinary Tour of Vegan Cuisines: Take viewers on a global culinary journey exploring vegan cuisines. Highlight the diversity of plant-based dishes across cultures, sharing recipes, cooking techniques, and the stories behind the dishes.

2585. DIY Off-Grid Solar Projects: Demonstrate how to complete various off-grid solar projects, from setting up solar panels and batteries to powering appliances. Discuss the basics of solar energy and tips for living off-grid efficiently.

2586. The Tradition of Handcrafted Pottery: Share the process and passion behind handcrafted pottery. Cover different techniques like wheel throwing and hand-building, glazing and firing processes, and the therapeutic benefits of working with clay.

2587. Revitalizing Public Spaces Through Art: Highlight projects that transform public spaces with art, from murals to sculptures and installations. Discuss the impact on communities and how viewers can get involved in public art initiatives.

2588. The History and Evolution of Writing Tools: Explore the history of writing tools, from ancient reed pens to modern digital devices. Discuss how each innovation has impacted the way we communicate and express ourselves.

2589. Challenges of Zero-Waste Living: Share the challenges and solutions encountered while attempting to live a zero-waste lifestyle. Provide practical advice, product recommendations, and motivational tips for viewers interested in reducing their waste.

2590. A Guide to Backyard Astronomy: Equip viewers with knowledge and tips for backyard astronomy, including choosing the right equipment, navigating the night sky, and capturing celestial phenomena with a camera.

2591. Reviving Traditional Textile Techniques: Explore and document traditional textile techniques from various cultures, such as batik, weaving, or block printing. Discuss their historical significance and modern applications in sustainable fashion.

2592. The Physics of Sports: Create a series that breaks down the physics behind popular sports and athletic movements. Explain concepts like momentum, force, and aerodynamics in an accessible way, using slow-motion footage and simple experiments.

2593. Building a Community Art Installation: Showcase the process of conceptualizing and constructing a large-scale art installation with community involvement. Highlight the collaborative effort, the challenges faced, and the impact on the local community.

2594. Sustainable Travel on a Budget: Share tips and experiences on how to travel sustainably while adhering to a budget. Cover eco-friendly accommodation, transportation, and activities that minimize environmental impact and support local economies.

2595. Homemade Eco-Friendly Cleaning Products: Demonstrate how to make effective cleaning products at home using natural, non-toxic ingredients. Discuss the benefits for health and the environment compared to commercial cleaning products.

2596. The Art of Precision Cooking: Dive into the world of precision cooking techniques, such as sous-vide, explaining the science behind cooking at precise temperatures and how it enhances flavor and texture in culinary creations.

2597. Restoring Ecosystems with Guerrilla Gardening: Document efforts to restore local ecosystems through guerrilla gardening, focusing on planting native species, creating pollinator-friendly spaces, and the role of guerrilla gardening in urban ecology.

2598. The Renaissance of Vinyl Records: Explore the resurgence of vinyl records, discussing their sound quality, the experience of collecting, and the community around vinyl. Include visits to record stores and interviews with collectors and audiophiles.

2599. A Year of Learning New Art Forms: Challenge yourself to learn and document a new art form each month, such as painting, sculpture, digital art, or photography. Share the learning process, the challenges encountered, and how each art form allows for different expressions of creativity.

2600. Urban Agriculture Innovations: Highlight innovative urban agriculture projects, like rooftop farms, indoor vertical farming, and community gardens. Discuss their impact on food security, urban greening, and community engagement.

2601. Exploring the World of Mushrooms: Delve into the fascinating world of mushrooms, covering identification, the ecological role of fungi, and their uses in cooking, medicine, and sustainable technologies.

2602. The Journey of Restoring a Historic Ship: Document the process of restoring a historic ship or boat, including the historical research, traditional craftsmanship involved, and the challenges of preserving maritime heritage.

2603. DIY Wind Power for Home Use: Guide viewers through setting up a small-scale wind power system for home use. Discuss the basics of how wind turbines work, site selection, and integrating wind power with home energy systems.

2604. Cultural Heritage Through Food: Explore cultural heritage by cooking traditional dishes from different countries and regions. Discuss the origins, cultural significance, and stories behind each dish, possibly featuring guest cooks from those cultures.

2605. The Art of Making Natural Incense: Show how to make natural incense from herbs, resins, and essential oils. Discuss the history of incense use across cultures and its applications in meditation, relaxation, and aromatherapy.

2606. Exploring Abandoned Places Safely and Respectfully: Share explorations of abandoned places, emphasizing how to do so safely, legally, and respectfully. Discuss the history and stories behind the locations and the allure of urban exploration.

2607. The Craft of Artisanal Baking: Dive into the world of artisanal baking, from sourdough bread to traditional pastries. Highlight the techniques, the science of baking, and the satisfaction of creating baked goods from scratch.

2608. Sustainable Aquascaping: Introduce viewers to the art and science of aquascaping within sustainable ecosystems. Discuss selecting plants and fish, maintaining water quality, and creating visually stunning underwater landscapes.

2609. The Impact of Climate Change on Local Ecosystems: Investigate and document the impact of climate change on local ecosystems. Include expert interviews, data analysis, and personal observations to highlight changes and potential solutions.

2610. Rediscovering Outdoor Games and Sports: Promote physical activity and outdoor play by rediscovering traditional outdoor games and sports. Share the rules, cultural backgrounds, and the health and social benefits of engaging in these activities.

2611. Crafting with Recycled Metal: Showcase the process of creating art or functional items from recycled metal. Highlight the tools needed, safety precautions, and the creative potential in materials often considered waste.

2612. The Secrets of Ancient Construction: Explore how ancient civilizations constructed their monumental buildings, temples, and structures without modern technology. Delve into the ingenuity behind these architectural marvels and attempt to replicate their techniques on a small scale.

2613. Zero-Waste Cooking Challenges: Challenge yourself or others to prepare meals with zero waste, showcasing how to utilize every part of the ingredients purchased and offering tips on composting and recycling kitchen waste.

2614. The Art and Science of Color Theory: Create a series delving into color theory, its principles, and its application in art, design, and everyday life. Include experiments and projects that help visualize how colors interact and affect mood and perception.

2615. Eco-Friendly Material Innovations in Fashion: Highlight the latest innovations in eco-friendly materials being used in the fashion industry, such as biodegradable fabrics and recycled textiles. Discuss the impact of these materials on reducing the industry's environmental footprint.

2616. The World Through Drone Photography: Share the beauty of landscapes, cityscapes, and natural wonders captured through drone photography. Offer tips on drone operation, photography techniques, and adhering to legal and ethical guidelines.

2617. Traditional Healing Practices from Around the World: Explore traditional healing practices and their cultural significance in various communities around the globe. Discuss the philosophy behind these practices and the modern interest in holistic healing methods.

2618. The Challenge of Building With Natural Materials: Document the process and challenges of building structures using only natural materials like wood, stone, and clay. Highlight the sustainability aspects and the connection to traditional building methods.

2619. Rediscovering Classical Music: Introduce audiences to the beauty and complexity of classical music. Discuss its history, key composers, and pieces, and demystify the genre for new listeners with engaging explanations and performances.

2620. Sustainable Living Through Minimalism: Share the journey towards a minimalist lifestyle, focusing on reducing clutter, simplifying life, and making more environmentally conscious choices. Discuss the impact on well-being and the planet.

2621. The Art of Paper Mâché: Dive into the world of paper mâché, showcasing how to create sculptures, masks, and decorative items using this versatile and eco-friendly medium. Share techniques, tips, and the endless creative possibilities.

2622. Exploring Urban Myths and Legends: Investigate urban myths and legends from various cities around the world. Delve into their origins, the truths (if any) behind them, and why they captivate the imagination of so many.

2623. A Beginner's Guide to Bird Watching: Offer a comprehensive guide for beginners interested in bird watching. Cover how to start, what equipment is needed, tips for identifying different species, and the joys of connecting with nature through birding.

2624. DIY Home Automation Projects: Showcase simple DIY projects for automating aspects of your home using readily available technology. Discuss the benefits of home automation, energy savings, and enhancing home security.

2625. The Renaissance of Analog Gadgets: Highlight the resurgence of interest in analog gadgets such as film cameras, vinyl record players, and typewriters. Discuss the appeal of analog in a digital world and the communities that cherish these gadgets.

2626. Creating a Sustainable Wardrobe on a Budget: Share tips and strategies for building a sustainable and ethical wardrobe without breaking the bank. Discuss thrifting, swapping, and upcycling as ways to be fashionably sustainable.

2627. The Joy of Making Handmade Greeting Cards: Showcase the process of creating handmade greeting cards, including various techniques like stamping, embossing, and watercolor. Discuss the personal touch and joy that handmade cards bring to both the creator and recipient.

2628. Eco-Friendly Solutions for Everyday Problems: Present eco-friendly and sustainable solutions to common household problems, from natural pest repellents to energy-saving tips and zero-waste alternatives for daily use items.

2629. Adventures in Foraging: Take viewers on foraging adventures, teaching them how to safely identify and harvest wild edible plants, mushrooms, and herbs. Discuss the nutritional benefits and culinary uses of foraged foods.

2630. The Cultural Significance of Masks Across the World: Explore the use and significance of masks in various cultures, from traditional ceremonies and festivals to their roles in theater and contemporary art.

2631. The Philosophy of Space Exploration: Delve into the philosophical implications and motivations behind human space exploration. Discuss topics such as the search for extraterrestrial life, the expansion of human civilization, and the ethical considerations of colonizing other planets.

2632. Crafting with Bio-degradable Materials: Showcase projects that use bio-degradable materials, emphasizing how to craft sustainably. Include tutorials on items ranging from home decor to personal accessories, highlighting the environmental benefits.

2633. The Evolution of Language: Explore the fascinating journey of how languages evolve over time. Discuss the influence of migration, conquest, and technology on language development and how dying languages can be preserved.

2634. Sustainable Urban Mobility: Highlight innovative solutions for sustainable transportation in urban areas. Discuss the benefits and challenges of implementing bike-sharing systems, electric public transport, and pedestrian-friendly city planning.

2635. Healing Gardens: The Therapeutic Power of Nature: Share the concept of healing gardens and their benefits for mental and physical health. Offer advice on creating a healing garden, including plant selection and design principles that promote tranquility and healing.

2636. DIY Upcycled Home Insulation Projects: Demonstrate how to improve home insulation using upcycled materials. Share practical tips for reducing energy consumption and creating a more sustainable living environment.

2637. Exploring Traditional Folk Music: Take viewers on a journey through the world of traditional folk music. Explore its roots, instruments, and the stories conveyed through songs, including performances and interviews with musicians.

2638. The Science of Photovoltaic Cells: Explain how photovoltaic cells convert sunlight into electricity. Discuss the technology behind solar panels, recent advancements, and the role of solar energy in combating climate change.

2639. The Renaissance of Public Libraries: Showcase the evolving role of public libraries in communities around the world. Highlight innovative services and programs that go beyond books, such as makerspaces, digital archives, and community outreach initiatives.

2640. Mindful Consumption in the Fashion Industry: Address the impact of fast fashion on the environment and society. Offer viewers sustainable fashion choices, including how to shop ethically, the importance of quality over quantity, and embracing second-hand and vintage clothing.

2641. The Art of Dry Stone Walling: Explore the ancient craft of building stone walls without mortar. Discuss the history, techniques, and the aesthetic and environmental benefits of dry stone walling in landscaping and architecture.

2642. Creating a Pollinator-Friendly City: Share strategies for urban areas to support pollinators. Discuss the importance of bees and other pollinators, how to create pollinator-friendly spaces, and the role of city planning in biodiversity conservation.

2643. A Beginner's Guide to Astronomy Software: Introduce viewers to software tools that enhance the stargazing experience, including planetarium software, apps for identifying celestial objects, and resources for amateur astronomers.

2644. Sustainable Event Planning: Offer tips for organizing events, from small gatherings to large festivals, in an environmentally friendly manner. Cover sustainable practices such as waste reduction, eco-friendly catering, and digital invitations.

2645. The Impact of Microplastics on Marine Life: Delve into the issue of microplastics in our oceans. Discuss their sources, how they affect marine ecosystems and what individuals and communities can do to reduce their impact.

2646. Reviving Indigenous Games: Highlight traditional games from indigenous cultures around the world. Discuss their cultural significance, rules, and efforts to keep these games alive in contemporary societies.

2647. Eco-Friendly Pet Toys DIY: Show viewers how to make eco-friendly toys for their pets using recycled or natural materials. Share ideas that are safe, fun, and help reduce the environmental pawprint of pet ownership.

2648. The Tradition of Tea Gardens: Explore the history and cultural significance of tea gardens. Discuss their design principles, the art of tea ceremony, and how to create a peaceful tea garden space at home.

2649. A Series on Ocean Conservation Heroes: Profile individuals and organizations making significant contributions to ocean conservation. Share their stories, achievements, and how viewers can support or get involved in preserving marine environments.

2650. Restoring Antique Books: Guide viewers through the delicate process of restoring antique books. Cover the tools, techniques, and precautions needed to preserve these treasures for future generations.

2651. The Art of Sourdough From Around the World: Explore different cultures' approaches to sourdough bread, highlighting unique techniques, ingredients, and the science behind sourdough fermentation. Share recipes and tips from various global traditions.

2652. Creating Wildlife Corridors in Urban Areas: Discuss the importance of creating wildlife corridors in urban environments. Showcase examples of successful projects, the benefits to biodiversity, and how viewers can advocate for or contribute to these green spaces in their communities.

2653. The Craft of Hand-Blown Glass: Delve into the intricate process of hand-blown glass, from gathering the molten glass to shaping and cooling the final piece. Highlight the skill and creativity involved, and the applications of hand-blown glass in art and everyday objects.

2654. Eco-Friendly Van Life: Share insights into living the van life sustainably. Cover topics such as solar power setups, minimizing waste, and tips for eco-friendly travel and living in small spaces.

2655. Revitalizing Traditional Culinary Techniques: Investigate and revive traditional culinary techniques that have fallen out of favor or been forgotten. From fermentation to smoking and curing, explore the history, health benefits, and flavors these methods bring to food.

2656. A Journey Through Quantum Physics: Make quantum physics accessible to a general audience by breaking down its concepts into understandable segments. Discuss its implications for technology, philosophy, and our understanding of the universe.

2657. The Renaissance of Mechanical Watches: Explore the enduring appeal of mechanical watches in the digital age. Delve into the craftsmanship behind watchmaking, the community of collectors, and what makes mechanical watches a coveted piece of technology and art.

2658. Urban Permaculture Design: Introduce the principles of permaculture design applied to urban settings. Share case studies of urban permaculture projects, benefits such as food security and community resilience, and tips for starting a permaculture garden.

2659. Historical Reenactment as a Hobby: Dive into the world of historical reenactment, covering various periods and the dedication to authenticity. Discuss how enthusiasts research, create costumes, and engage in events to bring history to life.

2660. The Science of Sleep and Dreams: Explore the latest research on sleep and dreams. Discuss the stages of sleep, the importance of sleep for health and well-being, and what scientists understand about why we dream.

2661. Building an Eco-Friendly Skatepark: Document the process of designing and building a sustainable skatepark. Cover the use of recycled materials, community involvement, and the positive impact such spaces have on local youth and skateboard culture.

2662. The Art of Preserving Memories: Share creative ways to preserve personal and family memories beyond traditional photo albums. Discuss scrapbooking, digital storytelling, and creating time capsules.

2663. Sustainable Fashion Through Textile Recycling: Highlight the process and importance of recycling textiles in combating fashion waste. Discuss how recycled materials are transformed into new fabrics and the role of consumers in promoting a sustainable fashion industry.

2664. The World of Competitive Chess: Delve into the competitive world of chess, from local clubs to international tournaments. Discuss strategies, the mental and emotional aspects of competition, and how chess has evolved in the digital era.

2665. Creating a Zero-Waste Bathroom: Offer tips and DIY solutions for creating a zero-waste bathroom. Cover eco-friendly products, homemade toiletries, and ways to reduce water and product waste.

2666. The Philosophy of Gardening: Explore gardening not just as a hobby but as a philosophical and mindful practice. Discuss how tending to a garden can offer insights into life, growth, and the impermanent nature of things.

2667. A Guide to Ethical Wildlife Photography: Provide tips for capturing wildlife through photography in an ethical and respectful manner. Discuss how to minimize disturbance, the importance of conservation, and how photography can contribute to wildlife protection.

2668. The Culture and Art of Tattooing: Explore the rich cultural histories of tattooing from around the world. Discuss the evolution of tattoo art, the significance of various symbols and designs, and the modern tattooing scene.

2669. Innovations in Clean Energy Technology: Showcase the latest innovations in clean energy technology, such as advanced solar panels, wind turbines, and energy storage solutions. Discuss the potential impact on reducing global carbon emissions and combating climate change.

2670. Exploring the Depth of Virtual Reality: Delve into the capabilities and future of virtual reality beyond gaming. Explore its applications in education, therapy, art, and how it's shaping new ways for people to interact, learn, and experience the world.

2671. Reviving Lost Languages: Explore efforts to revive and preserve languages on the brink of extinction. Highlight the cultural significance of language, challenges in revitalization, and success stories from around the world.

2672. The Art of Making Natural Pigments: Delve into the process of creating natural pigments from earth, minerals, and plants. Showcase how these pigments can be used in painting, dyeing fabrics, and other art forms, emphasizing their historical and cultural importance.

2673. Sustainable Living in Extreme Climates: Share strategies and innovations that enable sustainable living in extreme climates, from the icy Arctic to arid deserts. Discuss adaptations in architecture, energy use, and water conservation.

2674. Exploring the Mysteries of Deep Sea Life: Dive into the unknown world of deep-sea creatures and ecosystems. Discuss the challenges of deep-sea exploration, recent discoveries, and the importance of protecting these mysterious habitats.

2675. The Tradition of Story Quilts: Highlight the tradition of story quilts, where quilts are used as a medium to tell stories, commemorate events, or express cultural heritage. Share the history of this art form and how to create your own story quilt.

2676. Innovative Urban Transport Solutions: Explore innovative solutions being implemented in cities around the world to solve transport challenges. Include bike-sharing programs, electric buses, and urban cable cars, discussing their impact on city life and the environment.

2677. The Craft of Glassblowing: Introduce viewers to the mesmerizing craft of glassblowing. Cover the tools, techniques, and creative process involved in shaping molten glass into beautiful objects.

2678. A Year of Living Sustainably: Document the journey of adopting a more sustainable lifestyle over the course of a year. Share monthly challenges, successes, setbacks, and tangible impacts on personal carbon footprint and waste reduction.

2679. The Science and Art of Perfumery: Explore the intricate world of perfume-making. Discuss the science of scent, the process of creating a perfume, and the art of blending fragrances to evoke emotions and memories.

2680. Digital Detox Retreats: Showcase the concept of digital detox retreats. Discuss the benefits of disconnecting from digital devices, activities that promote mindfulness and relaxation, and tips for maintaining digital wellness in everyday life.

2681. The Evolution of Solar Energy: Trace the history and evolution of solar energy technology, from early innovations to the latest advancements in photovoltaic cells and solar infrastructure. Discuss the future potential of solar power.

2682. The Renaissance of Public Spaces: Document the transformation of neglected public spaces into vibrant community hubs. Highlight the importance of public spaces for social interaction, community events, and urban biodiversity.

2683. Zero-Waste Cooking Techniques: Share techniques and recipes for cooking without waste, emphasizing the use of whole ingredients, creative repurposing of leftovers, and homemade alternatives to packaged products.

2684. The Healing Power of Art Therapy: Delve into the practice of art therapy, discussing its benefits for mental health, techniques used, and how individuals can incorporate art therapy principles into their own creative practices for emotional well-being.

2685. Adventures in Urban Farming: Follow the journey of setting up and maintaining an urban farm. Cover the challenges of growing food in limited spaces, the benefits of urban agriculture, and how to engage the local community in farming activities.

2686. The World of Antique Restoration: Explore the delicate art of restoring antiques. Share the techniques, tools, and considerations involved in preserving historical integrity while breathing new life into vintage items.

2687. Cycling Across Continents: Document the experience of long-distance cycling across different continents. Discuss the preparation, challenges, and the cultural and environmental discoveries made along the way.

2688. DIY Eco-Friendly Art Supplies: Show viewers how to make their own art supplies from eco-friendly materials. Include recipes for paints, clays, and other mediums, highlighting the environmental and health benefits of DIY supplies.

2689. Exploring the Culture of Coffee: Take viewers on a journey through the global culture of coffee. From traditional coffee ceremonies to modern café trends, discuss how coffee is more than just a beverage in many societies.

2690. Building a Tiny Home in a Tree: Share the adventure of designing and constructing a tiny home in a tree. Cover the design process, structural considerations, and the unique challenges and joys of treehouse living.

2691. The Art of Eco-Friendly Packaging: Explore creative and sustainable packaging solutions for everyday products. Discuss the materials, design principles, and the impact of reducing plastic use on the environment.

2692. Revitalizing Community Through Public Art: Showcase projects where public art has transformed neighborhoods and fostered a sense of community. Highlight the artists, the process, and the stories behind the murals, sculptures, and installations.

2693. A Journey Through the World of Spices: Take viewers on a culinary adventure exploring the history, cultivation, and uses of spices around the globe. Share recipes that highlight the unique flavors and health benefits of various spices.

2694. The Evolution of Bicycle Design: Trace the history and technological advancements in bicycle design, from the earliest velocipedes to modern electric bikes. Discuss the impact of cycling on urban mobility and environmental sustainability.

2695. Restoring a Historic Greenhouse: Document the restoration of a historic greenhouse, covering the architectural significance, the challenges encountered in preserving its structure, and its role in educating the community about botany and sustainability.

2696. Sustainable Water Harvesting Techniques: Educate viewers on sustainable water harvesting methods for homes and gardens, such as rain barrels, green roofs, and greywater systems. Discuss the benefits of conserving water and reducing runoff.

2697. The Science of Mindfulness Meditation: Delve into the science behind mindfulness meditation, including its effects on the brain, mental health, and overall well-being. Share tips for starting a meditation practice and incorporating mindfulness into daily life.

2698. The Tradition of Handcrafted Wooden Boats: Highlight the craftsmanship involved in building wooden boats by hand. Explore the techniques, the types of wood used, and the cultural significance of wooden boats in maritime history.

2699. Exploring Ancient Libraries of the World: Take viewers on a tour of ancient libraries, discussing their history, architecture, and the treasures they housed. Explore what these spaces tell us about the cultures that built them and their approach to knowledge and learning.

2700. DIY Backyard Observatory for Amateur Astronomers: Show how to set up a simple backyard observatory for stargazing and amateur astronomy. Discuss the equipment needed, how to choose the best location, and tips for observing celestial events.

2701. The World of Competitive Gardening: Dive into the niche but fascinating world of competitive gardening, from giant vegetable contests to flower shows. Explore the dedication, techniques, and community behind this unique competition scene.

2702. Innovations in Biodegradable Materials: Showcase the latest innovations in biodegradable materials and their applications in products and packaging. Discuss the science behind biodegradability and the potential for reducing waste and pollution.

2703. The Art of Fermented Foods: Explore the world of fermented foods across different cultures. Discuss the fermentation process, health benefits, and how viewers can start fermenting foods at home with simple recipes.

2704. Creating a Butterfly Garden: Guide viewers through creating a garden that attracts and supports butterflies. Cover which plants to choose, how to maintain the garden, and the importance of pollinators in the ecosystem.

2705. The History and Culture of Board Games: Delve into the history of board games, exploring how they reflect cultural values, historical events, and human psychology. Share some of the oldest games and their modern equivalents.

2706. Sustainable Living in Tiny Spaces: Offer insights into maximizing space and living sustainably in tiny homes, apartments, and other small living spaces. Discuss space-saving furniture, decluttering, and minimizing energy use.

2707. The Renaissance of Pen and Ink Art: Explore the enduring appeal and techniques of pen and ink art. Highlight contemporary artists, the variety of styles and materials, and tips for beginners interested in this art form.

2708. Eco-Friendly Wedding Planning: Share ideas for planning a wedding that's both beautiful and environmentally friendly. Cover sustainable venues, ethical rings, local and seasonal food choices, and zero-waste decorations.

2709. The Impact of Light Pollution on Wildlife: Discuss how light pollution affects nocturnal wildlife and ecosystems. Share solutions for reducing light pollution and how individuals and communities can contribute to darker skies.

2710. Reviving Vintage Audio Technology: Showcase the process of restoring and enjoying vintage audio equipment, such as turntables, tube amplifiers, and reel-to-reel tape players. Discuss the unique sound quality and the nostalgia associated with vintage audio.

2711. The Science of Composting at Home: Delve into the science behind composting, including the types of compost systems, the biological process of decomposition, and how to troubleshoot common composting issues, promoting sustainability in everyday life.

2712. Rediscovering Ancient Martial Arts: Explore the history, philosophy, and techniques of ancient martial arts from around the world. Highlight their cultural significance and the modern-day practice of these traditional fighting arts.

2713. Eco-Friendly Interior Design: Share ideas and tips for eco-friendly and sustainable interior design. Discuss the selection of materials, furniture, and decorations that minimize environmental impact and create healthy, sustainable living spaces.

2714. The Magic of Stop Motion Animation: Take viewers behind the scenes of creating stop motion animation. Cover the creative process, from storyboard to sculpting models and frame-by-frame animation, highlighting the patience and precision required.

2715. Revitalizing Urban Rivers: Showcase efforts to clean and revitalize urban rivers in cities around the world. Discuss the environmental, social, and economic benefits of restoring natural waterways in urban environments.

2716. Building a Solar-Powered Workshop: Document the process of creating a fully solar-powered workshop or studio. Share insights on solar panel selection, energy storage, and managing power needs for tools and equipment.

2717. The Art of Digital Detoxing: Challenge viewers to reduce digital clutter and dependency. Share experiences, benefits, and tips for successfully disconnecting from digital devices and reconnecting with the physical world.

2718. Sustainable Fashion DIY Projects: Offer tutorials on DIY projects to upcycle old clothing or create new, sustainable fashion pieces at home. Discuss techniques like dyeing, sewing, and repurposing materials to reduce fashion waste.

2719. The World of Adaptive Sports: Highlight the incredible world of adaptive sports, showcasing athletes, competitions, and the adaptive equipment that makes participation possible, promoting inclusivity and resilience.

2720. Eco-Friendly Pet Ownership: Share strategies for raising pets sustainably, covering topics such as eco-friendly pet food, toys, bedding, and minimizing your pet's environmental pawprint.

2721. Exploring Abandoned Mines: Venture into the world of abandoned mines, discussing their history, the reasons they were abandoned, and safety precautions for exploring such locations, while highlighting the importance of preserving industrial heritage.

2722. Creating Art from Ocean Plastic: Highlight artists who create stunning pieces from ocean plastic. Discuss the environmental impact of plastic pollution and how art can raise awareness and inspire action to protect marine environments.

2723. The Basics of Ethical Hacking: Introduce the principles of ethical hacking, including the importance of cybersecurity, common vulnerabilities, and how ethical hackers help protect against cyber threats.

2724. Urban Gardening Innovations: Explore innovative urban gardening solutions like rooftop gardens, window farms, and hydroponic systems. Discuss how they contribute to food security, air quality, and urban greening.

2725. The Renaissance of Public Squares: Delve into the history and social significance of public squares around the world. Highlight their role in community life, cultural events, and as spaces for democratic expression.

2726. The Culture of Coffee Shops: Explore the unique culture and community found in coffee shops around the world. Discuss the history of coffee houses, their role as creative and social hubs, and how they've evolved over time.

2727. DIY Natural Beauty Treatments: Share recipes and techniques for creating natural beauty treatments at home. Cover face masks, hair treatments, and skin care using ingredients from the kitchen or garden.

2728. The Tradition of Oral Poetry: Delve into the tradition of oral poetry across different cultures. Explore its role in storytelling, historical record-keeping, and its influence on written literature.

2729. Innovative Water Conservation Techniques: Highlight innovative techniques and technologies for conserving water in agriculture, industry, and daily life. Discuss rainwater harvesting, greywater systems, and smart irrigation practices.

2730. Restoring Classic Arcade Machines: Share the process of restoring classic arcade machines, including electrical repair, cosmetic restoration, and the nostalgia and history behind iconic arcade games.

2731. The Science of Bread Making: Dive into the chemistry and biology of bread making. Explore the fermentation process, the role of different ingredients, and how variations in technique can affect the texture and flavor of the bread.

2732. Reviving Historical Fashion Techniques: Showcase traditional fashion and sewing techniques from various periods in history. Discuss how these methods can be adapted and incorporated into modern fashion design for sustainability and uniqueness.

2733. Building an Eco-Friendly Artist Studio: Document the journey of creating an artist studio that minimizes environmental impact. Cover the use of sustainable materials, energy-efficient lighting, and recycling or repurposing art waste.

2734. A Guide to Backyard Beekeeping: Provide an introductory guide to starting a backyard beekeeping hobby. Cover the basics of bee biology, hive management, and the environmental benefits of supporting pollinator populations.

2735. Exploring the World of Silent Films: Delve into the history and artistry of silent films. Highlight pioneering filmmakers, iconic movies, and how modern audiences can appreciate the storytelling techniques used in the silent era.

2736. Sustainable Travel: Exploring National Parks: Share tips and experiences from traveling sustainably in national parks. Discuss how to enjoy natural beauty responsibly, leave no trace principles, and support conservation efforts.

2737. The Art of Forged Metalwork: Introduce viewers to the craft of metal forging. Showcase the tools, techniques, and creative possibilities of transforming metal into functional items or artistic sculptures.

2738. Rediscovering Lost Crafts: Explore crafts that are in danger of disappearing. Highlight efforts to preserve these skills, the cultural significance behind them, and how enthusiasts are keeping these traditions alive.

2739. Innovations in Green Architecture: Highlight cutting-edge green architecture projects around the world. Discuss sustainable design principles, energy-efficient systems, and how buildings can positively impact the environment and human well-being.

2740. A Beginner's Guide to Astrophotography: Offer tips and techniques for beginners interested in capturing the beauty of the night sky. Discuss the basic equipment needed, setting up shots, and post-processing images.

2741. The Impact of Climate Change on Traditional Farming: Explore how traditional farming communities around the world are adapting to the impacts of climate change. Discuss sustainable farming practices that can mitigate these effects.

2742. Creating a Capsule Wardrobe: Guide viewers through the process of creating a capsule wardrobe that emphasizes quality over quantity. Discuss the benefits of minimalist fashion on personal style and the environment.

2743. Urban Biodiversity Projects: Showcase projects that aim to increase biodiversity in urban areas. Highlight initiatives like green roofs, wildlife corridors, and community gardens, and their role in creating healthier cities.

2744. The Tradition of Handmade Toys: Explore the art of making traditional handmade toys. Discuss the cultural significance, the joy of crafting, and how these toys can be a sustainable alternative to mass-produced items.

2745. DIY Sustainable Home Improvements: Share practical DIY projects for making homes more energy-efficient and environmentally friendly. Discuss insulation, water conservation, and using reclaimed materials.

2746. The Art and Science of Natural Dyes: Delve into the process of creating dyes from natural sources like plants, minerals, and insects. Discuss the history, techniques, and environmental benefits of natural dyeing.

2747. Adaptive Sports and Accessibility: Highlight the world of adaptive sports and the technology behind accessibility in athletics. Share stories of athletes, the challenges they overcome, and the importance of inclusivity in sports.

2748. Eco-Friendly Event Planning: Offer guidance on planning events, from small gatherings to large celebrations, in an environmentally friendly manner. Cover sustainable practices such as waste reduction, eco-friendly catering, and digital invitations.

2749. The Craft of Pottery Repair: Introduce the Japanese art of Kintsugi, where broken pottery is repaired with gold, and other pottery repair techniques. Discuss the philosophy behind embracing flaws and the beauty of imperfection.

2750. Sustainable Urban Design: Explore innovative urban design projects that focus on sustainability, from pedestrian-friendly city layouts to smart infrastructure. Discuss the impact of thoughtful design on community well-being and environmental health.

2751. The Art of Restoring Antique Maps: Dive into the meticulous process of restoring antique maps, highlighting the historical significance of these documents and the techniques used to preserve them for future generations.

2752. Eco-Friendly Backpacking Tips: Share strategies for minimizing environmental impact while backpacking in the wilderness. Discuss responsible practices such as leave no trace, sustainable gear, and protecting natural habitats.

2753. The Science Behind Musical Acoustics: Explore how musical instruments produce sound from a scientific perspective. Discuss the physics of sound waves, material science in instrument construction, and how musicians can manipulate acoustics for desired effects.

2754. Sustainable Fishing Practices and Aquaculture: Delve into sustainable practices in fishing and aquaculture, highlighting methods that help preserve marine biodiversity, ensure healthy fish populations, and support local communities.

2755. A Year in a Permaculture Garden: Document the journey of creating and maintaining a garden based on permaculture principles. Share seasonal activities, challenges, successes, and the garden's evolution over a year.

2756. Reviving Heirloom Seed Varieties: Highlight the importance of preserving heirloom seed varieties for biodiversity, flavor, and cultural heritage. Discuss how gardeners can participate in seed saving and exchange communities.

2757. The Art of Digital Minimalism: Explore the concept of digital minimalism, offering viewers strategies to reduce digital clutter, improve online habits, and find balance in a digitally saturated world.

2758. Exploring the World of Rare Books: Take viewers on a journey through the fascinating world of rare and antique books, discussing their history, the art of book collecting, and stories of the most sought-after volumes.

2759. Creating a Living Roof: Showcase the process of designing and installing a green roof. Discuss the environmental benefits, such as insulation, biodiversity, and stormwater management, along with maintenance tips.

2760. The Tradition of Shadow Puppetry: Explore the ancient art of shadow puppetry, including its cultural origins, storytelling techniques, and how to create and animate your own shadow puppets.

2761. Sustainable Urban Living Innovations: Highlight innovations that make sustainable urban living more accessible, such as smart city technologies, community sharing initiatives, and green transportation solutions.

2762. The Journey of Artisan Cheese Making: Share the art and science of making artisan cheese, from milk selection and curdling to aging and flavor development. Highlight traditional methods and the stories of artisan cheesemakers.

2763. Building a Community Microgrid: Explore the concept of a community microgrid, discussing its benefits for energy independence, resilience, and sustainability. Share case studies of successful microgrid projects.

2764. Rediscovering Traditional Games and Sports: Introduce viewers to traditional games and sports from various cultures that have been overshadowed by modern gaming. Discuss their rules, historical significance, and efforts to keep them alive.

2765. DIY Eco-Friendly Furniture: Demonstrate how to create furniture using sustainable materials and methods. Share projects that repurpose reclaimed wood, bamboo, and other eco-friendly materials into functional and stylish pieces.

2766. The History and Future of Space Stations: Delve into the history of space stations, from early concepts and the International Space Station to future plans for space habitats. Discuss the technological advances and challenges of living in space.

2767. Culinary Traditions of Indigenous Peoples: Explore the culinary traditions of indigenous communities around the world. Highlight their connection to the land, traditional ingredients, and the significance of food in cultural practices and ceremonies.

2768. The Impact of Urban Green Spaces: Investigate the role of parks, gardens, and other green spaces in urban areas. Discuss their benefits for mental health, community, and local ecosystems, and how cities can integrate more green spaces.

2769. Revitalizing Vintage Computers: Share the process of restoring vintage computers, from classic home computers to early laptops. Discuss the historical significance, challenges in finding parts and data preservation.

2770. Adventures in Language Learning: Document the journey of learning a new language, from the initial challenges to immersive practices and cultural exploration. Share tips, resources, and the personal growth experienced through language learning.

2771. The Magic of Biophilic Design: Dive into the concept of biophilic design in architecture and interior design, showcasing how integrating natural elements into living spaces can improve well-being and connect people more deeply with nature.

2772. Exploring the World's Ancient Forests: Take viewers on a journey through some of the world's oldest and most majestic forests. Highlight their ecological importance, the unique species they harbor, and the efforts to conserve these natural treasures.

2773. The Renaissance of Analog Photography: Explore the resurgence of interest in analog photography. Discuss the appeal of film in the digital age, the process of developing film, and tips for beginners interested in exploring this medium.

2774. Sustainable Urban Transportation Solutions: Highlight innovative solutions being implemented in cities around the world to promote sustainable urban transportation. Discuss electric public transit, bicycle commuting, and pedestrian-friendly city planning.

2775. The Art of Handcrafted Instruments: Showcase the craftsmanship involved in creating musical instruments by hand. Explore the materials, techniques, and passion behind custom guitars, violins, drums, and other instruments.

2776. Reviving Native Plant Landscapes: Discuss the importance of native plants in landscaping and ecosystem health. Showcase projects that have successfully reintegrated native flora into urban, suburban, and rural settings.

2777. DIY Renewable Energy Projects for Homeowners: Share simple DIY projects that homeowners can undertake to incorporate renewable energy solutions, like solar panels or wind turbines, into their homes, promoting energy independence and sustainability.

2778. A Culinary Journey Through Fermented Foods: Explore the world of fermented foods across various cultures. Discuss the health benefits, fermentation techniques, and share recipes for making sauerkraut, kimchi, kombucha, and more at home.

2779. The Importance of Coral Reefs and Their Conservation: Highlight the ecological importance of coral reefs, the threats they face, and ongoing conservation efforts. Discuss how individuals can contribute to coral reef preservation.

2780. The Evolution of Video Game Music: Delve into the history and evolution of music in video games. Explore how game music has grown from simple electronic tunes to complex orchestral scores and its impact on gaming and culture.

2781. Creating a Zero-Waste Kitchen: Offer practical tips for achieving a zero-waste kitchen, including reducing food waste, sustainable food storage solutions, and alternatives to single-use plastics.

2782. The World of Miniature Art: Explore the intricate and fascinating world of miniature art. Showcase artists who create tiny masterpieces and discuss the techniques, tools, and patience required for this unique art form.

2783. Innovative Water Saving Technologies for Agriculture: Highlight cutting-edge technologies and practices in agriculture that help save water, such as drip irrigation, soil moisture sensors, and water-efficient crop varieties.

2784. The Art and Tradition of Storytelling: Delve into the art and tradition of storytelling across different cultures. Discuss its role in preserving history, imparting lessons, and bringing communities together.

2785. Eco-Friendly Pet Care Practices: Share tips for eco-friendly pet care, covering sustainable pet products, environmentally responsible pet food choices, and ways to reduce pets' environmental pawprints.

2786. The Impact of Fast Fashion on the Environment: Explore the environmental impact of fast fashion, including resource consumption, waste, and pollution. Highlight sustainable fashion alternatives and ways consumers can make a difference.

2787. Urban Foraging: Introduce the concept of urban foraging, teaching viewers how to safely identify and harvest edible plants, fruits, and herbs in city environments while respecting public spaces and local regulations.

2788. The Journey of Restoring a Classic Car: Document the detailed process of restoring a classic car, from sourcing parts to mechanical repairs and bodywork. Share the challenges, successes, and the car's history and cultural significance.

2789. Exploring the Science of Bubbles: Dive into the science behind bubbles, from their physical properties and formation to their applications in technology, art, and entertainment. Include experiments and visual demonstrations.

2790. Championing Local Libraries: Showcase the vital role of local libraries in communities beyond just lending books. Highlight their services, community programs, and the importance of supporting these valuable institutions.

2791. Crafting with Reclaimed Wood: Showcase projects that utilize reclaimed wood, highlighting the beauty and sustainability of repurposing materials. Offer DIY tips for sourcing, preparing, and crafting furniture or decor items.

2792. The Science of Sound Healing: Delve into the principles behind sound healing, including how different frequencies affect the human body and mind. Highlight traditional instruments used in sound therapy and share testimonials on its benefits.

2793. Exploring Traditional Dwellings Around the World: Take viewers on a tour of traditional homes from various cultures, such as yurts, igloos, and adobe houses. Discuss their architectural features, materials, and how they're adapted to their environments.

2794. Sustainable Cooking Methods: Introduce viewers to cooking techniques that minimize energy use and waste, such as solar cooking, pressure cooking, and efficient meal planning. Share recipes that exemplify these methods.

2795. The Art of Calligraphy and Its Modern Resurgence: Explore the history of calligraphy, from ancient manuscripts to contemporary art forms. Offer tutorials for beginners and discuss how digital tools are blending with traditional techniques.

2796. Innovations in Eco-Friendly Packaging: Highlight recent advancements in sustainable packaging solutions, including biodegradable materials, edible packaging, and reusable systems. Discuss the impact on reducing plastic waste and pollution.

2797. The World of Plant-Based Medicines: Investigate the use of plants in traditional and modern medicine. Cover the science behind herbal remedies, how to safely use plant-based medicines, and the importance of preserving indigenous knowledge.

2798. Urban Wildlife Habitats: Show how urban areas can support wildlife through the creation of green roofs, butterfly gardens, and bird-friendly structures. Discuss the importance of biodiversity and how cities can coexist with nature.

2799. The Fascination with Tiny Houses: Delve into the tiny house movement, exploring the appeal of living minimally in small spaces. Highlight design innovations, the challenges of downsizing, and the lifestyle's environmental benefits.

2800. Restoring and Playing Vintage Video Games: Share the process of restoring vintage video game consoles and cartridges. Discuss the history of gaming, the nostalgia factor, and tips for collectors and enthusiasts.

2801. The Tradition of Handmade Papermaking: Explore the craft of making paper by hand, from sourcing sustainable fibers to the final pressing and drying process. Highlight the environmental advantages and the artistic aspects of handmade paper.

2802. Revitalizing Public Murals: Document the creation or restoration of public murals in urban settings. Discuss the collaborative process, the stories behind the murals, and their impact on community identity and beautification.

2803. Sustainable Fashion Upcycling: Showcase how to give old clothes a new life through upcycling techniques. Provide step-by-step guides for transforming thrift store finds into fashionable pieces, emphasizing creativity and waste reduction.

2804. The Role of Citizen Science in Conservation: Highlight projects where ordinary people contribute to scientific research and conservation efforts. Discuss how viewers can get involved in citizen science and the impact of their contributions.

2805. The Journey of Learning a Musical Instrument: Document the process of learning to play a musical instrument, from the initial struggles to milestones of progress. Share practice tips, motivational advice, and the personal benefits of music education.

2806. Exploring Underwater Ecosystems via Scuba Diving: Take viewers on a visual journey through diverse underwater landscapes, from coral reefs to shipwrecks. Discuss the importance of ocean conservation and responsible diving practices.

2807. The History and Craft of Bookbinding: Dive into the traditional craft of bookbinding, showcasing various binding techniques, the tools of the trade, and the care involved in preserving old and creating new books.

2808. Zero-Waste Beauty Routines: Share tips for creating a beauty routine that minimizes waste, featuring DIY skincare and makeup recipes, sustainable product choices, and advice for reducing plastic in the bathroom.

2809. Cycling Tours of Historic Cities: Offer guided cycling tours through historic cities, combining exercise with educational content about the city's history, architecture, and cultural landmarks.

2810. The Art of Bonsai: Introduce viewers to the art and discipline of bonsai, including selecting tree species, shaping techniques, and the philosophical aspects of patience and care in miniature tree cultivation.

2811. Urban Beekeeping and Its Impact on Cities: Explore the benefits and challenges of urban beekeeping, including how it supports local ecosystems, pollination in city gardens, and the production of local honey. Share insights from urban beekeepers and tips for getting started.

2812. Rediscovering the Art of Letter Writing: Encourage a return to the personal touch of handwritten letters. Discuss the history of letter writing, its impact on relationships and communication, and how to craft a meaningful letter in the digital age.

2813. Sustainable Travel Vlogs: Document eco-friendly travel experiences, showcasing how to explore the world responsibly. Highlight sustainable accommodations, transportation methods, and ways to minimize your carbon footprint while traveling.

2814. The Therapeutic Benefits of Gardening: Dive into how gardening can improve mental and physical health. Share personal stories, scientific research on the subject, and tips for creating a healing garden space at home.

2815. Exploring the World of Artisanal Salt: Uncover the craft of producing artisanal salt. Visit salt farms, learn about different methods of harvesting and processing salt, and explore the variety of flavors and uses in culinary arts.

2816. Innovative Community Recycling Initiatives: Highlight community-led recycling projects that are making a difference. Discuss the importance of recycling, innovative recycling methods, and how viewers can implement or support similar initiatives in their communities.

2817. The History of Astronomy Tools: Take viewers on a journey through the history of tools used in astronomy, from ancient astrolabes to modern telescopes. Discuss how these instruments have evolved and contributed to our understanding of the universe.

2818. Building a Sustainable Wardrobe from Scratch: Guide viewers on how to build a sustainable wardrobe, focusing on ethical brands, thrift shopping, and clothing care to extend the lifespan of garments. Share tips for making mindful fashion choices.

2819. Eco-Friendly Pet Care Solutions: Share strategies for raising pets sustainably, covering topics such as eco-friendly pet products, homemade pet food recipes, and reducing your pet's environmental pawprint.

2820. DIY Natural Home Fragrances: Teach viewers how to create their own natural home fragrances using essential oils, herbs, and flowers. Share recipes for homemade air fresheners, potpourri, and scented candles that avoid synthetic chemicals.

2821. Revitalizing Spaces with Vertical Gardens: Show how vertical gardens can transform indoor and outdoor spaces. Discuss the benefits of vertical gardening, suitable plants, and tips for installation and maintenance.

2822. The Rise of Eco-Friendly Technologies in Sports: Explore how sports are becoming more environmentally friendly through the use of sustainable materials, eco-conscious event planning, and initiatives to reduce the carbon footprint of teams and fans.

2823. Homemade Herbal Remedies: Introduce viewers to the world of herbal remedies. Share how to prepare simple herbal treatments for common ailments, emphasizing the importance of understanding herbs and their effects.

2824. The Craft of Traditional Wooden Toy Making: Showcase the art of making traditional wooden toys. Discuss the tools and techniques involved, the joy of handcrafted toys, and how they can be a sustainable alternative to plastic.

2825. Sustainable Urban Design Innovations: Highlight innovative urban design projects that focus on sustainability, from green buildings and energy efficiency to public spaces that encourage community and environmental health.

2826. Journey Through the Coffee Bean Lifecycle: From farm to cup, explore the entire lifecycle of coffee, including cultivation, harvesting, processing, roasting, and brewing. Discuss sustainable coffee farming practices and the art of coffee tasting.

2827. The Art and Science of Time-Lapse Photography: Teach viewers how to capture stunning time-lapse videos of natural phenomena, cityscapes, and more. Share tips on the necessary equipment, settings, and creative approaches.

2828. Restoring and Preserving Historical Documents: Highlight the importance of preserving historical documents. Show the restoration process, techniques used by conservators, and how these documents offer insights into our past.

2829. Eco-Friendly Crafting Materials: Explore alternative, eco-friendly materials for crafting projects. Discuss how to source sustainable supplies, and share projects that utilize recycled, upcycled, or naturally biodegradable materials.

2830. The Impact of Climate Change on Traditional Farming: Examine how traditional farming communities are adapting to the challenges posed by climate change. Discuss sustainable agricultural practices that can help mitigate these impacts and ensure food security.

2831. The Renaissance of Public Libraries: Showcase how modern public libraries are evolving beyond traditional roles to become dynamic community hubs, offering maker spaces, digital labs, and various educational programs.

2832. Zero-Waste Home Hacks: Share practical tips and tricks for reducing waste in everyday life, focusing on DIY solutions for common household items and sustainable swaps that can significantly reduce one's environmental footprint.

2833. The Art of Slow Living: Explore the philosophy and practices behind the slow living movement. Highlight ways to implement mindful habits into daily routines, emphasizing quality over quantity and the joy found in simplicity.

2834. Urban Acoustic Ecology: Delve into the study of sounds in urban environments, discussing how city soundscapes affect residents' well-being. Share experiences of sound walks and tips for finding tranquility in noisy settings.

2835. Reviving Indigenous Plant Knowledge: Highlight the importance of preserving indigenous knowledge of plants for food, medicine, and sustainability. Share stories of communities working to keep this knowledge alive and relevant.

2836. Sustainable Surfing: Explore how the surfing community is embracing sustainability, from eco-friendly surfboard materials to initiatives aimed at protecting ocean health and promoting environmental stewardship among surfers.

2837. The Chemistry of Cooking: Uncover the science behind cooking processes, such as why onions make us cry, the Maillard reaction for browning food, and the role of different ingredients in creating flavors and textures.

2838. Historical Costume Recreation: Document the process of researching, designing, and sewing historical costumes. Discuss the historical accuracy, techniques used in the past, and the challenges of recreating period attire.

2839. Eco-Friendly Party Planning: Offer tips for hosting parties and events in an environmentally friendly manner. Cover sustainable decorations, waste reduction, and creative, eco-friendly party favors and activities.

2840. The World of Citizen Science Projects: Introduce viewers to various citizen science projects they can participate in, from tracking local wildlife to contributing to global research on climate change, emphasizing the impact of collective data gathering.

2841. Exploring Traditional Healing Practices: Investigate traditional healing practices from around the world, discussing their cultural contexts, methods, and the integration of these practices into modern holistic health approaches.

2842. Innovations in Green Transportation: Highlight the latest innovations in green transportation technology, such as electric vehicles, hydrogen fuel cells, and advancements in public transit systems aiming to reduce carbon emissions.

2843. Backyard Biodiversity Projects: Share simple projects and practices to enhance biodiversity in backyards, such as creating insect hotels, planting native species, and setting up bird feeders, to encourage a variety of local wildlife.

2844. The Art of Preserving Family Recipes: Encourage viewers to preserve and share family recipes, discussing the importance of these recipes in maintaining cultural heritage and family history, along with tips for creating a family recipe book.

2845. DIY Upcycled Art Supplies: Demonstrate how to create art supplies from upcycled materials, promoting sustainability in the arts. Include ideas for making paints, brushes, and canvases from repurposed items.

2846. The Future of Space Tourism: Discuss the advancements and challenges of space tourism, including the companies involved, the potential environmental impacts, and the ethical considerations of commercial space travel.

2847. Crafting Traditional Musical Instruments: Showcase the crafting of traditional musical instruments from various cultures, highlighting the materials, craftsmanship, and cultural significance of each instrument.

2848. The Impact of Urban Gardening: Explore the social, environmental, and health impacts of urban gardening, including community gardens, rooftop farms, and window box gardens, on urban residents and communities.

2849. Exploring Micro-Homes and Compact Living Solutions: Delve into the trend of micro-homes and compact living, discussing the benefits of downsizing, innovative design solutions for small spaces, and the lifestyle changes involved.

2850. Sustainable Practices in Winemaking: Examine how wineries are implementing sustainable practices in viticulture and winemaking, covering organic farming, water conservation, and eco-friendly packaging.

2851. The Craft of Artisanal Candle Making: Dive into the world of making artisanal candles, focusing on natural waxes, essential oils for scent, and the art of creating unique, eco-friendly candles at home.

2852. Exploring the Mysteries of Deep Earth: Uncover the fascinating science studying the Earth's deep interior, from seismic studies to deep drilling projects, and what these reveal about our planet's history and dynamics.

2853. Reviving Traditional Woodworking Techniques: Showcase the beauty and skill behind traditional woodworking techniques. Highlight craftsmen who use classic methods to create furniture, art, and everyday objects, emphasizing the value of handmade craftsmanship.

2854. Sustainable Fashion: From Idea to Wardrobe: Follow the journey of a sustainable garment from the initial design concept through to the final product. Discuss the challenges and rewards of creating fashion that's both stylish and kind to the planet.

2855. The Psychology of Space and Organization: Explore how the organization and design of personal spaces impact mental health and productivity. Offer tips for creating environments that foster well-being and creativity.

2856. Eco-Friendly Travel Gadgets: Introduce viewers to innovative gadgets and accessories designed for eco-conscious travelers. Highlight products that are durable, rechargeable, or made from sustainable materials.

2857. The Art of Precision Coffee Brewing: Delve into techniques for brewing the perfect cup of coffee, covering various methods like pour-over, French press, and espresso. Discuss the importance of bean selection, grind size, water temperature, and timing.

2858. Conservation Efforts for Endangered Languages: Highlight the importance of preserving endangered languages and the efforts being made around the world to save them. Share stories of communities revitalizing their linguistic heritage.

2859. The Evolution of Digital Art: Explore the rise of digital art, from early pixel art to contemporary 3D modeling and virtual reality experiences. Discuss the tools and technologies that have shaped this art form and its impact on the art world.

2860. Building a Sustainable Community Kitchen: Document the creation of a community kitchen focused on sustainability. Discuss how such kitchens can support local food production, reduce waste, and bring communities together over healthy, homemade meals.

2861. The Science of Plant-Based Nutrition: Examine the nutritional science behind plant-based diets, discussing the health benefits, essential nutrients, and how to ensure a balanced and nourishing diet.

2862. Historic Shipwrecks and Underwater Archaeology: Delve into the world of underwater archaeology through the exploration of historic shipwrecks. Discuss the techniques used in underwater excavations and what these sites can tell us about our past.

2863. The Challenge of Plastic-Free Living: Share the journey of attempting to live without single-use plastics. Highlight the difficulties encountered, alternatives discovered, and the overall impact on waste reduction.

2864. Adventures in Urban Homesteading: Document the experiences of starting an urban homestead, from backyard chickens and beekeeping to growing a vegetable garden and implementing rainwater harvesting systems.

2865. Reviving the Art of Natural Perfumery: Explore the process of creating perfumes using only natural ingredients. Discuss the history of perfumery, the art of scent composition, and how to extract and blend natural fragrances.

2866. Sustainable Practices in Craft Brewing: Highlight how craft breweries are implementing sustainable practices in brewing, packaging, and distribution. Discuss the use of local ingredients, water conservation efforts, and community engagement.

2867. The Renaissance of Penmanship: Celebrate the art of beautiful handwriting in the digital age. Offer tutorials on improving penmanship, exploring styles from cursive to calligraphy, and the benefits of writing by hand for cognitive and motor skills.

2868. Innovations in Sustainable Architecture: Showcase innovative projects in sustainable architecture that push the boundaries of eco-friendly design. Discuss energy efficiency, green materials, and the integration of nature into built environments.

2869. Exploring the World of Insect Cuisine: Investigate the practice of consuming insects as a sustainable protein source. Share recipes, nutritional benefits, and address common misconceptions about entomophagy.

2870. The Cultural Significance of Traditional Textiles: Delve into the world of traditional textiles, exploring their cultural significance, the techniques used in their creation, and the stories they tell about the people and places they come from.

2871. The Art of Eco-Friendly Printmaking: Explore traditional and innovative printmaking techniques that minimize environmental impact. Highlight non-toxic processes, recycled materials, and natural inks in creating stunning prints.

2872. Restoring Ecosystems with Native Plants: Delve into projects that focus on restoring natural ecosystems using native plants. Discuss the importance of native flora for biodiversity, combating invasive species, and supporting local wildlife.

2873. The Evolution of Bicycle Design and Culture: Trace the history of bicycles from their inception to the present day, highlighting key design changes, the rise of cycling culture, and the bicycle's role in promoting sustainable transportation.

2874. The Renaissance of Public Markets: Showcase the resurgence of public markets and their role in supporting local farmers, artisans, and communities. Explore how these markets serve as hubs for sustainable living and cultural exchange.

2875. DIY Solar-Powered Gadgets: Provide tutorials on creating useful solar-powered gadgets for everyday use. Discuss the basics of solar technology, materials needed, and the environmental benefits of harnessing solar energy.

2876. Exploring the Depths of Caves: Take viewers on a journey into the world of speleology, exploring magnificent caves and the unique ecosystems they host. Discuss cave formation, the thrill of cave exploration, and the importance of conserving these hidden worlds.

2877. The Craft of Natural Jewelry Making: Highlight the process of making jewelry from natural materials like stones, wood, and metals. Share techniques for sourcing and working with these materials sustainably and ethically.

2878. Green Roof Gardens: Explore the benefits and challenges of creating green roofs in urban environments. Discuss the insulation, biodiversity, and stormwater management benefits of rooftop gardens, and how to start one's own.

2879. The Science of Clean Energy: Explain the science behind different forms of clean energy, such as solar, wind, hydro, and geothermal. Discuss how these technologies work, their potential to reduce carbon emissions, and the future of energy.

2880. Heritage Crafts Revival: Document the revival of heritage crafts that are at risk of disappearing. Explore crafts like basket weaving, pottery, and blacksmithing, highlighting the artisans keeping these traditions alive and the importance of preserving craftsmanship.

2881. Sustainable Cooking Fuels: Investigate alternative, sustainable cooking fuels such as biogas, ethanol, and solar cookers. Discuss their environmental impact, how they're made, and their potential to replace traditional cooking fuels in different parts of the world.

2882. Mindful Tech Consumption: Offer insights into mindful consumption of technology, emphasizing the importance of digital detoxes, sustainable tech habits, and how to make more environmentally friendly gadget choices.

2883. The Global Impact of Fast Fashion: Dive into the environmental and social impacts of the fast fashion industry. Discuss the lifecycle of fast fashion garments, sustainable alternatives, and how consumers can make more ethical fashion choices.

2884. Revitalizing Urban Spaces with Art: Showcase projects that use art to transform and revitalize urban spaces. Highlight community murals, sculpture gardens, and temporary installations that bring beauty and conversation to neglected areas.

2885. Sustainable Aquaponics Systems: Introduce viewers to the principles of aquaponics, combining fish farming with hydroponic gardening. Discuss the benefits, challenges, and how to set up a small-scale aquaponics system at home.

2886. Adventures in Ethical Wildlife Photography: Share guidelines and experiences for capturing wildlife through photography ethically and responsibly. Discuss the importance of respecting wildlife, minimizing disturbance, and using photography for conservation awareness.

2887. Zero-Waste Beauty Routines: Demonstrate how to adopt a zero-waste beauty routine, featuring DIY skincare and makeup products, and tips for reducing packaging waste in personal care products.

2888. The Art of Creating Sustainable Festivals: Explore how festivals around the world are becoming more sustainable. Discuss measures for waste reduction, energy efficiency, and community engagement in creating eco-friendly event experiences.

2889. Innovations in Recycling Technology: Highlight recent technological advancements in recycling, such as AI sorting systems, advanced composting techniques, and new methods for recycling plastics and electronics.

2890. Exploring the Tradition of Tea Gardens: Delve into the history and cultural significance of tea gardens. Explore their design, the varieties of tea grown, and the role these gardens play in the production and enjoyment of tea.

2891. The Art of Sustainable Landscaping: Explore techniques and principles behind sustainable landscaping, highlighting water conservation, native plant use, and creating wildlife habitats in residential and public spaces.

2892. Reviving Classical Music for Modern Audiences: Showcase efforts to make classical music accessible and relevant to today's audiences, including innovative concert formats, blending genres, and educational outreach.

2893. Eco-Friendly DIY Pet Accessories: Offer tutorials on crafting sustainable pet accessories, such as toys, beds, and feeding stations, using upcycled materials and eco-friendly fabrics.

2894. The Science of Sleep and Environment: Delve into how environmental factors affect sleep quality. Discuss the role of light, noise, temperature, and bedroom design in promoting restful sleep and overall health.

2895. Virtual Reality in Education: Explore the potential of virtual reality technology in enhancing educational experiences. Highlight immersive VR applications for teaching history, science, art, and more.

2896. Sustainable Urban Drainage Systems (SUDS): Investigate the design and benefits of Sustainable Urban Drainage Systems in managing rainwater in cities. Discuss how SUDS prevent flooding, improve water quality, and enhance urban landscapes.

2897. The History and Techniques of Mosaic Art: Trace the history of mosaic art from ancient times to the present. Offer DIY tutorials for creating mosaics and discuss the therapeutic benefits of this intricate art form.

2898. Innovations in Sustainable Packaging: Highlight the latest innovations in sustainable packaging solutions, focusing on biodegradable, compostable, and reusable options. Discuss the challenges and potential impact on reducing packaging waste.

2899. The Renaissance of Public Speaking: Explore the art of public speaking and its significance in the digital age. Share tips for effective communication, overcoming fear, and the role of storytelling in engaging audiences.

2900. Wildlife Conservation Volunteering: Share experiences and opportunities for volunteering in wildlife conservation projects. Highlight the impact of conservation efforts on endangered species and ecosystems.

2901. The Tradition of Handcrafted Pottery: Delve into the world of handcrafted pottery, showcasing the skills, techniques, and cultural significance of pottery across different cultures. Include tutorials for beginners interested in the craft.

2902. Sustainable Living in Off-Grid Communities: Explore life in off-grid communities, focusing on their sustainable practices, renewable energy use, and the sense of community and resilience developed in these environments.

2903. Exploring Ancient Trade Routes: Take viewers on a journey along ancient trade routes, such as the Silk Road and Spice Routes. Discuss the historical, cultural, and economic impacts of these trade networks.

2904. The Craft of Artisan Bread Making: Showcase the art and science of making artisan bread, including sourdough starters, fermentation processes, and various baking techniques to create crusty, flavorful loaves.

2905. Eco-Friendly Wedding Ideas: Offer inspiration and ideas for planning an eco-friendly wedding. Discuss sustainable venue choices, catering options, decor, and ways to minimize the environmental impact of wedding celebrations.

2906. Reviving the Art of Shadow Theatre: Introduce viewers to the traditional art of shadow theatre, including its history, storytelling techniques, and how to create shadow puppets and perform your own shows.

2907. Sustainable Practices in Coffee Production: Explore sustainable practices in coffee production, from shade-grown coffee to fair trade policies. Discuss the environmental and social benefits of sustainable coffee farming.

2908. The Beauty of Urban Ruins and Abandoned Places: Share explorations of urban ruins and abandoned places, discussing their history, the allure of decay, and the stories behind these forgotten spaces.

2909. Homemade Eco-Friendly Cleaning Solutions: Demonstrate how to make eco-friendly cleaning solutions at home, emphasizing natural ingredients, effectiveness, and reducing the use of harsh chemicals in household cleaning.

2910. The Role of Art in Community Healing: Explore how art projects and initiatives can facilitate community healing and dialogue in the aftermath of tragedy or conflict. Highlight case studies and the impact of these art-based interventions.

2911. Revitalizing Cities Through Green Infrastructure: Explore how cities worldwide are integrating green infrastructure, like parks, greenways, and living walls, to combat urban challenges such as air pollution, heat islands, and biodiversity loss.

2912. The Art of Book Sculpture: Showcase artists who transform books into intricate sculptures, discussing the creative process, inspiration behind their work, and the conversation between literature and visual art.

2913. Sustainable Seafood Practices: Delve into the importance of sustainable seafood, including how consumers can make responsible choices, the impact of overfishing on marine ecosystems, and spotlighting initiatives promoting ocean health.

2914. Exploring Soundscapes in Nature: Take viewers on an auditory journey through various natural soundscapes, discussing the importance of sound in ecosystems, its effects on wildlife, and efforts to preserve natural acoustic environments.

2915. Ancient Grain Revival: Highlight the revival of ancient grains in modern cuisine, discussing their nutritional benefits, environmental resilience, and how to incorporate grains like amaranth, quinoa, and spelt into daily meals.

2916. The Rise of Eco-Tourism: Explore eco-tourism destinations and practices that prioritize conservation, community involvement, and sustainable travel experiences, highlighting how tourism can contribute positively to environmental protection and local economies.

2917. The Science of Biophilic Design in Workspaces: Examine how incorporating elements of nature into office and workspace design can boost well-being, productivity, and creativity, supported by scientific research and case studies.

2918. Traditional Fermentation Techniques Around the World: Discover traditional fermentation techniques and their cultural significance across different societies. Share recipes and processes for making fermented foods and drinks, emphasizing their health benefits.

2919. DIY Eco-Friendly Textiles and Fabrics: Teach viewers how to create or source eco-friendly textiles for DIY fashion and home decor projects. Discuss natural dyes, sustainable fabric choices, and techniques for minimizing environmental impact.

2920. Urban Agriculture and Food Security: Highlight urban agriculture initiatives that enhance food security, from rooftop gardens to community-supported agriculture (CSA) programs. Discuss their role in local food systems and community resilience.

2921. Adaptive Reuse in Architecture: Explore projects where old buildings are repurposed for new uses, highlighting the sustainability aspects of adaptive reuse, challenges faced during transformation, and the blend of historic preservation with modern design.

2922. The Craft of Handmade Musical Instruments: Showcase the intricate process of crafting musical instruments by hand, from traditional stringed instruments to innovative creations. Highlight the artisans' skills, materials used, and the acoustic science involved.

2923. Photographing the Night Sky: Offer tips and techniques for astrophotography, capturing the beauty of the night sky. Discuss equipment, settings, and locations best suited for stellar photography, including how to photograph celestial events.

2924. Zero-Waste Lifestyle Challenges: Document the journey of attempting to live with zero waste, sharing personal experiences, challenges, successes, and tips for minimizing one's environmental footprint through mindful consumption and waste reduction.

2925. The Art of Stained Glass Creation: Dive into the world of stained glass art, from its historical significance in sacred spaces to contemporary applications. Share the process of designing, cutting, and assembling stained glass pieces.

2926. Innovative Water Conservation in Gardening: Present innovative gardening techniques that conserve water, such as xeriscaping, drip irrigation, and using water-retaining soil amendments. Highlight the importance of water-wise gardening in response to climate change.

2927. Exploring the History of Maps and Cartography: Delve into the fascinating history of maps and cartography, tracing how maps have shaped our understanding of the world. Discuss ancient mapmaking techniques, iconic maps, and the role of maps in exploration and navigation.

2928. The Philosophy Behind Minimalist Living: Explore the philosophical underpinnings of minimalist living, discussing how reducing possessions can lead to increased focus, freedom, and fulfillment, and sharing strategies for adopting a minimalist lifestyle.

2929. Reviving Vintage Cameras and Techniques: Share the joy of restoring vintage cameras and using them to capture images, highlighting the unique qualities of film photography, the process of film development, and tips for beginners interested in analog photography.

2930. Sustainable Practices in Winemaking: Investigate sustainable and organic winemaking practices, focusing on vineyard management, biodiversity, and environmentally friendly packaging. Highlight wineries leading the way in sustainability.

2931. The Role of Urban Trees in City Living: Explore the benefits of urban trees for air quality, mental health, and biodiversity. Highlight initiatives for urban reforestation and the challenges of maintaining green spaces in densely populated areas.

2932. Crafting with Upcycled Materials: Showcase creative projects that repurpose upcycled materials into art, home decor, or fashion. Discuss sourcing materials, the process of transformation, and the environmental impact of upcycling.

2933. The Future of Sustainable Transport: Delve into emerging technologies and initiatives aimed at creating sustainable transportation solutions. Cover electric vehicles, bike-sharing programs, and innovations in public transit.

2934. Traditional vs. Modern Farming Techniques: Compare traditional farming techniques with modern agricultural practices. Discuss the sustainability, efficiency, and environmental impacts of each approach, highlighting the balance between innovation and tradition.

2935. Eco-Friendly Home Renovations: Share tips and ideas for renovating homes with sustainability in mind. Discuss energy-efficient appliances, sustainable building materials, and design choices that reduce a home's environmental footprint.

2936. The Art of Nature Journaling: Introduce viewers to nature journaling as a way to connect with the natural world. Share tips on observing, sketching, and writing about nature, highlighting the benefits for mindfulness and creativity.

2937. Restoring Natural Habitats: Document restoration projects aimed at returning natural habitats to their original state. Discuss the challenges involved, the importance of restoring ecosystems, and the positive impact on biodiversity.

2938. Exploring the World of Natural Wines: Delve into the natural wine movement, covering the winemaking process, the characteristics that distinguish natural wines, and the debate within the wine community about definitions and standards.

2939. Zero-Waste Gardening Techniques: Offer guidance on creating a zero-waste garden, including composting, choosing sustainable garden products, and methods for minimizing waste in garden maintenance and harvesting.

2940. The Revival of Analog Gaming: Explore the resurgence of interest in analog games, such as board games, card games, and tabletop RPGs. Discuss the appeal of physical games in the digital age and the communities that form around them.

2941. Sustainable Water Use in Home Gardens: Share strategies for conserving water in residential gardens, including rainwater harvesting, drip irrigation, and selecting drought-resistant plants.

2942. The Impact of Fashion on Water Resources: Investigate the fashion industry's impact on global water resources, covering issues like water pollution from dyeing processes and the water footprint of cotton production. Highlight sustainable fashion alternatives.

2943. Building Community Through Food Co-ops: Showcase the role of food co-operatives in building community, supporting local farmers, and providing access to healthy, sustainable food options.

2944. DIY Eco-Friendly Home Cleaning Products: Teach viewers how to make their own eco-friendly cleaning products using natural ingredients. Share recipes for all-purpose cleaners, laundry detergents, and dish soaps that are safe and effective.

2945. The Tradition of Oral Histories: Highlight the importance of oral histories in preserving personal and community stories. Discuss methods for recording and preserving these narratives for future generations.

2946. The Science of Compostable Plastics: Explore the development and use of compostable plastics. Discuss the science behind these materials, their environmental benefits, and the challenges associated with composting them properly.

2947. Urban Farming Innovations: Highlight innovative urban farming projects and technologies, such as vertical farms, aquaponics systems, and rooftop gardens, that are transforming food production in city environments.

2948. The Cultural Significance of Tea Ceremonies: Delve into the history and cultural significance of tea ceremonies in various cultures. Explore the rituals, etiquette, and philosophical aspects of these ceremonies, and their role in social and spiritual life.

2949. Adaptive Clothing Design: Showcase innovations in adaptive clothing design for individuals with disabilities. Highlight designers and brands that are making fashion more inclusive, focusing on functionality, style, and accessibility.

2950. Sustainable Practices in Art Supplies and Creation: Explore sustainable practices in the art world, from eco-friendly art supplies to methods for reducing waste in art creation. Share tips for artists looking to make their practice more environmentally friendly.

2951. The Journey of a Zero-Waste Chef: Document the challenges and successes of a chef striving to achieve a zero-waste kitchen. Share insights on sustainable food sourcing, minimizing food waste, and creative recipes that use every part of an ingredient.

2952. Revitalizing Traditional Textile Arts: Explore the revival of traditional textile arts like weaving, embroidery, and dyeing. Highlight artisans keeping these crafts alive, the cultural significance behind the techniques, and workshops or classes available for beginners.

2953. Eco-Friendly Adventure Sports: Showcase adventure sports that emphasize environmental stewardship, such as leave-no-trace hiking, eco-conscious mountain biking, and sustainable surfing. Highlight how enthusiasts can enjoy adrenaline-pumping activities while protecting the planet.

2954. Innovative Urban Cooling Solutions: Discuss innovative solutions being implemented in cities to combat the urban heat island effect. Explore green roofs, reflective surfaces, urban forestry projects, and community initiatives aimed at reducing city temperatures.

2955. The Science and Art of Natural Light in Photography: Offer tips and techniques for using natural light to create stunning photographs. Discuss the golden hour, diffused lighting, and how to adjust settings for the best natural light shots.

2956. Sustainable Living on a Boat: Share the lifestyle of individuals or families living sustainably on a boat. Cover how they manage energy use, waste, and water, along with the joys and challenges of life at sea.

2957. The Renaissance of Public Speaking and Debate Clubs: Highlight the importance of public speaking and debate clubs in fostering effective communication skills, critical thinking, and civic engagement among youths and adults.

2958. Conservation Efforts in Urban Wildlife: Explore conservation efforts aimed at protecting wildlife in urban settings. Highlight initiatives to create wildlife corridors, protect native species, and engage city dwellers in wildlife conservation.

2959. The Art of Making and Playing Didgeridoos: Delve into the cultural significance, crafting process, and playing techniques of the didgeridoo. Highlight its origins with Indigenous Australian cultures and its influence on global music scenes.

2960. Sustainable Practices in the Cosmetics Industry: Investigate how the cosmetics industry is embracing sustainability. Discuss eco-friendly packaging, natural ingredients, cruelty-free testing, and brands leading the way in environmental responsibility.

2961. Historical Restoration Projects on Social Media: Showcase how social media platforms are being used to document and promote historical restoration projects, engaging the public in the preservation of cultural heritage.

2962. Mindfulness and Sustainability in Fashion: Discuss the intersection of mindfulness and sustainability in fashion choices. Explore how a mindful approach to consuming fashion can lead to more sustainable practices and reduce the environmental impact of clothing.

2963. The Global Impact of Community Gardens: Examine the social, environmental, and economic impacts of community gardens around the world. Share stories of how these gardens bring communities together, provide fresh food, and transform urban spaces.

2964. Ethical Dilemmas in Artificial Intelligence: Delve into the ethical considerations of developing and implementing artificial intelligence. Discuss issues around privacy, bias, job displacement, and the future relationship between humans and AI.

2965. Reviving Lost Folk Songs and Ballads: Highlight efforts to revive and preserve lost or forgotten folk songs and ballads. Share the process of researching, recording, and performing these pieces, emphasizing their cultural and historical importance.

2966. The Craft of Custom Pen Making: Showcase the art and business of crafting custom pens, from selecting materials like wood and resin to the precision machining and finishing processes that create unique writing instruments.

2967. Eco-Friendly Innovations in Packaging Design: Explore innovations in packaging design that reduce waste and environmental impact. Highlight compostable materials, reusable systems, and minimalist designs that challenge conventional packaging.

2968. The Role of Art in Mental Health Recovery: Investigate how engaging in art can support mental health recovery and well-being. Share stories and research on art therapy, community art projects, and personal expressions through art as a form of healing.

2969. Sustainable Event Management: Offer insights into organizing events sustainably, covering eco-friendly event planning, minimizing waste, sustainable catering options, and engaging attendees in green practices.

2970. Wild Foraging and Ethical Practices: Educate viewers on the practice of wild foraging for edible plants and mushrooms, focusing on safety, identification, and ethical considerations to ensure sustainability and respect for natural habitats.

2971. The Intersection of Technology and Traditional Crafts: Explore how modern technology is being used to preserve and innovate traditional crafts, from digital weaving patterns to 3D-printed ceramics, highlighting the fusion of old and new techniques.

2972. Reviving Community Through Food Co-operatives: Document the impact of food co-operatives in revitalizing communities, providing access to healthy, local food, and fostering a sense of belonging and mutual support among members.

2973. The Art and Science of Coffee Cupping: Delve into the world of coffee cupping, the practice used by coffee professionals to evaluate coffee aroma, taste, and body. Share insights on how to cup coffee at home and what to look for in a good brew.

2974. Exploring the World's Sacred Groves: Take viewers on a journey to explore sacred groves around the world, discussing their cultural, religious, and environmental significance and the efforts being made to preserve these ancient natural sanctuaries.

2975. The Renaissance of Letterpress Printing: Showcase the revival of letterpress printing, emphasizing its tactile beauty, craftsmanship, and the community of artists keeping this traditional printing technique alive in the digital age.

2976. Sustainable Living through Homesteading: Share stories of individuals and families who have embraced homesteading, focusing on their sustainable practices, the challenges they face, and the rewards of self-sufficient living.

2977. Eco-Friendly Innovations in Footwear: Highlight innovations in sustainable footwear, from shoes made of recycled materials to those designed with biodegradable components, showcasing how the industry is moving toward more environmentally responsible practices.

2978. The World of Competitive Birdwatching: Introduce viewers to the niche but fascinating world of competitive birdwatching or "birding". Discuss the rules, the skills required, and how these competitions contribute to conservation efforts.

2979. Photography as a Tool for Environmental Awareness: Discuss how photography can be used to raise awareness about environmental issues, showcasing powerful images that have sparked change and highlighting photographers who focus on conservation.

2980. Upcycling Electronic Waste into Art: Showcase artists and makers who transform electronic waste into stunning pieces of art or functional objects, discussing the creative process and the message behind repurposing tech waste.

2981. The Cultural Significance of Public Baths: Explore the history and cultural significance of public baths across different cultures, from Turkish hammams to Japanese onsen, discussing their social role and architectural beauty.

2982. Urban Space Activation: Highlight creative ways urban spaces are being activated to promote community engagement, from pop-up parks and street art installations to community-led markets and outdoor cinemas.

2983. The Science Behind Sustainable Building Materials: Delve into the science and technology behind sustainable building materials, discussing innovations like hempcrete, mycelium bricks, and recycled plastic blocks, and their impact on green construction.

2984. Traditional Healing Gardens Around the World: Explore the concept of healing gardens, from the medicinal gardens of medieval monasteries to contemporary therapeutic landscapes, discussing their design principles and healing properties.

2985. The Evolution of Puppetry as an Art Form: Trace the history of puppetry from its ancient origins to modern-day performances. Highlight the diverse styles of puppetry, the craftsmanship behind puppet making, and puppetry as a storytelling medium.

2986. Innovative Approaches to Public Transportation: Examine innovative approaches cities are taking to improve public transportation, from autonomous buses and smart ticketing systems to initiatives aimed at increasing accessibility and reducing congestion.

2987. The Role of Libraries in the Digital Age: Discuss how libraries are adapting to the digital age, transforming into multifunctional spaces that offer digital lending, makerspaces, and community programs alongside traditional book lending.

2988. Crafting Artisan Spirits: Take viewers behind the scenes of crafting artisan spirits, from small-batch distilleries to homemade infusions, highlighting the creativity, science, and tradition involved in spirit production.

2989. Conservation Photography Expeditions: Share expeditions of photographers who focus on conservation, capturing images that tell compelling stories about the planet's endangered species and threatened habitats.

2990. The Impact of Microclimates on Gardening: Explain the concept of microclimates and how understanding them can significantly impact gardening success. Share tips for identifying and leveraging microclimates in backyard gardens or community spaces.

2991. Reviving Historic Gardens: Document the restoration of historic gardens, sharing their history, the restoration process, and the challenge of maintaining their original design while adapting to modern conservation practices.

2992. The Art of Natural Ink Making: Explore the process of making inks from natural materials like berries, nuts, and minerals. Highlight the historical significance of ink making and offer tutorials for viewers to create their own eco-friendly inks.

2993. Sustainable Practices in Textile Art: Showcase artists who incorporate sustainable practices into their textile art, from using recycled materials to natural dyes. Discuss the environmental impact of textiles and how artists are making a difference.

2994. Innovative Urban Composting Solutions: Explore innovative solutions to urban composting challenges, highlighting community composting programs, in-home composting technologies, and policies that support waste reduction and soil health.

2995. Eco-Friendly Children's Toys: Delve into the world of eco-friendly children's toys, discussing the importance of sustainable materials, non-toxic paints, and designs that encourage imaginative play without harming the environment.

2996. The Revival of Artisanal Fishing Techniques: Highlight the revival of traditional, sustainable fishing techniques that have minimal impact on marine ecosystems. Share stories from communities around the world where these methods are making a comeback.

2997. Exploring the Acoustic Ecology of Cities: Investigate the unique soundscapes of urban environments and the study of acoustic ecology. Discuss how city sounds affect residents' well-being and the initiatives to map and improve urban soundscapes.

2998. Sustainable Landscape Photography: Offer tips for landscape photographers to practice their craft sustainably, including minimizing environmental impact while shooting, ethical wildlife photography practices, and promoting conservation through their work.

2999. The Science of Plant-Based Meats: Examine the science behind the creation of plant-based meats, discussing the technology used to mimic the texture and flavor of animal meat, nutritional aspects, and the environmental benefits of plant-based diets.

3000. DIY Solar Water Heating Systems: Provide viewers with a guide to building their own solar water heating systems for home use. Discuss the principles of solar thermal energy, materials needed, and the potential savings on energy bills.

3001. The Role of Art in Urban Regeneration: Explore how art projects and initiatives can drive urban regeneration, transforming neglected spaces into vibrant areas. Highlight successful case studies where art has been a catalyst for community revitalization.

3002. Adventures in Seed Saving: Share the importance of seed saving for biodiversity and food security. Offer tutorials on how to save seeds from various plants, and stories from gardeners and farmers dedicated to preserving heirloom varieties.

3003. Crafting with Sea Glass: Showcase the beauty of crafting with sea glass, from jewelry making to home decor. Discuss how to responsibly collect sea glass and the creative process behind transforming these ocean treasures into art.

3004. Eco-Friendly Personal Care Routines: Share tips for creating personal care routines that are both effective and eco-friendly. Highlight natural skincare recipes, sustainable beauty brands, and ways to reduce plastic waste in the bathroom.

3005. The Impact of Climate Change on Winter Sports: Explore how climate change is impacting winter sports, from skiing and snowboarding to ice climbing. Discuss the challenges faced by athletes, resorts, and the measures being taken to adapt.

3006. Reviving Community Orchards: Highlight the benefits and joys of community orchards, from promoting local food security to fostering social connections. Share stories of how these orchards are being established and maintained by communities.

3007. Innovations in Bicycle Design for Sustainability: Explore innovations in bicycle design aimed at enhancing sustainability, such as bamboo bikes, electric assist technology, and models designed for heavy cargo transport.

3008. Sustainable Design in Tiny Home Living: Delve into sustainable design principles in tiny home living, covering energy efficiency, space-saving innovations, and the use of eco-friendly materials in construction and decor.

3009. The Tradition of Hand-Carved Wooden Canoes: Share the tradition and craftsmanship of hand-carving wooden canoes, discussing the cultural significance, techniques used, and the connection between builders and the waterways.

3010. Green Solutions for Pet Waste Management: Offer solutions for eco-friendly pet waste management, including biodegradable waste bags, composting pet waste safely, and community initiatives to handle pet waste responsibly.

Made in United States
Troutdale, OR
04/26/2024

19477177R00170